IN ONE'S OWN SHADOW

IN ONE'S OWN SHADOW

An Ethnographic Account
of the Condition of Post-
reform Rural China

XIN LIU

UNIVERSITY OF CALIFORNIA PRESS
BERKELEY LOS ANGELES LONDON

University of California Press
Berkeley and Los Angeles, California

University of California Press, Ltd.
London, England

© 2000 by
The Regents of the University of California

Library of Congress Cataloging-in-Publication Data

Liu, Xin, 1957–
In one's own shadow : an ethnographic account of the condition
of post-reform rural China / Xin Liu.
p.   cm.
Includes bibliographical references and index.
ISBN 0-520-21993-7 (alk. paper). —ISBN 0-520-21994-5 (alk. paper)
1. Shaanxi Province (China)—Rural conditions.   2. Shaanxi Province (China)—Social life
and customs.   3. Rural development—China—Shaanxi Province.
4. Social change—China—Shaanxi Province.   I. Title.
HN740.S54L58   2000
306'.0951'43—dc21   99-31248
                                                           CIP

Manufactured in the United States of America

09   08   07   06   05   04   03   02   01   00   10   9   8   7   6   5   4   3   2   1

To Mayako

Contents

Illustrations

Maps

Figures

Tables

Photographs (following page 106)

1. A view of the village
2. The wheat fields in summer
3. Spring plowing
4. Weaving in the courtyard
5. The wedding bread
6. The courtyard door
7. Sacrifice to the sedan chair
8. Burning paper (money) at the grave

Preface

The modernizing process in contemporary China, perhaps not unlike similar processes in other parts of the world, past or present, was carried out according to a developmental map of moral geography, which indicated a number of newly invented social positions. In rural China, two contrasting regions were carefully marked out on this map: "the poor and backward areas" on the one hand and the areas that "got rich first" (i.e., were developed) on the other. The term "poor and backward areas" (*pinkun diqu*) has become a standard political phrase, denoting places where developmental work is needed and connoting the sense of social retardation associated with such places. They are set against areas that "got rich first" (*xianfuqilai*), an official slogan commonly used since the late 1970s. Those residing in the "poor and backward areas" were often considered incapable of making any changes *for* and *by* themselves. They remained in the shadow of the modernizing process; they were the unspeaking objects of the official slogan "to realize four modernizations!" (*shixian sihua*); they were passive but necessary, for the very process of development was possible only when such people were waiting to be modernized.

However, to be in the shadow of the modernizing process is not to claim a fixed social position, represented by a single definite socioeconomic group; instead, it is a transitional moment, experienced by many people (in different degrees) at different stages of economic development. The character of this transitional moment of existence is historically and culturally specific. To adequately understand the condition of Chinese society in transition, I believe we must first critically examine this mode of social being *as becoming*. Such is the purpose of this book. It is an ethnographic account of the very experience of becoming modernized in rural Shaanxi, a province in northwestern China, in the last decade of the twentieth century. It focuses on the process of experiencing a historically specific form of modernization by a particular group of rural residents in China, burdened with a revolutionary past.

For two reasons, I have chosen the term "post-reform" rather than "post-Mao" or "post-socialist" to define rural China. First, it is, in fact, a phrase employed by both Chinese sociologists and local people themselves. For in their view the economic reform in the countryside, though it has not yet been completed, took effect in the early 1980s when household production, known as "the agricultural responsibility system," was reintroduced. Second and perhaps more important, either "post-Mao" or "post-socialist" would implicitly contradict my argument that a great number of Maoist or socialist elements have been incorporated into the cultural practices of the present.

In a general sense, the notion of practice occupies a central place in the organization of my arguments. Two implications of this theoretical orientation are particularly significant. First, my writing focuses on experience and performance in the actual act of everyday practice, by which I mean to emphasize that many aspects of everyday action are not articulated or perhaps not even articulable. Second, the meanings of these practices are not always consciously known by the agents themselves. To imitate Michel Foucault, I may say that people know why they do this or that, they also know how to do this or that, but they do not know what they do does.

Two inquiries are central to this book. The first is concerned with how macrohistorical forces of transformation are incorporated into everyday practices in rural China in the last decade of the twentieth century to form a unique moment of social existence. Everyday practices are the fruits of larger forces of society, but at the same time these practices also transform those forces in ways that reflect the specific historical situations in which they are adopted. These adoptions in a given locality constitute, to borrow a term from Wittgenstein, "a form of life," which may be defined in this context as the everyday appropriation of macrosocial transformation. Instead of applying "a form of life" to a cultural pattern, I use the term to indicate the *formation* of a mode of historical experience: that is, something being "formed" as a moment of existence in the context of larger social forces. In this sense, the economic reform in the past two decades may be understood as "re-form(ation)" of historical elements derived from three main social sources: the traditional, the revolutionary, and the modern. The first part of the book is devoted to the question of how the constituent elements of everyday life in northern rural Shaanxi were "re-formed" in the 1990s.

My second major line of inquiry is concerned with the relationship between the form of a cultural practice and its content; or, to use instead structuralist terminology, the inquiry is about the relationship between the signifier and the signified in a context of social change and cultural continuity. A series of detailed ethnographic examples will illustrate a key characteristic of the cultural production of symbolic forms in rural China: that is, the discrepancies between what a performance or a symbol means and what it does or may do in everyday practice. By using this old pair of concepts—form versus content—I intend to demonstrate the historical contingency of certain cultural forms, as they were "re-formed" in post-reform rural China.

In collecting ethnographic materials and writing this book, I have received help from many people. My gratitude is first of all due to the people in Zhaojiahe, with whom I worked as an ethnographer. In particular, I would like to thank Zhao Xicang and my three hosts, Wanbin, Zunxi, and Famin, whose understanding and help were crucial to my fieldwork. In order to protect their anonymity, personal names in this book are spelled according to *putonghua* pronunciations, which differ from their local sounds.

For academic help and assistance, I am most grateful to Mark Hobart and Elisabeth Croll, University of London, under whose guidance I was able to be trained to become an anthropologist. For their valuable assistance in reading and commenting on different chapters of the book, I thank Stephan Feuchtwang, Stuart Thompson, Alan Dundes, Nancy Scheper-Hughes, Nelson Graburn, Laura Nader, Elizabeth Perry, Mariane Ferme, and Herbert Phillips. Aihwa Ong's friendship and support have been crucial to my intellectual development since I joined the department at Berkeley. Over the past three years, three historians in Berkeley—Frederic Wakeman, Wen-hsin Yeh, and Irwin

Scheiner—have influenced me in ways that they themselves may not even be aware of. I would also like to take this opportunity to thank Sangjik Rhee, Vivienne Huang, Zhang Huaibing, Ulla Munch Jörgensen, and Aamer Hussein for their friendship and support during my years of study in London.

James L. Watson and Judith Farquhar provided two very detailed, suggestive readings of the manuscript for the University of California Press. Although their comments were different, both were crucial to helping me sharpen my argument in revising the manuscript. In particular, I must thank Judith Farquhar for her helpful suggestions on the rendering of some local Chinese terms and phrases. In the process of preparing the manuscript for publication, Sheila Levine, editorial director of the Press, gave me much valuable advice, which helped me tremendously in preparing the book. I would also like to thank Suzanne Knott and Alice Falk of the Press for their invaluable editorial assistance.

The Sino-British Friendship Scholarship (SBFS) provided me with the initial opportunity to become an anthropologist. The Humanities Research Fellowship of the University of California at Berkeley allowed me time and gave me the resources to complete the final revision.

Notes on the Text

Chinese Units of Measure

Length

1 *li*	= 0.50 kilometer
1 *chi*	= 0.33 meter

Area

1 *mu*	= 0.08 hectare
1 *li*	= 0.01 *mu* = 0.1 *fen*

Weight

1 *dan*	= 50.0 kilograms
1 *jin*	= 0.5 kilogram

Official Exchange Rates, U.S. Dollars and Chinese Yuan

1980	1 dollar = 1.5 yuan
1985	1 dollar = 2.7 yuan
1986	1 dollar = 3.5 yuan
1990	1 dollar = 4.8 yuan
1992	1 dollar = 5.5 yuan

1993   1 dollar = 5.8 yuan
1994   1 dollar = 8.6 yuan

1996   1 dollar = 8.4 yuan

Romanization

Most names and words are written in Mandarin, romanized according to the pinyin system. A few crucial terms in the local dialect have been spelled to replicate the original sounds.

Exotic Familiarity

"Dead Brains"

In early December 1991, a local morning train left Xi'an as usual. Xi'an, the capital of Shaanxi, is famous for its spectacular ancient tombs, where the first emperor of China[1] lay with his buried "army"— an unbelievably large number of ceramic warriors and horses. This trove, recently excavated, has been increasingly seen by the government of the People's Republic as a glory of Chinese civilization. Against a freezing wind, the train slowly headed northeast, passing a few towns and small cities still covered with undiluted smog from the coal being burned by hundreds of thousands of households as they just finished their breakfast; it traveled through a blanket of unawakened winter wheat fields that stretched out on a vast plain, the Weihe Plain,[2] leaving the noise and busy life of the provincial capital behind. Further northeast, one could feel more the idleness of winter in rural Shaanxi. Occasionally, through the windows of the train, one could see a few people traveling by bicycle along narrow dirt roads that connect villages and townships. After passing through scenery that changed little for more than seven hours, the train arrived at Qifeng, a small village station at the edge of the Weihe Plain. Passengers, most of them in their traditional cotton-padded black suits, had been waiting in front of the exits before the train fully stopped, as if they were in a hurry. As soon as the doors opened, people rushed past each other—jumping off the train onto the platform, clapping on the shoulders those who had waited in the wind as they shouted and exchanged greetings.

Twice a day this train stopped at the Qifeng station, providing the

Map 1. Location of Zhaojiahe.

main long-distance transportation for a population of a few hundred thousand in this area. If one continued on this train, one would soon reach Hancheng, a medium-size city that few people outside this region know. Further north, Yan'an, the communist base in the 1930s and 1940s, is situated on the northern Shaanxi plateau. This area lies roughly between Yan'an and Xi'an—that is, between the cradle of the communist revolution and the symbol of Chinese imperial history (see maps 1, 2, and 3).

That December morning was the first time I had taken this train, the first time I had traveled to northern Shaanxi, an area in which I had neither personal nor family connections, a region I had rarely dreamed of visiting, although I at one time lived in a city not far away.[3] As an ethnographer of my own society, I strained to watch for unfamiliar things, ready to take notes on anything that seemed strange, and wondered how—and if—my reactions would be different if I had been born in this area, or if I were entirely alien to the culture. So far, nothing seemed "exotic" except an old man beside me on the train who

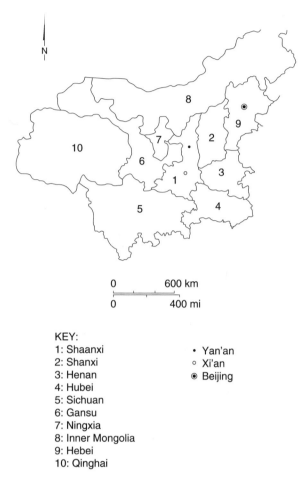

KEY:
1: Shaanxi
2: Shanxi
3: Henan
4: Hubei
5: Sichuan
6: Gansu
7: Ningxia
8: Inner Mongolia
9: Hebei
10: Qinghai

• Yan'an
○ Xi'an
◉ Beijing

Map 2. Shaanxi and its neighboring provinces.

smoked a water pipe, which looked like an old-fashioned pistol, elegantly blowing the smoke into my face from time to time.

Someone was supposed to meet me at the station to accompany me to Zhaojiahe, the destination of my fieldwork, a rural community that was not indicated on any maps—at least not on the maps to be found in Xi'an or any other cities. But nobody appeared. Having noticed my hesitation, three young people kindly agreed to be my guides to the village. These young people, two men and one woman who had been brought up in this area, had recently found jobs in Xi'an and were re-

Map 3. Geographic divisions of Shaanxi.

turning to visit their families. We left the train station and stepped into neatly arranged winter wheat fields. Passing a few small quiet villages, we soon faced the huge Dayu Valley. Only then did I realize that the train station sat on a plateau between two enormous valleys. This plateau is part of the Weihe Plain in central Shaanxi. Although this area is not "mountainous," people living in the valley often describe it as "mountain ravines" (*shangou*). Many rural communities lie at the bottoms of these valleys (see map 4). In order to reach Zhaojiahe, we needed to walk down one side of the valley and climb up the other.

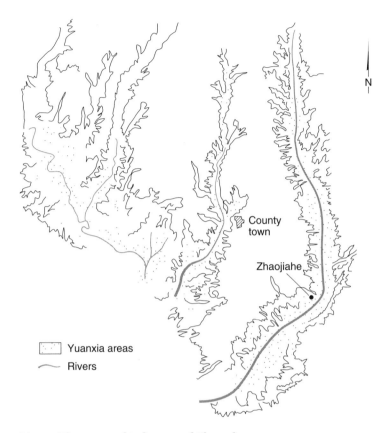

County
town

Zhaojiahe

N

Yuanxia areas

Rivers

Map 4. The topographic features of Chengcheng county.

Anyone traveling here for the first time would be amazed by its topographic complexity: roller-coaster dirt roads, twisted, sometimes even dangerous, often with two or three inches of dust on their surface, were intertwined with the terraced fields stretching out on both sides of the valley.[4] The valley was breathtakingly beautiful when one stood overlooking the narrow dirt roads embroidered on not-yet-very-green buds of winter wheat fields. However, walking these little roads was much less romantic than the view, particularly if one had luggage.

With some amusement, I commented to my companions on the dust and on the strange yet fresh feeling of walking through ankle-deep dust powder. Jianhui, who had recently started work in Xi'an, made a calm but surprising comment: "Those mountainous people (*shanliren*) are dead brains (*sinaojin*); they do not know how to build roads, and they are indeed very backward (*luohou*)." Without irony he stressed the words "dead brains" and "backward." Who are the "dead brains"? People in *this* area, or all peasants?

As our conversation continued, my companions questioned me about the purpose of my visit. Not willing to engage in a long discussion about anthropology and fieldwork, I tried to answer vaguely and briefly, telling them that I wanted to have a look at today's rural life. The young woman, who earlier had not seemed to have any interest in our conversation, suddenly burst in: "What the hell is worth looking at in this fucking poor *shangou* (mountain ravine)?" She did not mean ill, but simply could not understand what motivated my visit to such a place, a place from which they had managed to escape. What underlay her outburst was a social philosophy characteristic of the 1990s. In the last decade of the twentieth century, there was a massive flow of people and goods across local, regional, and national boundaries, unprecedented in the history of the People's Republic of China. People began to travel much more frequently and farther than ever before; but the flow of people was supposed to follow the rules of a particular "power geometry," to use Doreen Massey's term (1994), and was shaped by the desire to "get rich first."[5] Therefore, the direction of movement was expected to be from poor localities to rich regions, from rural areas to urban centers, from the inland to coastal areas where better economic opportunities have been created by the penetration of transnational capital, and, on a larger scale, from China to the West. People are not expected to travel in the opposite direction,[6] unless there is a personal reason—for instance, to visit one's relatives. The question of where one comes from and where one goes has become central in the making of social relations. One could hardly be right to travel in a wrong direction, as in my own case, since travel has been given a meaning, associated not with *looking at* something but with *looking for* something: wealth.

It is in the very production of this moral geography that the "dead brains" can be located in space.[7] Locations are marked according to their degree of development; because development occurs over time, some people are thus seen as less "backward" than others (Hobart 1993). The most backward are the "dead brains": people who are not only poor but also incapable of making changes in life. They cannot even build a proper road. They are passive in the strict sense of the term.

After crossing a stream at the bottom of the Dayu Valley, we began to climb up the other side. Halfway up the hill, when I was hardly able to catch my breath, came a wave of strange sounds. After we ascended another layer of terraced fields, an astonishing scene appeared. On a main village road, a group of young people were running fast and yelling loudly as they carried on their muscular shoulders a colorful sedan chair. A heavy cloud of dust followed their progress; the vivid, beautifully painted, eye-catching colors of the sedan chair looked like a mirage in the mist of dirt. I stood in the middle of the road, watching the parade with my mouth wide open. Not until a few minutes later, when I saw another group of people following the chair—wearing white gowns, wailing and sobbing—did I realize that the beautiful sedan chair must have carried a dead body instead of a smiling bride.

After a long, tiring journey on the hilly dirt roads, I was finally in front of two rows of mud-walled houses. The three young people left for their own destinations. This is Dawa, one of the three dwelling clusters of Zhaojiahe that lean on the western bank of the Dayu Valley. Looking at the village architecture at close range, one sees that houses are built into the hills like caves. The "cave dwelling," which is characteristic of the vernacular architecture in northern rural Shaanxi, is called *yao* in the local dialect. Because the houses are built into the shapes and curves of the hills, both for convenience and safety, the entire community seems to be carved into the slope of the valley. From a distance, one can hardly notice their delicate architecture, though one may sometimes find a few abandoned old cave houses scattered on the hills, looking like huge open mouths without any teeth.

Zhao Wanbin, my first host in the community, whose eldest son was my contact in Beijing, stood in a large, vaulted, dark cave room with gray bricks exposed, holding his newly born granddaughter in his arms. He smiled at me and acknowledged my arrival without saying anything. Behind him on the wall, I noticed in the dim light a grinning, half-naked actress staring at me over my host's shoulders from a vividly printed calendar. Wanbin's wife, Yin'ai, immediately started to make a bowl of noodles for me as a welcoming meal. To offer a guest something to eat is a social norm. Social relations are largely defined and reiterated by exchanges of food and banquets.

Zhaojiahe is a single-surname village, which is not unusual in this area.[8] It is under the administration of Leijiawa township, Chengcheng county, the Weinan district of Shaanxi province (see map 5). The whole community is divided into several groups (*cunmin xiaozu*), which are in turn organized in three dwelling clusters, consisting of about two hundred households in all. According to the village household registration, there were 860 residents in 1992; but some people claimed that the true figure should have been at least 10 percent higher, because a number of villagers trying to avoid direct conflict with the government's birth control policies managed not to record their children. All except one household were farmers, and their main crops were wheat and cotton.

People in this area view residential communities as social units defined by agnatic ties. Though communities can be named in many ways, most take the surname of a dominant cluster of agnates. For instance, Zhaojiahe literally means "Zhao family river." Because a stream constantly flows through the bottom of the valley, many rural communities in the neighborhood—such as Yangjiahe, Houjiahe, Majiahe, and Dangjiahe (see map 6)—are similarly named. Their surnames (Zhao, Yang, Hou, Dang, etc.), which distinguish one group from another, often indicate a still-existing descent group,[9] which forms the core of a community. Each of these communities is no more than half a mile from another; and most of them bear an identical contour and appearance, although they vary greatly in size.[10]

The stream in the valley serves as an important resource for irrigation, but it can cover only a small proportion of the land that belongs to Zhaojiahe. A large amount of arable lands, stretching out on both sides of the valley, depend on rainfall as their only possible source of water. Indeed, people in this area worry a great deal about the water needed for agricultural production. One local proverb puts it: "What one eats depends on rainfall (*kaotian chifan*)." It is true that there are more droughts than floods in this area; as another local proverb says, "Out of ten years there will be nine droughts (*shinian jiuhan*)." In the years before the Communists came to power, people organized certain "rituals" to pray for rains when droughts occurred;[11] but this kind

HUANGLONG

BAISHUI

Wangzhuang

HEYANG

Zhuangtou

County town

Leijiawa

Zhaojiahe

PUCHENG

Chengjiao

Jiaodao

DALI

N

Map 5. Chengcheng county.

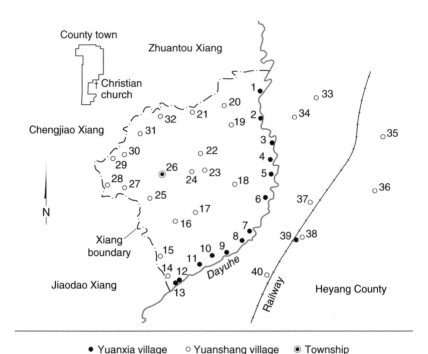

Map 6. Zhaojiahe and its neighboring villages.

• Yuanxia village	○ Yuanshang village	◉ Township

1: Liujiahe	11: Ximajiahe	21: Shenhou	31: Beilizhuang
2: Beimencunhe	12: Huitouju	22: Linshang	32: Liangjiazhuang
3: Nanyangjiahe	13: Yuchang	23: Potizhuang	33: Jingyi
4: Dangjiahe	14: Jinjiaqiao	24: Miaowa	34: Xipo
5: Zhaojiahe	15: Zuojiapo	25: Baochengzhuang	35: Hejiazhuang
6: Dawa	16: Baocheng	26: Leijiawa	36: Dongfen
7: Houjiahe	17: Linchuan	27: Mengjia	37: Qincheng
8: Yuanjiahe	18: Poti	28: Zhenjia	38: Qifen
9: Xiao Zhaojiahe	19: Beimencun	29: Tianjiazhuang	39: Qifen Station
10: Dongmajiahe	20: Chengqiangtou	30: Nanlizhuang	40: Dujiadian

of activity, denounced as feudal superstition by the Maoist government, was severely attacked during the Great Leap Forward (1958–59) and abandoned soon after. Yet rains, which are most likely to come in summer, often bring with them destruction and land erosion. Even a modest rain can cause serious erosion, creating ravines that destroy roads and fields.[12] Little dirt roads were often blocked by debris after a summer rain, and a huge gully might appear in the middle of a road overnight. I was told that sometimes a donkey or a cow, commonly used as draft animals, slipped into a ravine after a rain; because there was no way to get the animal out, it was left there to die.

Though it is a large practical concern, water does not seem to have a significant symbolic or social function in daily life. For instance, in important ceremonies such as weddings or funerals, when various kinds of symbols are employed in conjunction with both ritualized and spontaneous actions, water or its image has almost no place. Here as in many other parts of northern rural China, people rely on wells for the water they consume daily. Each household has a water vat that stores a few day's worth of water, used almost exclusively for drinking and cooking. Bathing is not an essential part of life in this area. In the past, people took baths only twice in their life: once after birth and once before their wedding.[13]

In contrast, the significance of the soil is emphasized in everyday life. The soil of this region is known as the "loess." The whole region is covered by, as Theodore Shabad (1972, 225) put it, "a mantle of yellow wind-laid silt," which is generally believed to come from the Ordos Desert of Inner Mongolia. The concern about the soil goes far beyond its basic role in agricultural production: association with the loess constitutes a crucial part of one's sense of self and belonging. Local people believe that their soil is better than that of others, because it produces the best flour. In the mid-1970s, there was a severe drought and a shortage of grain in this area. To help, the government sent wheat flour that had been imported from Canada. One woman recalled, "We did not like Canadian flour, because it was too crispy (*meijin*). The steamed bread made of the Canadian flour was not as tasty as that made of our own. Ours is much more sturdy." An old man then interrupted, "You know why? The soil is different."[14]

Many other aspects of life also depend on the loess—housing, for instance. In the past, most houses were simply caves dug into the hills, and they were called *tuyao:* that is, "soil or earthen cave dwellings." It was possible to build such houses only because of the specific quality of the soil. Housing conditions have improved since the 1950s, and most houses are now *zhuanyao,* or "brick cave dwellings." Nevertheless, bricks are still made by local people themselves from the loess, which is not only the most appropriate construction material but also free and convenient, available almost everywhere, surrounding each house.

Heavy, plastered mud walls, of exactly the same color and texture as the ground, are built to divide one house from another. If one stood in the middle of a dwelling cluster, one could sometimes see nothing but the loess. Houses, grounds, public squares, roads, and fields are linked by and through this soil, in lighter or darker shades of yellow.

If one walked around in this community, one might find a few trees, usually scattered around rows of cave houses; occasionally a cow or donkey, enjoying the sunshine if there was any; hardly any dogs; perhaps a few trotting hens looking for additional food; and often groups of young or old women sitting in front of their doors, giggling and chatting with each other. The only open space in Zhaojiahe is a public square at the center of the main dwelling cluster, where funerals and wedding receptions take place. The square is surrounded by a few buildings: the community headquarters, an elementary school, and a small retail shop (see map 7). Since the early 1980s, the headquarters has seldom been used; in the Maoist past it was the center of political gatherings, of endless mass meetings and study sessions.

People in this community were nostalgic, often passionately so, and denied that the present had any merit. They claimed that they loved the years of the Maoist revolution. Both publicly and behind their doors, they openly showed their contempt for Deng Xiaoping (who died in 1997), the architect of economic reform and the paramount leader of the Communist Party after Mao Zedong. People have become increasingly dissatisfied with current changes, even though their material life has been greatly improved. The virtue of the past seems to grow out of fear of the present. People in this community believed that they were the ones who have been left behind in the national race for wealth. Soon after my arrival, my host Wanbin came to talk to me about his concern and dissatisfaction with the present.

The present society is wholly "rancid."[15] Now everything is money. But it doesn't work. During Mao's time, if you did something wrong, you would have to make a self-criticism at a mass meeting. People didn't want to lose face, so there was little wrongdoing. Now, there are so many laws but none of them works. If you have money, you can always get away with whatever crimes you commit. People have become so greedy that we peasants always get cheated. When Chairman Mao died, we all worried about what would happen afterward. Deng came out; everything turned out to be so bad. Everything collective is collapsing; nobody cares. One looks after oneself. In the past, cadres

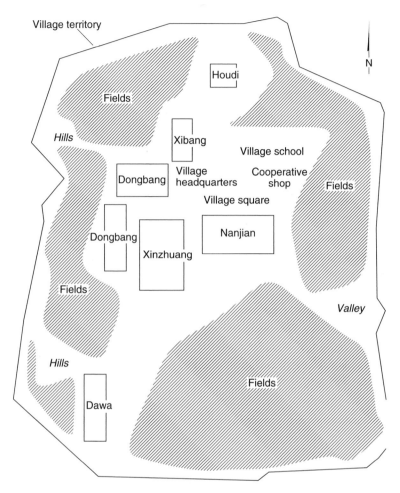

Map 7. Villager groups in Zhaojiahe.

were elected and chosen by the masses. Now they are simply appointed by the local government. All the officials and cadres are corrupt. They only want to make money for themselves. Damn it!

There are several notes of disheartenment in this commentary, which may be seen as a "collective representation" of the sentiment against the present. First is a cry for the loss of collectivism, once urged on the population so feverishly by the Maoist government. This complaint reflects a deeper concern over the perceived lack of any "moral economy" that could sustain a certain order in the community.[16] Individuals are now on their own, but the rules and assumptions for a changed vision of society and community are not yet clear. Thus the present appears to be full of uncertainty (e.g., Croll 1994). The Maoist era, viewed in retrospect, can be seen as a dreamworld—not for what it had actually offered but for what it had promised. One may well argue that many people suffered during the radical years of the Maoist revolution, but that misses the point here: under the rule of the Maoist regime, individuals may have been punished but they were never *ignored,* and people in this community now have a strong feeling of being neglected and isolated. As James Scott (1976) has shown, in peasant communities, when everyone is starving, each individual feels less hungry than he or she would otherwise. Nothing is more dangerous than being alone.

Second, social stratification, even though much less evident in this area than in the southeastern coastal areas, was strongly felt in Zhaojiahe. Money produces distinctions and differences. The differentiation in wealth is believed to be the reason for an increasing number of crimes—theft and robbery in particular. What is worse is that criminals may be able to avoid punishment if they can afford the fines levied. Thus the law and the punishments it specifies are ineffective in stemming the growth in crime. According to local people, punishment should be applied not simply to the misconduct—the crime—but to the person responsible, the criminal. Here, the metaphysical relationship between a person and his or her action needs to be problematized. These villagers saw the very nature of a person as embedded in his or her behavior as social practice.[17]

Third, local people claimed that they have lost control over the selection of local officials and cadres, who are the instrument of the state.[18] The Maoist era was remembered as a happy time of "democracy," when the voices of the masses were heard.[19] The two decades of economic reforms have taken away any possibility of their controlling processes of change, the local people insisted. That loss, rather than rampant corruption itself, is now the main cause of their despair.

In this area "the present" began in 1981, when collective land was distributed to each household in the name of the "agricultural responsibility system" and the family again became the basic unit of production and consumption.[20] Economic growth has been evident since then; so has the growth of its discontents. The economic differences between "brothers" (*zijiawu*; see chapter 2) have grown; individuals have also become greater threats to each other. Concerns about safety dominated daily conversations in the 1990s. Anyone who grew something different from others had to pay extra attention to his crops. For instance, during the summer people had to sleep in the fields with their watermelons, watching out for possible thieves.[21] The Maoist past would be always brought up whenever safety was mentioned. "Which period is better?" Wancheng, the group head of Dawa, yelled; "In Mao's time, if you left your hoe behind, you could certainly find it in the same place the next day. Nobody would touch it. Nobody would dare touch it. Where you left it, you would definitely find it at the same spot. But nowadays, even if you keep your things carefully in your own house, they will still be stolen!"

In order to reinforce the need to be cautious, a few stories, perfectly rehearsed, were passed around; they served as psychological protection against the fearful present. One of these stories, which I was told several times, is worth recording here:

An old man from a nearby village, who planned to sell his donkey in an open market in the town, knew there were many *zeiwazi* (thief babies) in that area. *Zeiwazi* would follow those who just made a transaction and steal the money from them. All transactions were conducted in cash. People had to carry cash with them, sometimes a large amount of money, to go to market. A good donkey in 1992 was worth about five hundred yuan, which was a small fortune for many families. The old man was very courageous and extremely cautious. He found himself a big rope, and brought it with him to the market. He wore a traditional cotton-padded black jacket over a homemade cloth shirt. As soon as he had sold the donkey, he immediately placed his money underneath his shirt. For its safety, he left his money close to his belly, and then tied the rope tightly around his waist. He told others, "I want to see how *zeiwazi* could reach my money," and walked away to enjoy himself. When the old man walked along the steps going up to a cinema, a cigarette butt was thrown down his back, under his collar. He started to scream and had to untie his rope in order to get rid of the cigarette butt burning his skin. People surrounded him and some helped. The old man took off his jacket and shirt, throwing the cigarette butt away, and then, suddenly, he realized that his money was already gone. He cried his heart out.

This story was often performed amusingly with exaggerated effects, taken up by one person and then another. It encapsulates well all the

discontent that Wanbin's comments had expressed. As the story implies, good people are alone and isolated; thieves work collectively. No
one can escape being robbed, no matter how carefully one prepares.
More important, there is no guarantee that any punishment will fall
on the evildoers: the present society is so inefficiently organized and
managed that it denies its people any protection. Officials or cadres play
no role in this story; in the everyday affairs of the local community,
they were often viewed as nuisances.

These villagers felt extremely uncomfortable about being a "peasant" (*nongmin*) in the 1990s (see Cohen 1993), because they believed
that "peasants" are always cheated and discriminated against outside
their own communities. People in Zhaojiahe insisted that poor people
had received respect and power during the years of the Maoist revolution. "But nowadays," I was told by an angry woman, whose daughter failed to secure a job in town, "everyone will cheat peasants. If you
go to the market, you will always get cheated. They sell the worst thing
to you, and ask you to pay more than others, simply because you are a
peasant! During Mao's time, who dared? 'Mass repression' (*qunzhong
zhuanzheng*)!"

No time seems more pleasant than the Maoist past, the local people
of this area agree. My intent is to document in detail a set of historically situated strategies and tactics for dealing with everyday life that
are shared by this particular group of rural residents: that is, those who
are seen as being "backward," those who are nostalgic about the Maoist
past and suspicious of the present, those who see themselves as being marginalized by the regime of modernization, those who claim to
be hopeless victims of social change, those who are fearful about their
future—in short, a people of little significance.

Host and Hostage

A truthful account of the circumstances of fieldwork, an honest description of the relationship between the ethnographer and the subjects of his or her study, is crucial if the reader is to evaluate the published ethnography.[22] Though I had originally trained in economics and
applied statistics in China, a fellowship unexpectedly brought me to
study anthropology in Britain in 1990, leaving behind a city where the
effects of the Tiananmen Incident still lingered.[23] I had at first planned

to do research on the social function and organization of literacy and orality, but this subject turned out to be of little relevance to my field experience. Just as "theory is not determinant of ethnography" (Fardon 1990, 3), so too thematic preparation may not be determinant of the ethnographer's actual experience.

As soon as I returned to Beijing in the winter of 1991, I started to search for a field site. I decided to work in a rural community in part because I had no previous experience of country life. By studying a form of life that was not intimately familiar to me, I hoped that I would be able more easily to play the role of an anthropologist: that is, to be at least an "insider's outsider" (Rabinow 1977, 157).[24] While I was looking for a place to start, a friend of mine introduced me to her home village—Li Zhuang in Hebei province, which was about two hours by train from Beijing. My hasty visit to the village was welcomed by a group of local officials and cadres, as it seemed that everyone had been informed that a Beijing cadre had arrived. A welcome banquet was prepared with roast chickens bought from a nearby market. Our conversation quickly turned to possible investments for this community, which had already shown much success in industrial development. After a few rounds of drinks, I suddenly realized that I was thought of as someone who had the potential to bring further business to the community. Nice food but difficult to swallow—this was not what I had expected. I was hoping to find a place where I could participate in the everyday life of ordinary families. I left Li Zhuang the following morning.

This trying experience made me begin to realize that even for a native scholar studying his own society, choosing a field site was highly problematic. It also pushed me further in considering how I might carry out my research from the perspective of "the cheese and the worms" (Ginzburg 1980)[25]—that is, from a perspective not cast in the official language of development and modernization, a perspective that is not easy to discover in the existing ethnographic representations of Chinese society.[26] After my return to Beijing from Li Zhuang, the university where I used to teach kindly offered me their research base, a rural community called Dachengzhuang in a suburb of Beijing. A number of research projects had been carried out in this community, and the university was willing to provide me with years of statistics that they had collected. I paid a visit to the officials of Fangshan county, whose administrative authority covered Dachengzhuang. While they were very gracious and willing to have me there, they insisted that I should stay in a county hotel ten kilometers away from the village. They even offered me a bicycle in case I needed to travel in the area. By no means was I able to convince them that what I wanted to do was to live with "peasants." The chief official said to me, "What is the point of living with them? Whenever you want to talk to them, we can bring them here to *report* to you."

Peasants were supposed to be described, portrayed, and represented by others, either government officials or university professors. They were denied any role in the production of knowledge about them. The very absence of their voices in the discussion of their own problems indicates an epistemological regime that demarcates "to know" from "to be known." My university colleagues in Beijing, many of whom were infatuated with discovering new methods of quantitative analysis—focusing on macrosocial change and often traveling between urban centers—also frowned at me when they heard that I wanted to live with "peasants" for a year. Some suggested that I could go for one or two weeks at most, while others insisted that even that was an absurd idea. One young professor asked me, "What can you get by living with peasants—I mean, apart from some lice?"

My chance to get some lice finally came when I happened to meet Zhao Xicang, a graduate student in Beijing whose family was living in rural Shaanxi. I requested permission to visit Zhao Xicang's parents. Zhao Xicang's father, Zhao Wanbin, soon replied and assented. Wasting no more time, I left for this "unofficial" community; I stayed there from the winter of 1991 to the summer of 1992.

This introduction to the community profoundly affected my role as an ethnographer and the nature of work I was able to carry out. At the beginning, because of my vague claim of interest in rural life, people conceived of me as a journalist or someone whose purpose was deliberately hidden for some reason. My host's neighbors thought that I was investigating rural corruption and thus some people, particularly cadres, kept their distance from me in the first few weeks of my fieldwork. My initial association with Wanbin, which was purely a coincidence, certainly created a distance between me and the community's leadership group. Wanbin, who was himself a member of the Communist Party, was one of the most vicious critics of the community leaders.

People were disappointed to discover that I was in fact not a journalist and had no intention of investigating rural corruption, real or alleged. But I was still viewed as possessing social connections and power. That I was from Beijing and abroad, an outsider who should and could have demonstrated economic privilege, made me special in their eyes. I stayed with several families, for short or long periods, after a confrontation with Wanbin that resulted in my moving out of his house.[27] Three of these hosts, including Wanbin, were particularly significant. Zunxi, my second major connection, was a public figure in the community. At the age of sixteen he went to work as a carpenter in Xi'an. Ten years later, after a workplace accident that injured his back, Zunxi returned to Zhaojiahe to live with his paralyzed mother. Other members of Zunxi's extended family also had experience working in cities or towns. Zunxi and his brothers were seen by others as people who knew the values and fashions of the outside world. In daily conversations, they were frequently called on to explain what was going on in Xi'an or other places.

My third main connection was Famin; none of his close relatives had been successful in pursuing any kind of work other than farming. He and his four brothers were all farmers in Zhaojiahe, and five of his six sisters were married to local men. Famin was viewed as a "typical," "honest" person who knew little about the outside world. Yet he also enjoyed a high genealogical rank; thus despite his relative youth (he was in his early thirties), Famin was one of the most senior members of this community. Even an old man in his seventies might have to address Famin as "grandfather." This status did not bring him any economic advantage or political authority; it only guaranteed that his family celebrations, such as weddings or funerals, were always a local attraction.

Although my fieldwork covers a very wide range of experiences with local people, both within and outside this community, these three hosts provide the main point of reference in my analysis. This focus is explained in part by the greater extent of my interactions with them. In addition, my experiences with them were—to borrow a term from Clifford Geertz—often "thicker" than with others.

The community's perception of my status and presence tended to change as I moved from one household to another. At first, I was given many privileges; for example, I was asked to take the most important seat when dining. Later, I was much less frequently treated as a formal guest. Though initially I was perceived as someone whose judgments could have serious consequences for them, in the last few weeks of my fieldwork I was often ignored. By moving between houses, I crossed a crucial threshold and stepped into the intimate world of domestic control and power. Such involvement profoundly affected my angle of observation and style of writing. No longer a hostage of their hospitality, I became in many ways subject to their domestic control and authority.

Some common constraints in the study of rural Chinese society also applied in my case. For instance, because it is still seen as socially inappropriate for an unmarried young woman to talk to an unrelated male, my conversations with unmarried women were limited to relatively formal contacts with some female schoolteachers. However, I had numerous opportunities to observe how sexual meanings were produced and reproduced in everyday life—through the arrangement of domestic space, for example. In addition, this study of a rural community in Shaanxi does not allow me to draw conclusions about China as a whole. There is no such identity as "Chinese peasant," perfectly shaped as we wish, just as there are no local identities whose boundaries are not blurred and constantly modified. Social selves, not unlike genetic selves, are partially connected and imperfectly represented. No two individuals are exactly the same, but everyone is related through some mode of reproduction, either distant or close, that depends on a series of historical and cultural conditions (see Strathern 1991). Thus my writing provides only a partial representation of the changing condition of post-reform Chinese society—capturing the macrosocial transformation in a mode of everyday behavior and performance.

Everyday Practice

Participating in daily life both in public and in the intimacy of the domestic world of my hosts, I was exposed to a form of everyday power, often exercised without any direct mediation of language, that determined how "dead brains" were produced in the reproduction of society.[28] A few days after my arrival in Zhaojiahe, I was invited to attend a wedding. As usual, a temporary dining hall was set up in the bridegroom's courtyard, and as guests arrived they joined the feast, which had started in the early morning. Important relatives such as the bride's parents were invited to sit at a particular table at which better food was served. Food plays an important function in producing differences, by which the hierarchy of social relations is constantly reiterated. It was as noisy and lively as the other weddings I later experienced or as those inscribed by earlier anthropologists into our imagination of Chinese society (see Freedman 1979b). As the feast continued, the bridegroom and bride, glasses in hand, visited each table and took turns persuading guests to drink or eat more. At some tables their persuasion was more symbolic than at others. Guests also demanded, often with pretended exaggeration, that the newlyweds should drain their own glasses. If the couple refused to do so, they would be required to kiss in front of the guests; otherwise they were not allowed to move on as duty prescribed. After having made the rounds a few times, the bride was obviously becoming drunk, and was afraid to revisit those tables dominated by young people. People laughed and joked about her reluctance to return where guests had forced her to accept more alcohol or more kisses. Nothing seemed unusual—yet a dramatic event was to follow. Before people started to leave in the afternoon, a middle-aged man named Huangshan (as I learned later) stood up and walked slowly but with determination to a table, next to the door, that held food, clothes, wine, and other gifts received from the guests. After staring at the table for a few seconds, he suddenly pulled it over. As a bottle of wine splashed on the ground, flooding a swarm of unprepared ants who had also been enjoying their banquet, Huangshan told the astonished group that the new couple had not shown the minimum amount of "propriety" (*lijie*). He declared that he was an uncle of the bride, but the new couple did not—as custom demanded—come to his table at least three times during the meal. Both the groom's and bride's parents immediately came over, apologizing and trying to calm Huangshan down. He yelled at everyone who came close to him, causing a disturbance—but nothing more. The wedding feast had resumed before I was able to understand what had happened, or even to move closer to the people who were arguing at the center of the courtyard. Nobody seemed to be angry; Huangshan himself went back to his table to continue his meal, as happy as he had ever been.

Something must have escaped my observation. I missed seeing how his discontent developed prior to the event and why it was resolved so easily. One person later commented: "Oh, Huangshan has always been such a bad-tempered man. He makes trouble from time to time, but he is not harmful." Others disagreed. For instance, my host blamed the parents of the bridegroom for not preparing better food for other guests—that is, for those who believed that they should have been treated more distinctively. Still others claimed that Huangshan, who in recent years had become quite well-off by developing an orchard, simply wanted to demonstrate the power of his wealth. Old women tended to explain the event by referring to the history of conflicts between the two families, pointing to a dispute some years ago that Huangshan had had with the parents of the bridegroom over an issue related to irrigation. Discussion and interpretation of such an event can easily run in a circle of perspectives, just as anthropological arguments often do, with everyone pointing to a particular reason in a particular context and suggesting different possible directions. I doubt very much whether one could find what James Scott in his analysis of "the arts of resistance" (1990) has called a "hidden transcript" that makes it possible to look at this kind of incident with any interpretive certainty. What is crucial here, in my view, is a particular notion of "situation": that is, actions, absorbed in everyday knowledge, are carried out according to a set of implicit rules and meanings (e.g., see Douglas 1975b), which are in turn transformed as a result of such actions. This is what I will call "everyday practice."

A major concern of my writing, informed by such occasions as Huangshan's outburst, is to write macrosocial transformation into a mode of everyday practice: that is, to describe how changes in China's economy and society are embodied in a gradual process of unconscious modifications of behavior and consciousness.[29] Such an orientation not only refuses the telescopic perspective of viewing social life "from the twelfth floor" (Erikson 1989, 532), which has been very common in studies of Chinese society (particularly of the Maoist years),[30] but also attempts to give the notion of "everyday practice" some theoretical significance.

Pierre Bourdieu has seriously—if not entirely successfully— attempted to develop a number of analytical tools, hoping to produce a "theory of practice" (Bourdieu 1977, 1990; see also Bourdieu and Wacquant 1992; Calhoun, LiPuma, and Postone 1993). Bourdieu's idea of practice, which derives from his incessant effort to break down the dualistic assumptions inherent in Western epistemology, particularly the opposition of objectivism and subjectivism, is relevant to my writing in two respects. First, Bourdieu argues that practice is always situated: it always bears a specific set of temporal and spatial relations.[31] Second, practice is not entirely consciously orchestrated. Nothing is purely accidental, but neither is it wholly intentional. Improvisation and strategy—or, as Michel de Certeau has emphasized, "tactics" (1984, xix)—are the essence of practice. Thus practice is characterized by fluidity and indeterminacy; it is like a game, to use Bourdieu's metaphor (1990, 66–68, 80–82).

In order to understand Bourdieu's theory of practice, we should look briefly at one of his key analytical notions, "habitus": produced by "[t]he conditionings associated with a particular class of conditions of existence," these are "systems of durable, transportable dispositions, structured structures predisposed to function as structuring structures" (Bourdieu 1990, 53). According to Bourdieu, habitus is "constituted in practice and is always oriented towards practical functions" (52). In other words, habitus generates practice, which in turn constitutes habitus. On the one hand, habitus is "predisposed to function as structuring structures"; on the other, outcomes in the practice generated by habitus are not predetermined by the actors' conscious aims. Habitus is rather "an internal law through which the law of external necessities, irreducible to immediate constraints, is constantly exerted." Putting it in another way, Bourdieu sometimes calls it "the internalization of externality." The habitus, which is itself a product of history, "produces individual and collective practices—more history—in accordance with the schemes generated by history." He uses the phrase "system of dispositions" to indicate this quality of habitus; it is "a present past that tends to perpetuate itself into the future by reactivation in similarly structured practices" (54). Furthermore, the habitus is located, both bodily and mentally, in human agents. This embodiment is implicit and may not even be articulable (see Taylor 1993).[32]

Practice is not a result of conscious determination. The effects of action always exceed or are richer than its intention (see Asad 1993, 15). The crucial point here is that something exists only *in* practice—only in the ways of talking, the ways of doing, the ways of behaving, and so on. The habitus of everyday practice, as Richard Jenkins puts it, "is not just *manifest* in behaviour, it is an integral *part* of it (and vice versa)" (1992, 75, emphasis in the original).[33] Despite Bourdieu's effort to undermine the foundations of Western epistemological dualism, some critics of his work have pointed out that he himself often takes an objectivist stance (J. Thompson 1991, 11; Jenkins 1992, 91–92). This stance sometimes induces his "theory of practice" to take shelter in the shadow of transactionalism. In other words, he may slip into an analysis of transactions between individuals or groups of individuals in terms of the "logic" of their strategies and tactics.[34]

Michel Foucault has provided some interesting insights through his actual analyses of different kinds of practices, particularly the institutional and the disciplinary.[35] Two of his ideas are particularly useful here. First, dispersion constitutes a key element in Foucault's notion of practice. Dispersion means not only that there are always multiple forces engaged in practice but, more important, that the very nature of practice lies in its diversity and multiplicity (see Foucault 1972, 3–17; Best and Kellner 1991, 42–45). It is the notion of "discursive practice" that allows Foucault to relate madness to reason, discipline to normalizing strategies, sexuality to the technique of self, subjection to power, and power to knowledge (see Dreyfus and Rabinow 1982; Merquior 1985). Second, Foucault always treats practice as a historical construct—not in a conventional sense, taking historical events as interrelated sets of meaningful successions or processes, but in understanding history itself as contingent and unpredictable. Practice is contingent, and there are no predetermined laws that can be detected beforehand and outside it (see Foucault 1972, 1977). Specifically, in Foucault's view, as to some extent in Bourdieu's analysis, time no longer appears as an external coordinate according to which practices are carried out; rather, time (as well as space) is constituted and reconstituted as and in practice (see Foucault 1979, 1980). There is an uncertainty in practice, for it transforms itself in the very moment when it is actualized.

Underlying this interest in the notion of practice is an enduring concern among Western scholars to seek a compromise between society as a whole and the individual's action. Anthony Giddens attempts to bridge structure and human agency in his notion of "structuration" (1984), whereas Charles Taylor (1985) notes that in society much agency is linked neither to single individual humans nor great collectivities but to shifting, historically constituted complex forms. Earlier,

R. G. Collingwood distinguished instruments (what, or who, carries out action) from agents and patients. "Agents" command that an action be carried out, take responsibility for that action, or both (Collingwood 1942, 8). Agents are often "complex," composed of more than one person: for example, they might be households or relative-based groupings. Such groupings are commonly somewhat fluid, changing from situation to situation, and thus are not identical with corporate groups. "Patients" are those on whom others carry out actions. They differ from objects of the action in that they are conscious. Agency, instrumentality, and patiency are not given in nature but are recognizable only through discursively situated practices. Different people and groups in any instance are likely to have different, contested accounts of agency. As Mark Hobart puts it, "agency and patiency are situational, overlapping, ironic and under-determined" (1990a, 96).

Such notions have also influenced anthropology. As Sherry Ortner has pointed out (1984), the idea of practice has been a significant organizing symbol in anthropology since the late 1970s. My engagement with this theoretical orientation is meant to be critical of two common tendencies in writings about Chinese society.[36] First, often very little room is left to discuss the social unconscious, which cannot be discovered in any documents but exists only in a mode of behavior or practice. Instead, a great deal of attention has been given to contemporary China's political organizations and ideologies.[37] My writing, though also concerned with such organizations and ideologies, aims at accounting for how they are embodied in everyday experience and performance. Second, ethnographic writings about contemporary China generally assume that certain social positions, such as those of cadres or local officials, are structurally stable in relation to the state or to other social groups. This assumption tends to allow ethnographies of, for example, rural China to focus on a political relationship centered around such groups as the village cadres.[38] In contrast, I describe the practices in and through which a certain subject position is formed or constituted. Thus, I argue that agents, instruments, and patients are situationally defined—and those social positions are constantly changing.

This book is divided into two parts, each consisting of three chapters. The first part is devoted to a description of the macro sources of his-

torical influence that render everyday action and experience meaningful. In the case of rural China, three are identifiable: the traditional,
the revolutionary, and the modern. These provide useful categories of
theoretical analysis; but in actual social and cultural practice the elements of everyday life are often so complexly combined that they cannot be traced back to a single "source." In identifying these major historical influences, I introduce the sociocultural context in which this
particular group of rural residents lives and struggles. The second part
of the book focuses on certain moments of everyday practice as articulations of the elements derived from these macro sources. In the
course of action, these elements become expressions of experience, becoming meaningful—both as reasons for and consequences of action—
to the agents whose subject positions are modified precisely because
of this particular actualization. Though each moment is unique, we can
identify some as characteristic of post-reform rural China. In these
chapters I provide an ethnographic description of certain "typical" moments of such articulations.

As in other parts of rural China, the idea of kinship, largely coming
from the traditional source of historical influence, plays an important
role in structuring a vision of social relationships by defining both individual and collective identities and shaping individuals' attitude and
sentiment toward each other. In chapter 2, I discuss the traditional concept of kinship in the context of a marriage crisis that has followed the
economic reforms in this community. Patrilineal descent and virilocal
marriage had survived the encounter with the Maoist revolution, but
they were forced to give way in the 1980s. Endogamy, which in earlier
times would have been taken as incestuous, has become a social norm
in the 1990s. I argue that this is one of the changes that reflects a shift
in how these people conceptualize the relationship between the self
and the other.

Marriage is a central concern for the people in this part of rural
Shaanxi, and in chapter 3 I examine its practice in the 1990s. As a
process of negotiation and a mirror of social change, marriage incor-
porates a set of elements that are at once traditional, revolutionary, and
modern. This chapter shows that in its everyday appropriation of such
historical influences, marriage "digests" these elements—and digestion
is a crucial metaphor. What and how to eat are questions essential to
the social and cultural life in this region. Food, as well as its prepara-

tion and presentation, serves symbolic functions central to the organization and expression of both individual and collective feelings. Food as a system of signification will be discussed in chapter 4. Within such a system, social distinction and cultural difference are produced and reproduced on various daily occasions.

In chapter 5, I turn to describing a number of everyday experiences and performances, such as bargaining and swearing, in order to capture certain typical moments of social life and provide an ethnographic account of the condition of post-reform rural China. Chapter 6 explores two "ritualized" moments of cultural practice carried out on ceremonial occasions. Weddings and funerals, in more elaborate forms revived under the more "liberal" policies of the post-Mao state, have become a primary theater of collective action. The question of collectivity, its consciousness and form, is discussed in relation to two particular issues: the uses of violence and what I call the "pliability" of emotion. The fundamental question here concerns the relationship between the social and the individual body—that is, how they are mutually conditioned and reinforced.

Chapter 7 deals with politics, particularly with some cumbersome efforts made by the local authorities trying to reintroduce political struggles of the Maoist kind in the 1990s. Focusing on the implementation of birth control policies and an unsuccessful attempt to carry out a "second socialist education movement" in the early 1990s, I argue that the Maoist political ground has collapsed. The infrastructure necessary to support that form of politics no longer exists, even though political slogans of the Maoist variety may still have currency. In other words, the ideological content of Maoism remains relevant, but it no longer takes any practical form. The game is now, at least in part, in the hands of "dead brains." In the last decade of twentieth-century China, we witnessed the emergence of a new type of subjects who stood for the "backward otherness" created by and in the modernizing process. Yet these new subjects, who were always in the shadow of development, represent a negation of the negation of the Maoist revolution—a mode of self crucial to the constitution of Chinese modernity.

Part One

The Culture of Predicament

The Uses of Confusion

Resisting Ideology

Kinship in Practice

Zhaojiahe consists of a descent group based on agnatic ties; a common ancestor can be traced through a written genealogy, which has been kept in a relatively good form.[1] All other material forms of traditional kinship, such as family temples,[2] were either destroyed or transformed into something else during the radical years of the Maoist revolution. For instance, the main family temple was turned into a village school during the Great Leap Forward. We may wonder why the genealogy was left intact. What was the effect of the Maoist revolution on the traditional institution and ideology of kinship in this particular community? How can the past be understood in light of the present transformation in the name of development and modernization?

As James Watson has argued (1982, 1986), anthropological models of Chinese kinship are basically drawn from field investigations in South China, focusing on the lineage organization that is characterized by corporate ownership of shared assets, particularly in the form of land.[3] The general theoretical assumptions that support these models come from the pioneering work of Maurice Freedman (1958, 1966),[4] whose innovation opened up a new field of investigation (J. Watson 1986, 274–75). Kinship is no longer simply viewed in terms of principles of descent and schemes of classification, but in terms of the control and allocation of resources and formation of segmented descent groups (Ebrey and Watson 1986, 1–2). Freedman's framework, which itself borrowed concepts from E. E. Evans-Pritchard's ([1940] 1969) and Meyer Fortes's (1945, 1953) work on segmented descent groups in Africa, so strongly influenced later research that it became, in Watson's words, a "lineage paradigm."[5]

Lineage in southeastern China, as Freedman viewed it, is a corporate group that both celebrates its group solidarity through common property ownership and differentiates its members according to wealth. To quote Emily Ahern: "The resulting segments are ritually demarcated by worship of the ancestor in whose name the corporate estate was established, perhaps in a hall built for that purpose; they are economically demarcated by the share that the members of each segment may have in the income from the corporate property" (1976, 1). A main contribution of Freedman's model is in showing how the mechanism of segmentation within the group is a dynamic response to a larger social context shaped by economic and political differentiation and domination. A key element in this analysis is its focus on property and its ownership. As Burton Pasternak writes, "Freedman's generalised lineage model derives from the nature of Chinese property relations. The lineage does not exist if it is not incorporated. Internal segmentation too requires the establishment of corporate foci" (1985a, 190).

Lineage organization in North China does not fit this model.[6] As Myron Cohen argues, "Although many elements of northern lineage organisation are found also in the southeast and elsewhere in China, they are combined in the north into a distinctive arrangement of cemeteries, graves, ancestral scrolls, ancestral tablets, and corporate groups linked to a characteristic annual ritual cycle" (1990, 509). In contrast to the common ownership found in southeastern China, in the north "the fixed genealogical mode most readily served as an expression of solidarity in the absence of significant corporate holdings" (510). The annual cycle of genealogical activities involves a series of activities that celebrate an "associational solidarity"; its four major elements are performances centered on graves, the establishment of tablets and scrolls, the celebration of New Year, and the commemoration of Qingming.[7]

The fiercest attack on Freedman's paradigm comes from some Taiwanese scholars. For instance, Allen Chun argues that Freedman did nothing but use structural functionalism to systematize a view of Chinese kinship relying on earlier works by certain native Chinese scholars.[8] Freedman provided no empirical evidence to support his argument, and his conclusions are basically wrong because he failed to understand that "Chinese kinship is based on native concepts whose fundamental meanings must be understood in their proper linguistic and symbolic context and that the specific institutions within which these concepts are embedded are at the same time subject to the influence of sociopolitical and intellectual forces and therefore may change with the times" (Chun 1996, 432). Chun both favors linguistic-symbolic over structural-functional approaches and stresses that sensitivity to history is essential for effective analysis of Chinese kinship. According to Chun, Freedman's model is popular for two reasons. First, it feeds an illusion that Chinese society can and should be understood from the ground up. Freedman suggests that it is possible to grasp Chinese society at large, including its social structure and the political authority of the state, by making the household and family the basic units of analysis and scrutinizing everyday life.[9] Second, this model supports anthropologists' belief that agnatic and territorial organizations are based on the same rational principles. Thus the calculating man can be well situated in both family and lineage (Chun 1996, 430).

Chun's own account of the Chinese lineage organization covers the past three millennia, pointing to two transformations as crucial. The first was the transformation of the ancient system, during the Zhou dynasty if not earlier, of kingly succession based upon primogeniture, territorial sacrifice, and multiple lines of descent into a system of unilineal agnatic community and equal inheritance of land. The second was the revival of the ancient system by neo-Confucian scholars, who reconceptualized ancestor worship in their attempt to promote localized lineage as a pattern of social organization (Chun 1996, 432–37). Against Freedman's model, Chun argues that the creation of localized lineage reflects not only large historical forces but also a deliberate top-down process by the elite as they reworked the native categories of kinship.

While Chun's general statement that Chinese kinship has to be understood in its own historical and cultural context is entirely unobjectionable, his particular remedy seems inadequate. One commentator rightly points out that Chun's model has two major problems: "The first is the paradoxical ahistoricity of his 'historical' account, which ranges freely across Chinese history since the Ch'in and beyond the seizes on textual quotations which he believes accumulate into a theory of the development of the lineage. In doing this he reproduces the very problem to be found in Freedman's thesis—its lack of historical and geographical specificity. . . . The second problem is precisely that Chun's approach is textual. . . . Fascinating as his historical account is, it tells us nothing about practice" (Clammer 1996, 441).

Some of Chun's points had been argued earlier by other Taiwanese scholars. For example, Q. Chen (1985), trying to launch a radical critique of the Western theory of Chinese kinship, claims a distinction between genealogical aspects of descent principles and functional aspects of group activities.[10] According to Chen, it is a mistake to take *jia, zu,* and *zong* (commonly translated "family," "lineage," and "clan") as core concepts in explaining Chinese kinship. He sees the emphasis on these terms as being rooted in Western anthropological premises rather than the reality of Chinese society. Chen stresses instead a genealogical aspect of descent, a "pure genealogical mentality" (*chun xipu linian*), that cannot be reduced to its functions.[11] This should be the starting point of analysis, he insists.[12]

My objection to this critique of Freedman's paradigm is twofold. First, despite Chun's putative focus on the interplay between culture, ideology, and practice, there is little space in his account for a discussion of the *practice* of kinship. The term "practice" indicates the very process in and through which a sense of self or a form of subject is produced. This process, never complete, is always caught in a moment of becoming. In my writing "practice" thus contrasts with "ideology," which always represents a completed articulation of a particular social consciousness, whether officially promulgated or not. Second, rather than objecting to Freedman's model as a "bottom-up" approach, I argue that Freedman and his followers have not gone far enough in this direction, precisely because they often move too quickly from describing a "calculating man" to generalizing about the social structure as a totality. Moreover, Freedman's bottom-up approach and Chun's top-down approach take the same epistemological stance: both are concerned with kinship as an ideological system. This sense of kinship is defined not by the people analyzed but by the analyzers, and thus reflects what Pierre Bourdieu calls "intellectualism." "Intellectualism," he explains, "is inscribed in the fact of introducing into the object the intellectual relation to the object, of substituting the observer's relation to practice for the practical relation to practice" (1990, 34). What seems to be urgent, therefore, is to provide an account of kinship in practice, from the perspective of the practitioner—perceived as a set of strategies rather than as an ideology.

Zijiawu: A Material Sense of Self

A crucial notion of kinship, *zijiawu*, was brought to my awareness by a mistake I made in the beginning of my fieldwork. I frequently referred to members of this community as others' "relatives" (*qinqi*). After a while, some villagers became impatient: "What the hell are you talking about?! We are not relatives, we are *zijiawu!*" Embarrassed, I began to realize a basic classification of social relationship: relatives are only those connected by affinal (or marriage) ties; *zijiawu* are those connected by descent.

The term *zijiawu* consists of three Chinese characters: *zi, jia,* and *wu*. The character *zi* can be translated as "my"; *jia* is often translated as "family." The key word *wu*, which literally means "room" or "house," denotes brotherhood. Together, they denote "my family brothers"—a central concept of practical kinship.[13] The core of the idea of kinship in Zhaojiahe is the notion of *wu*. Its possible meanings vary, but it essentially stands for both the house and the domestic group at once.[14] The domestic group is often defined as "the basic unit of production, consumption, and political authority, whose members normally reside together and share a common budget for everyday expenses" (Ebrey and Watson 1986, 5). *Wu* indicates such a group.[15]

A crucial difference between the Chinese term *jia* and the English term "family" has long been noted. Martin Yang pointed out that there was no overt differentiation in meaning between "family" and "home" in Chinese. As he noted, "The same word [*jia*] stands for both—people living under the same roof, for a group of people is not a family unless they have a permanent house, one which they own" (M. C. Yang 1945, 46). The notion of *jia* indeed implies a sense of home—that is, a shelter that the family members share. Without such a place, these individuals can hardly be seen as constituting a family. Nevertheless, it does not follow from there being no differentiation in meaning between "family" and "home" in Chinese that there is no difference between "home" and "house." In the second pair, the English distinction holds: the latter term invokes an image of the concrete, material form of the building, whereas the former tends to convey an image of a place or a shelter in its abstract sense. This is to say that the implicit image associated with *wu* is different from that linked to *jia*.

Let us consider *wu* and *jia* as "metaphors" in which a sense of self is accommodated.[16] Roman Jakobson's celebrated discussion of the distinction between metaphoric and metonymic processes in language can be of some use here.[17] A metaphor is based on some *likeness* between a word and its substitute—for example, "culture is a text"—while a metonym is based on an *association* between the words.[18] For instance, for "interpretive anthropology" we can metonymically substitute "Clifford Geertz," the name of one of its main advocates. Jakobson sees metaphor and metonymy as two basic modes that characterize language's binary process of selection and combination. According to Saussurean structural linguistics, meaning is produced by two fundamental linguistic actions: a "horizontal" movement, by which words are combined in a sequence, and a "vertical" movement, by which particular words are selected from the available storehouse of vocabulary. The mode of operation in the first is metonymic; in the second, metaphoric. The opposition between metaphor and metonymy may be seen as corresponding to the very fundamental opposition between synchronic and diachronic modes of language. Therefore, we have the following (adapted from Hawkes 1977, 78):[19]

Selective/Paradigmatic Synchronic Dimension
(Metaphor)

Combinative/Syntagmatic Diachronic
Dimension (Metonymy)

This interaction is played out on a large scale; as Robert Scholes points out, "Jakobson finds this distinction between metaphoric and metonymic processes in language discernible not only at the level of individual expressions in language but at the level of larger patterns of discourse as well" (1982, 20).[20]

In a sense, both *jia* and *wu* may be said to be at once metaphoric and metonymic, for each uses the shelter in which the members of a family reside to refer to a domestic group. But the former is so construed that the similarity between who one is and where one lives is emphasized—"home" is *like* "family"; the latter instead directly invokes an association between the concrete building and the people who live in it, drawing on a relationship of contiguity.[21] Brotherhood is an extension of the very fact of sharing a house. In other words, a sense of brotherhood derives from sharing a house rather than from any likeness between a house and a group of brothers.

Such a form of identity explicitly constitutes the meaning of self in the material arrangement of life, directly asserts that self bears a material form. Genealogy therefore does not trace ties that bind individuals consanguously but instead records a hierarchy of houses that enables people to understand who they are and how they are related. Genealogy for the villagers is less a way of tracing origins (a topic that they had little interest in talking about) than a confirmation of one's acceptance by a *wu*. Genealogy does not authenticate the origin but provides a "pedigree" of the houses. These houses are not ancestral halls but places in which people take shelter; they are considered to be property.

Those who are excluded from one's *wu* can only be relatives (*qinqi*), not *zijiawu*. Men are supposed to remain in the *wu* in which they were born; women are supposed to move between "houses" at marriage. Thus, affinal relations are "metaphoric" in that they are selected from a pool of possible individuals in other communities; "brothers," as males are commonly called, are instead in a relationship of a "metonymic" kind, because they are related by virtue of sharing the same house. Contiguity here has two consequences: first, each brother can only be defined in relation to another (i.e., their relationships are always interdependent and hierarchical); second, social distance is measured by the physical distance between different houses. Brothers of the same parents tend to be the closest neighbors; brothers of the same grandfather often take one section of a dwelling cluster; brothers of the same great-grandfather often fill an entire dwelling cluster; and so on. As a result of family divisions, there are many groups of brothers between the two poles of the descent—between the whole community as one big *zijiawu* and each *wu*. All the subgroups of brothers between these two poles are referred to as *zijiawu*, whose specific meaning thus always depends on the context in which the word is spoken.[22]

Such an idea of kinship is practiced under a number of social and economic constraints, difference in wealth being central among them. As Freedman suggested (1958, 19–32), among the powerful and rich members of a lineage a vertical sense of connection was more significant; whereas among the poor members the horizontal relationship, such as that between husband and wife, was of greater importance.[23]

It was within such a differentiated social space that the ideology of kinship was imposed; it was on the very elastic notion of *zijiawu* that the ideology of kinship was differentially received. In the pre-Communist era, an elite group in Zhaojiahe used to gather in the family temple, with its door firmly closed, to decide on official names for each member of this community, to compile the genealogy, and to determine the way in which ancestors were to be remembered. They were deeply concerned about the origin of their surname, taking seriously what was written in the preface of their genealogy: "for animals know their parents and a stream must have its genesis."[24]

The structure and ideology of the pre-Communist order of kinship were attacked and largely destroyed by the Maoist government, and after the land reform (1949–52) the influence of the elite group in this community was largely eliminated.[25] After only a short period of household production, the process of collectivization began. In the late 1950s the Great Leap Forward led to the establishment of the people's communes. Local farmers were called on to work outside their own communities, helping to construct public projects far away from their own interests and vision. In such a radical process of collectivization, what was left to differentiate one person from another was the house that each still possessed. Indeed, the house became the only marker of identity. A sense of self could be maintained only through the maintenance of the house, and thus the house was to become the only possible means of producing social distinction and difference. Precisely because collectivization allowed people little control over what they produced and consumed, the house was reinforced as a symbol of self.

In their economic structures, the Maoist and the traditional society show some striking similarities; both were characterized by a cellular structure of rural communities (see Donnithorne 1972). But collectivization weakened *zijiawu* as an organizing principle of practical kinship. The cellular structure was maintained from the outside; inside each rural community, contiguity in relationships was now confined to that between the house and its members. In other words, within the household, contiguous relationships were strengthened; beyond the household, relationships between agnatic kin were weakened. The house, rather than any larger kin groups, was to become the embodiment of self.

Yuanzi: Courtyard and Storage Economy

Anthropologists have long noticed that the Chinese family can play very different institutional roles. As Cohen notes, "the property-holding unit known in Chinese as the *chia*—which has generally been identified as the 'family'—was actually a kin group that could display a great deal of variation in residential arrangements as well as in the economic ties that bound its members together" (1970, 21).[26] Arthur Wolf and Chieh-shan Huang, drawing on material from rural Taiwan, make it clear that "what is usually taken to be one institution is in fact a composite of three institutions: the *ke,* the descent line, and what Margery Wolf calls 'the uterine family'" (1980, 57). The *ke* is the stove that signifies the domestic group. The descent line is mainly concerned with property relations, which are organized according to patrilineal principles. The "uterine family" is constituted by a circle of relationships based on those between mother and child.[27] In what follows, I reverse the logic of such arguments to show how these different aspects of "family" are embodied in the material arrangement of the house. In this region the house, or *wu,* means two things: *yuanzi* in general and *yao* in particular.

Yuanzi, the courtyard, signifies the property relations among brothers. *Yuanzi* is what one possesses. As an old man, whose brother had left the community, once said: "I do not know what I should do. I cannot leave this place, because my *yuanzi* is here. My brother has asked me several times to move to the city where he lives, but I cannot simply leave. What about my *yuanzi?* He can leave but I cannot. Our 'family property' (*yuanzi*) is here." When people refer to how much someone owns, they tend to speak in terms of how much his *yuanzi* is worth. Discussions of family divisions focus on how to divide a *yuanzi.*

A *yuanzi* is a compound consisting of a series of shelters, rooms, and other homestead structures. In northern rural Shaanxi, *yao* (i.e., cave dwellings), rooms, and various kinds of shelters are built in a circle around a central yard. Both in its spatial arrangement and its social functions, each *yuanzi* varies little from one household to another. The *yuanzi* of my host in Zhaojiahe, shared with his father's brother's widow, can serve as an example.[28] Wanbin and his wife, Yin'ai, have four adult children and two granddaughters. When I was there, his second son, Xincang, and Xincang's wife were living with Wanbin. This was perceived by other members of the community to be a good family, because Wanbin was said to be a hardworking farmer and Yin'ai a diligent wife. Wanbin himself admitted that his family was "moderately prosperous" (*bijiaohao*).

Wanbin's family occupies the lower part of the courtyard (see figure 1); his *yuanzi* consists of a big *yao*, two small *yao*, two rooms, a cow shed, an outside kitchen, a small backyard, a cart shelter, and a tool storage shed made of straw. The big *yao*, which was used as bedroom by Wanbin, his wife, his mother, and his granddaughters, was the family center, and I will discuss its interior arrangement in detail below. Important daily activities all took place there, including both cooking and eating, with all their symbolic meanings and functions in the organization of the family's cultural and social world. The *yao* was also the place for sewing and weaving, which used to be necessary extensions of agricultural production. Children, who often provided adult entertainment and recreation, were literally brought up in the *yao*. Visitors or guests must be received, entertained, and looked after in the *yao*. Above all, the *yao* was a storage room in which grain and other valuable goods were carefully kept.

Outside the big *yao* in Wanbin's *yuanzi* was a small kitchen for cooking in summer. Two small *yao* were built in 1978 when Xincang was preparing to get married. One of the small *yao* was Xincang and his wife's bedroom, and the other was used as a storage room; two bicycles, raw cotton in big plastic bags, several pieces of furniture, and chemical fertilizers were kept in it. Next to them was a cow shed, with two small rooms beside it. The left one was used, again, for storage (it held hoes, spades, other handy tools, and plastic bags); the other room was prepared for overnight guests. Two straw sheds next to the backyard held a cart and other heavy agricultural tools such as plows. In front of these sheds was a deep cellar, covered by a huge stone, in which fresh vegetables were stored. Dry straw for the cow was kept at the inner end of the backyard. Toilets, called *maozi* in the local dialect, were located farthest from the main *yao*.

An outsider easily sees that storage is one of the most important functions of a courtyard. Everything must be saved, and storing everything in good order lies at the heart of everyday production and consumption. For most peasants, collectivization had reduced their risks to survival and increased their security. Except for the years immediately fol-

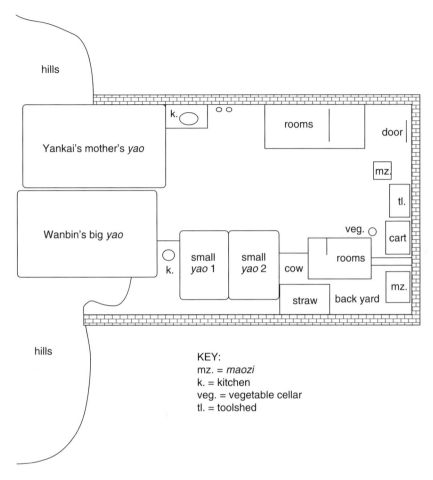

Figure 1. Wanbin's *yuanzi*.

lowing the Great Leap Forward, when a severe famine spread across the country, their basic needs were secured by the people's commune. Though some forms of economic inequality continued, income differences within each rural community were on average much less significant than before. As production was taken over by the collective and taken out of the individual's control, managing consumption became the focus of each family's attention. Individuals—or, more precisely, individual families—competed to manage their houses better. Using well what one received from the people's commune, rather than trying to find alternative sources of production within or outside the community, became an important way to accumulate social capital. The management of the courtyard can thus be seen as a means of competing for prestige and everyday power.

To be sure, storage may have been an important concern for people in this area before collectivization. But variations among households in income and ownership of property had been much greater then. Some owned land and others were simply tenants. Some families had horses and other means of production; others relied almost entirely on renting out their labor. In other words, several economies had existed side by side, and each family's strategies for success varied according to its economic condition. During the period of the people's commune, in contrast, the income of each household—which was distributed in the form of grain and other agricultural products—depended solely on the labor it contributed to the collective production. Under such conditions, the courtyard came to serve a greater symbolic function, taking the place of property ownership: to arrange what one was given by the collective in a good order was the only way of differentiating oneself from others (on the importance of a good courtyard in marriage negotiations, see chapter 3).

As a result, the *wu* was significantly strengthened as a basic social unit. Contrary to the intent of collectivization, property relations never ceased to function as an important aspect of family; they were intensified as the courtyard received new emphasis as a symbol of material relations. However, the ideological aspect of kinship, which had been largely maintained through the authority of and control by the elite (often called the "gentry class" in the anthropological literature on China), was largely eliminated. By taking over all the collective activities, the people's commune dominated social life outside the *wu;* at the same time, the commune reinforced the practical aspect of kinship by preserving the *wu* as a total unit of consumption.

Yao: Domestication of Self

The *yao*—the heart of a *yuanzi*—is shaped like a loaf of bread (see figure 2). The *yao* is always built into a cliff; only its "face" (*yao mianzi*) can be seen. There are three openings on the front side of a *yao:* a double door, a top window, and a main window. It is always at the inner-

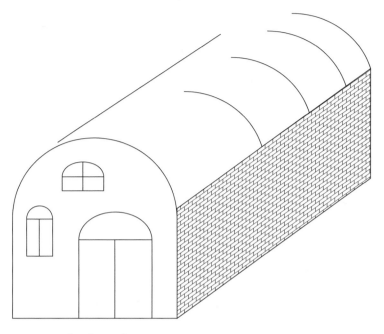

Figure 2. The shape of a *yao*.

most part of a *yuanzi*. Someone inside a *yao* can see the outside clearly; but because the inside is dark and the outside bright, someone outside cannot easily see in.

Significant social and cultural activities are all carried out inside the *yao*. The term is also employed in daily life to indicate a domestic group whose members share a common budget and reside together. The *yao* assumes a multiplicity of social and economic functions embracing all the possible needs of a family. Some people claimed that even if some natural disaster prevented further agricultural production, their families would still be able to survive for another year or two inside their own *yao*. Although the *yao* is only part of their world in a material sense, it is the primary symbol of a cosmological order by which social relations and cultural distinctions are maintained.

I will again look to my host for an example, again stressing that the same principles organize the interior space of all the houses in the region's rural communities. Wanbin's *yao* (figure 3) is about fifty square meters in area, roughly ten meters in length and five meters in width. Beside the door was a huge brick bed (called a *pei* in this

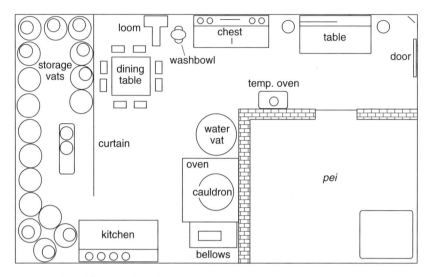

Figure 3. Wanbin's *yao:* interior arrangement.

region),[29] here as always built under the main window and occupying a large space in the *yao*. Wanbin's bed was big enough to accommodate seven or eight people at the same time, and this was by no means exceptional. A *pei* is often seventy to eighty centimeters high, with two small openings in its front to allow access to an internal heating system (figure 4), primarily fueled by wheat straw. A brick fence about fifty centimeters high forms a kind of wall around the bed, leaving only a small front indentation through which people get on and off.

A big brick oven was built next to the bed, and a large cauldron for daily cooking sat on the oven. The kitchen, a huge plank on which cooking equipment and ingredients were kept, was next to the oven. Opposite the oven was a square, short-legged table where daily meals were served for the male members of the family. A table and two chairs occupied the space opposite the bed. This was the main table of the house. A red chest for the storage of family valuables such as sweets, cloth, and cash was beside the main table. On the other side of the chest was a washbowl, set on a bench; next to the bowl was a loom. Further inside, a plastic curtain hid the inner third of the *yao*. Behind the curtain were huge vats for storing wheat and other kinds of grain. On top of the vats were jars for flour or steamed bread.

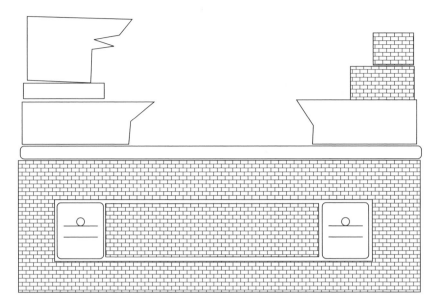

Figure 4. The front of a *pei*.

Bed : table :: female : male

The *yao* is divided along its width into two halves, signified respectively by the bed and the table (or tables). It is not necessary for any internal constituents to be oriented in a particular direction. There is no correspondence, for instance, between sunlight and the placement of bed or table.[30] For people in this region, what is important is to build a contrast *within* the house. The table must be in the same half as the door, but the door can be on either the right or the left side of the house. The bed half merges with the dark, curtained inner third of the interior space where grains and steamed bread are kept. One can interpret the bed half as "hidden," because it must not be visible through the door to someone outside. During the day, the double door is usually left open, thus allowing the table half to be joined with the outside— the open courtyard space. People at the table can look through the door and watch who is coming into the courtyard or what is happening outside it.

The bed, connected to the oven and next to the water vat, is the only place that can be heated when the weather turns cold. The bed half, warm and hidden, is the place for water, fire, and the oven; the place for cooking and spinning; the place for sleep, sexual intercourse, child-birth, and the training of children. The wedding rites will end when the bride "takes over" the bed and "occupies" it. A funeral starts with a ceremony to remove the dead person from the bed to the mourning hall. In short, the bed signifies the essential events of life. The opposite side of the house, the table half, is the place for recreation and entertainment, the place for receiving guests as well as hens and, occasionally, dogs. No animals are allowed to get onto the bed, but they are sometimes allowed to stay underneath the table. Hens sometimes come into a *yao*, but they are allowed only in the table half. Guests, like hens, are kept almost exclusively around the main table space, where they are offered cigarettes and tea.

To the eyes of an outsider, the warm, hidden bed half of the house appears to have the same relation to the unheated, open table half as female roles have to the male. The bed half, which women occupy, is the place of family intimacy; the table half, which men take up, is the place of public interaction. Discussions of village affairs are often carried out around the table, whereas bride price is usually negotiated on the bed or near the oven. During the day, the bed is used exclusively by women. Sexual behaviors are, both metaphorically and literally, confined to the bed. Furthermore, the bed is also the place where food is prepared. The steamed bread, the main daily source of nutrition, is always prepared on the bed. From the perspective of continuing the *yao*, making love and preparing food have the same function.

The sexual division of domestic space cannot be demonstrated more clearly than when a meal is being served. While eating, men are supposed to sit down at the table and not move from their seats; women are supposed to move around the bed, looking after the children and passing the food to the male members of the family. Women's tasks center within the house, and they are bound in a space that is domestic and intimate. During the years of the people's commune, however, women indeed went out of their houses and joined men in agricultural production; and in the vast rural areas of North China, they have continued to play important roles in agricultural production (Judd 1994). What was the effect of the wider social change on the sexual division of labor within each household? How can we understand the seeming persistence of the tendency to confine women to intimate, private space?[31]

The sexual division of labor within each house still exists because of a combination of traditional and revolutionary historical influences. Though the Maoist revolution shook the foundation of the ideology of kinship, it was simply destructive: it failed to deliver any alternative models for imagining change or guiding how the practice of kinship might be modified. Despite the authorities' radical claims of a revolution in social relations, people in this part of rural China found no other models of domestic life available during the Maoist years. One reason was that the material conditions of life remained "traditional." For instance, when communication channels between villages or townships (which had often been difficult) were almost completely blocked because local market systems were closed down (see Skinner 1964–65, 1985), the local people could dwell on nothing but what they had been used to. No one was allowed or willing to restore the traditional ideology of kinship, but in effect everyone contributed to the intensification of its practice as it became perhaps the only available local knowledge, implicit and inarticulable. The destruction of family temples did not automatically create a new vision of how to conduct everyday life, nor did improved housing conditions significantly alter the gendered space within each house. Local people insisted that the quality of building materials significantly improved during the Maoist revolution; but to an outsider, the style of building and the mode of life appeared to have changed strikingly little.

Inside : outside :: host : guest

Another social distinction embodied in the practice of domestic space is drawn between the inside (*li*) and the outside (*wai*). Determining who is *in* one circle and who is *outside* it has social significance in a wide range of cultural activities. For instance, invitations to a funeral must be sent in an order that makes the hierarchy of social relations clearly visible: the closer one is to the deceased, the earlier one should be informed of the event. People spent hours talking about how someone's relatives had refused to witness the removal of a body simply because the offended parties believed they should have been informed earlier than others. This is no minor matter: the dead cannot be removed from the bed to the mourning hall until all important relatives are present, and in the summer delaying a funeral can be disastrous.

Therefore, local people carefully decide the order in which messages about family events should be sent out, not only because the information itself is seen as social capital but also because social relationships are produced by this very choice to include some and exclude others.

The house (i.e., the *yao*) can be seen as divided along its length into three relatively equal parts. Nothing important or valuable is supposed to be kept in the outer third of the house, which is next to the door. A chest or two, usually placed opposite the oven and the water vat, often mark the middle third of the house. Behind a curtain lies the dark, private inner third of the house. The outer third of the house is the place for receiving acquaintances and neighbors. Both hosts and guests are careful about how they respectively offer and take up particular space in the house. If the visitor is female, she will be invited to stay on the bed, together with all other women in the house. Male visitors are invited to sit beside the table opposite the bed and are often offered cigarettes or tea. Neighbors are supposed to stay next to the door. If it is mealtime, some food may be passed to the visitor. Formal guests, such as local officials or important relatives from other communities, must at least be offered a formal meal, and therefore they are invited to sit down with the male family members in the middle zone of the house. No guests are allowed to enter the space behind the curtain.

Arranging the dining seats is part of domestic practice. There are three possible positions: facing the door, facing the curtain, and facing the walls. The "prime seat" (*zhuwei*), which faces the door (an inside position that allows one to look out), is supposed to be taken by the head of a family, the father. Because the seats facing the walls are positioned half inward and half outward, they are often left for guests. The most junior member of a family is supposed to choose the seat facing the curtain; it may also be given to an insignificant guest, such as a neighbor who visits frequently. Important or highly respected guests are sometimes invited to take the prime seat, thereby reversing the spatial relationship between guest and host. To allow an outsider to take an insider's position signifies that the guest is held in highest esteem.

The seating arrangement depends on the location of the door, which makes possible the clear differentiation of inside/insider and outside/outsider. There is but one door into a courtyard or a *yao*. The door into the walled courtyard is small, often too narrow for two people to use at the same time and too low for a tall person to walk through up-right. All the cultural and social meanings of such a door are displayed when the bride attempts to get into the bridegroom's house, the place for the wedding ceremony. The bride will be stopped in front of the door by a group of young people, and she literally has to fight her way into the courtyard (see chapter 6).

The spatial plan is closely associated with the particular shape of the house. It is difficult to imagine that people growing up and living in such structures would not be affected to some degree by the social and cultural values embedded in the ordering of daily space. It is even harder to imagine that people in this region would have failed to use—consciously or not—the forms with which they were familiar to assert control and authority. Consider the community headquarters, which was built during the Great Leap Forward as part of an unprecedented political agenda. Although the headquarters was intended to accommodate the needs of newly introduced economic collectivism, providing an office for the cadres as well as a place for political meetings and gatherings, its architecture was the same as that of an ordinary house, except its yard in front of a pair of *yao* was bigger. Various kinds of mass meetings were held there in the past, but the most popular and frequent were attended only by those who had been categorized as the poor and lower-middle-class peasants.[32] Members of this group, who formed a large majority of the residents, were supposed to enjoy new political and economic equality. But when they came into the headquarters, they were naturally differentiated according to the rules they were familiar with and constantly practiced in their own houses. The cadres usually occupied the seats around the table, facing outside; others, most of whom carried their own benches, took the outer third of the house space; and women sat on the bed. This is simply an unconscious application of the domestic spatial hierarchy to a new form of social organization.

A sketch of the fields of social relations, modeled on the division of domestic space, can sum up this discussion (see figure 5). It is organized by four oppositions: *zijiawu* versus relatives, men versus women, insider versus outsider, and host versus guest (perhaps a special case of insider versus outsider). One should note that these oppositions, which in fact are always overlapping, here are abstractions for the sake of analysis. In most cases, local people cannot provide a systematic explanation

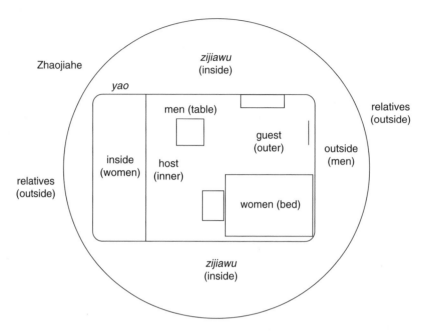

Figure 5. The fields of social relations.

for such social categories without referring to an actual situation. Because the ideology of kinship was incorporated in the practice of domestic space, it illustrates what we may call "practical ideology."

The observation that the fields of social relations in rural China are
organized according to a number of dualist assumptions is not new (e.g.,
see S. Potter and J. Potter 1990, 252–54). However, researchers seem
not to have noticed that these long-standing oppositions continued to be
used to conceptualize social relations even after the traditional ideology
of kinship was destroyed by the Maoist revolution. My argument is that
the practical aspects of traditional kinship were in fact strengthened by
the revolution, as the house became a stronger symbol of self. The
arrangement of domestic space, often accomplished without conscious
thought, allowed traditional elements to be combined with large-scale
societal changes. We witness a double trajectory: on the one hand, the
idea of *zijiawu* (my family brothers) as a key organizing principle of traditional kinship was damaged by collectivization; but on the other hand,
the very core of this principle, the idea of *wu*, was strengthened by the
establishment of the people's commune. In other words, a discrepancy

emerged between the organizing principles of the social body and those of the individual body. Although the social body was undergoing a radical transformation, the individual body continued to be contained within the space of the domestic, with little or no hope of breaking out. In the 1980s and 1990s, this discrepancy resulted in a marriage crisis.

The Marriage Crisis

Is there anything more frightening to a rural community than being no longer able to recruit brides from its conventional bride exchange circles? Is there anything more terrifying to a Chinese farmer than imagining a future without posterity? Is there anything more threatening to rural life than the loss of its ability to make allies through affinity? People in this community felt themselves in crisis in the early 1990s. After more than a decade of economic reforms, they began to face increasing difficulty in recruiting brides.[33]

It has been noted that a residential propinquity remains a precondition for mate selection in rural China.[34] In the case of Zhaojiahe, most brides were, or had been, recruited from its neighboring villages, within a radius of not more than a few kilometers. These neighboring communities can be divided into two main categories: *yuanshang* (those who live on the plateau) and *yuanxia* (those who live in the valley). The term *yuan* can be literally translated as "plateau," while *shang* and *xia* are "up" and "down," respectively. As a *yuanxia* community, people in Zhaojiahe blamed their trouble on the faster economic development in the *yuanshang* areas in the past two decades, which has made women in *yuanshang* reluctant to marry into the *yuanxia* communities.

Table 1 shows the numbers of brides recruited from different neighboring communities, which can be divided into two groups. The first eight listed—Qincheng, Yuanjiahe, Poti, Dangjiahe, Liujiahe, Zhaojiahe, Xipo, and Beimen—represent the core circle of bride recruitment. Social interaction and economic cooperation are most frequent and intensive among them (see map 6). The second group, made up of the remaining communities and provinces, is less significant to people in Zhaojiahe, in terms of marriage and all other social interactions. Bride recruitment depends on custom as well as propinquity. Brides are more likely to be recruited from places to which more daughters have already been sent.

TABLE 1. Bride Recruitment by Locality

	1940–49	1950–64	1965–79	1980–92	Total
Qincheng°	9	13	13	3	38
Yuanjiahe	3	3	13	10	29
Poti	2	4	11	5	22
Dangjiahe	2	2	9	4	17
Liujiahe	2	1	3	10	16
Zhaojiahe	0	0	2	12	14
Xipo°	0	1	3	4	8
Beimen	4	2	1	0	7
Lizhuang	0	1	1	3	5
Hejiazhuang°	1	2	2	0	5
Miaowa	3	2	0	0	5
Linchuan	1	1	2	0	4
Wancunxiang°	2	1	1	0	4
Henan†(p)	4	0	0	0	4
Leijiawa	0	1	1	1	3
Yangzhuang‡	0	0	1	2	3
Majiahe	0	1	1	0	2
Jiaoxicun°	1	0	1	0	2
Guchi°	0	1	0	1	2
Yangjiahe	0	0	1	1	2
Gansu†(p)	0	0	0	2	2
Zhuangdouxiang‡	0	0	2	0	2
Chengqiangdou‡	1	0	1	0	2
Linshang	0	0	1	1	2
Potizhuang	0	0	1	0	1
Sanhecun°	0	0	0	1	1
Baocheng	0	0	1	0	1
Guanjiahe‡	0	0	1	0	1
Liujiawa‡	0	1	0	0	1
Yulin†	1	0	0	0	1
Loujiawa‡	1	0	0	0	1
Zhaozhuang‡	0	0	0	1	1
Dali†	1	0	0	0	1

(table 1. continued)

	1940–49	1950–64	1965–79	1980–92	Total
Pucheng†	0	1	0	0	1
Yaodou‡	0	0	0	1	1
Shangdong†(p)	0	0	0	1	1
Dujiadian°	0	0	0	1	1
Lujingzhen°	1	0	0	0	1
Zhipao°	0	0	0	1	1

SOURCES: Household Registration (1990) made by the village accountant and household interviews that I conducted in 1991–92.
NOTES: Italics mark villages that are not in the Dayu Valley.
° villages that belong to Heyang county.
† villages or places that belong to other counties or provinces.
‡ villages that do not belong to Leijiawa Xiang (township) but belong to Chengcheng county.
(p): province.

All the communities of the first group are spread along the Dayu Valley; three of them—Qincheng, Poti, and Beimen—are located in *yuanshang.* Qincheng, a *yuanshang* community, has provided the most brides (thirty-eight) for men in Zhaojiahe, but the numbers have clearly been declining since 1980. Overall, the percentage of the *yuanshang* brides since 1980 has decreased (see table 2). Up to the mid-1960s, more brides came from Qincheng than any other community; but then the percentage started to decline from about 50 percent to a little more than 23 percent during the Cultural Revolution (1966–76). It is striking that during the period of economic reforms, the brides from Qincheng fell even more dramatically: to 6.3 percent. Poti, another *yuanshang* community, experienced an increase during the Cultural Revolution, when it provided one-fourth of all brides in Zhaojiahe, but a significant decline to 10.4 percent in the period of the economic reforms. Beimen, the last *yuanshang* community in this group, simply supplied no brides in the 1980s. The total percentage of brides recruited from these three *yuanshang* communities ranges from 68.2 percent (before 1949) to 73.1 percent (1950–64), 45.4 percent (1965–79), and finally 16.7 percent (1980–91).

The increasing difficulty of finding brides from the *yuanshang* areas

TABLE 2.   Bride Recruitment
from the Eight Major Villages (percentages)

	1940–49	1950–64	1965–79	1980–92	Total
Qincheng	9 (40.9)	13 (50.0)	13 (23.6)	3 (06.3)	38 (25.2)
Yuanjiahe	3 (13.6)	3 (11.5)	13 (23.6)	10 (20.8)	29 (19.2)
Poti	2 (09.1)	4 (15.4)	11 (20.0)	5 (10.4)	22 (14.6)
Dangjiahe	2 (09.1)	2 (07.7)	9 (16.4)	4 (08.3)	17 (11.3)
Liujiahe	2 (09.1)	1 (03.8)	3 (05.4)	10 (20.8)	16 (10.6)
Zhaojiahe	0	0	2 (03.6)	12 (25.0)	14 (09.3)
Xipo	0	1 (03.8)	3 (05.4)	4 (08.3)	8 (05.3)
Beimen	4 (18.2)	2 (07.7)	1 (01.8)	0	7 (04.6)
	22 (100.0)	26 (99.9)	55 (99.8)	48 (99.9)	151 (100.1)

SOURCES: Household Registration (1990) made by the village accountant and
household interviews that I conducted in 1991–92.
NOTES: Italics mark villages that are not in the Dayu Valley.
Because of rounding, percentages may total more or less than 100.0.

was said to be the reason for practicing endogamy. As tables 1 and 2
show, there was no bride recruited within Zhaojiahe before the mid-
1960s; two cases of intra-village marriages occurred in the late 1970s.
But a remarkable change took place in the 1980s: twelve brides—that
is, one-fourth of the total number recruited—came from within Zhaojiahe itself. The single-surname rule, which used to prohibit marriage
within the community, no longer held. I heard a number of reactions
to and interpretations of this change. Young people who had left the
community predicted that it would bring about genetic deterioration
and would ultimately destroy the village. Those who lived in Zhaojiahe often argued that the Marriage Law did not prohibit people of the
same surname from marrying each other, if the biological connection
was more than five generations ago. As Wanyou, an old man in his sixties, once said, "My daughter was the first one who married within the
village, but my daughter's father-in-law and I have long been 'out of
five generations.' The government says that people should not marry
within five generations, but we are not. We are out of five generations."[35] But in fact, few people knew exactly where they stood in the
village genealogy.

Wanyou lived in Dawa, a next-door neighbor of my host, Wanbin. Both Wanyou's second daughter and his granddaughter were married within Zhaojiahe. Wanyou's daughter, Fenlian, was married to Jianliang of Dongbang, another group of villagers located in the main cluster. Fenlian and Jianliang were classmates in high school and married in 1979. Wanyou explained, "After my son's death in 1974, there were not enough people in my house. My wife died a long time ago. There was always a shortage of hands in my house. Therefore, I talked to some go-betweens and told them my difficulties. I asked them to look out for my Fenlian. But my consideration was that I wanted to marry Fenlian nearby. In case I needed her help, I could reach her. This was the reason that I married Fenlian to Dongbang." Wanyou was very proud of himself. "I provided such a good example. Nowadays, there are more intra-village marriages. They all follow my suit. The girls from *yuanshang* do not want to come to our Zhaojiahe anymore. What can we do? We have to marry our daughters somehow. We cannot let our daughters stay home."

Wanyou's statement clearly refers to practical concerns regarding marriage. Such concerns are no longer regulated by a larger consensus outside the house. It is well known that in traditional China a mate was chosen by a family rather than by any larger groups of kin; but in the past the general rules of marriage, such as virilocal residence and village exogamy, were laid out by the lineage rather than by individual families. As already noted, the Maoist revolution eliminated the elite group that had provided local authority, thus clearing out an ideological space. Now a family can decide not simply on a particular mate but also on the rules of marriage themselves, which have become open to negotiation. This is the significance of the emergence of the conjugal family as a central social organization in post-Mao rural China (see, e.g., Yan 1996).

Wanyou's argument also echoes a general complaint heard among the people in Zhaojiahe: women from *yuanshang* areas have become unwilling to marry into *yuanxia* communities, mostly for economic reasons. Nevertheless, he does not explain why Zhao villagers have to choose partners within their own village instead of looking for partners in other *yuanxia* communities. Anthropologists often credit the Maoist revolution with making endogamy more acceptable in rural China. For example, in Chen village, a lineage community in Guangdong, a marriage revolution in the 1960s allowed Chen villagers to marry within their own community. Although before the land reform Chen villagers had been poorer than the members of their neighboring communities, they had little difficulty in recruiting brides: they could always find even poorer families whose daughters would be willing to marry into Chen village. But after every family was given a piece of land, the poor families in other communities were no longer poor in comparison; therefore their daughters became reluctant to be married into Chen village. This was the primary cause of village endogamy there (Chan, Madsen, and Unger 1992, 186–91).

Though Zhaojiahe could have suffered the same misfortune, it did not. Farmers in the *yuanxia* area were in fact more productive during the years of the people's commune, because they could use the river to irrigate parts of their lands. Because they were in the valley, in other words, *yuanxia* had better water resources than *yuanshang*—and at that time, water was the most crucial, if not the only, factor in determining agricultural production. Now, after two decades of economic reforms, the grounds of competition have shifted. With the introduction of the so-called socialist market economy, transportation and communication have become most important in securing economic health and advantage. Many explanations for the marriage crisis were based on a belief that the economic and social gap between *yuanshang* and *yuanxia* would inevitably increase. These accounts are obviously inadequate, because they do not explain why the villagers could not marry women from other *yuanxia* communities. To repeat myself: this change in choice of mate reflects a fundamental shift in the structure of the society, as the rules of the marriage game are no longer controlled exclusively by an independent group.

Such a change in marriage practice may cause confusion. A typical problem is that people could no longer address each other properly. As a mother of three daughters once told me, "I myself call Fenlian 'mother' (*niang*), because Fenlian's husband is my husband's father's brother. But my daughter calls her 'sister' (*jie*), because they were in school together. So, who am I? Is Fenlian my daughter? In that case, my husband should be my son, shouldn't he?" Under these conditions, the concept of *zijiawu* as a collective whole is impossible to maintain. Despite the villagers' extraordinary ability in managing the confusion at present, it has become impossible to arrange an ethical space from the perspective of *zijiawu* as a whole. In geographical terms, they are still recognized as being from Zhaojiahe; but an ethical order derived from the notion of *zijiawu* can no longer hold. The confusions in usage simply indicate that a new ethical or moral space is emerging. In the next chapter, we will examine how such confusions as these are negotiated in marriage, which mirrors such changes.

3

Marriage as a Mirror of Change

Central to my inquiry in this chapter is the question of cultural continuity and social change. In particular, I examine the effect of the Maoist
revolution on traditional cultural practices and institutions, as well as
the nature of recent changes introduced under the name of modernization.[1] Rural China in the past few decades has gone through an unusual path of development, comprising a bizarre mixture of "traditional,"
"revolutionary," and "modern" elements. At each moment, a distinct
combination of these elements revealed the constantly shifting economic
policies and political orientations of the state. The economic reforms
beginning in the late 1970s seem to have brought back a wide range of
traditional practices, such as ancestral celebrations and popular religious
rituals, that had been forbidden if not entirely obliterated by the Maoist
government. How can one understand such "inventions of tradition"?
Helen Siu asks, "Have traditional cultural assumptions survived the encounter with the Maoist revolution to come back in full circle in the
1980s? Or . . . [are] what we observe today mere fragments of tradition
reconstituted for coping with contemporary existence, which continues to be shaped by the priorities of the socialist state?" (1989, 1).

This chapter addresses such questions by examining marriage as a
process by which divergent historical influences are absorbed into
everyday practice. I focus on the changes in marriage practice as a
reflection of macrosocial transformation. In his analysis of the impact
of economic reforms on marriage in rural China, Stevan Harrell argues that the reforms have produced a double effect, and changes in
marriage practice should be expected to follow several paths (Harrell

1992; see also Davis and Harrell 1993). On the one hand, some changes may result in a return to traditional practices forbidden or strongly discouraged by the Maoist government, such as early marriage and high bride-price or dowry,[2] because people have been allowed greater freedom in making these choices since the late 1970s. On the other hand, as Harrell writes, "Other changes . . . might result from the opening up of economic opportunities that were never there before, either before or during the collectivist era" (1992, 323).[3] He suggests several hypotheses (323–25). First, age at marriage in rural China in general is expected to fall, because the government has abandoned the effort to induce people to get married late.[4] Moreover, as decollectivization has reduced the government's capability to monitor people's compliance with its policies, they may return to the pre-Communist practice.[5] Second, village endogamy should become less appealing in general, a change that is again a return to the pre-Communist norms. Third, uxorilocal marriage, which was encouraged by the state during the radical years of the Maoist revolution,[6] would decline in those areas where it was not traditionally a favored practice (where it had been favored, it would continue as before). Finally, as the government's "antifeudal" policies were softened, bride-price and dowry would increase.[7] "In particular," Harrell declares, "in areas where dowry declined with the elimination of competition for status based on property in the collective era, it will increase faster than bride-price. At the same time, the predicted direction of modern change would also be in the direction of higher bride-price and dowry, for the simple reason that families now have more surplus wealth than ever to invest in signs of social status" (1992, 325). An underlying assumption here is the acceptance of Jack Goody's argument (1973) that dowry rather than bride-price sustains social stratification.[8]

Harrell's predictions provide a useful outline of the current situation. But precisely how macrosocial transformation was incorporated into a unique set of marriage practices remains an open question. My focus in this chapter is on analyzing marriage to show how a unique moment of rural existence results from constantly shifting economic and political realities. We will examine how traditional, revolutionary, and modern elements of practice combine to constitute one moment of post-reform rural existence.

The Language of Marriage

In Zhaojiahe, unmarried young people do not discuss their future marriage. Even if they wish to, they are not able to do so, because the language of marriage belongs to the parents.[9] There are two key phrases that parents employ: *songxifu* and *mainuzi.* Each consists of three Chinese characters. *Xifu* means "wife"; *nuzi* is used for "daughter," though it literally means "girl." *Song* and *mai* are verbs. In its literal sense, *song* is "to send," but its deeper connotation is "to give" or "to provide";[10] *mai* is "to sell." Thus *songxifu* means "to provide a wife (for one's son)"; *mainuzi* means "to sell a daughter (to someone else)." When talking about a son's marrying, a villager might say, "My son is old enough (to be married), so I have to think about 'giving him a wife.'" Or: "Look at that terrible family; their son is already twenty-five, and they still cannot 'provide the son a wife.' What a shame!" Of their daughter, parents might say, "It is no problem to 'sell a daughter' nowadays, and many families want to 'sell their daughters' to urban residents." Or: "Look at that family, how clever they are! They 'sold their daughter' to another person and got twice as much as they had been promised previously by the first."

The verb "to marry" in Chinese is gendered. For instance, in Mandarin *jia* refers to the marriage of a woman;[11] *qu,* the marriage of a man. Both terms imply the virilocality of marriage: *jia* is "to marry out" (to depart from one's natal family); *qu* is to "marry in" (to allow the bride to move into one's family). Moreover, men and women can use these terms of themselves. A woman might say "Wo yao *jia* ren le" (I am going to get married); or a man might say "Wo yao *qu* xifu" (I want to marry). But the phrases used in Zhaojiahe are of a different kind. *Songxifu* and *mainuzi* cannot be used by and of oneself, for it makes no sense to say that one *provides* oneself a wife or *sells* oneself as a wife. Such language implies the involvement of a third party. Those who marry and those who control the language in which marriage is discussed are supposed to be separate. In such a manner, marriage is registered as a matter of importance to the family.[12]

The two verbs *song* and *mai* are commonly used in daily life. Someone who wishes to visit a relative will say, "We need to *send* some steamed bread to the relative" (*Gai gei wa* song *dian mo*). Steamed bread, called *mo* in the local dialect, is the main food of the region, and different types of *mo* are supposed to be exchanged among relatives on different social occasions. These exchanges are reciprocal in the strict sense of the word, though the exchange is usually not immediate but postponed. In talking about these visits it is necessary to employ the term *song*, which signifies that reciprocal relationship between relatives. Those who control the family economy and resources—that is, the parents—are in the position to talk either about sending steamed bread to relatives or about providing wives to their sons. These two activities are not rhetorically differentiated: thus "to send" or "provide" a wife to one's son suggests a reciprocal relationship between the two generations that imposes responsibilities on each.[13]

The verb *mai* indicates a special kind of transaction. For daily needs such as cooking oil, sugar, and so forth, people usually bargain with traveling traders who bring their goods to the village on either a bicycle or a donkey cart. On these occasions, people do not actually "buy" goods; instead, they engage in barter. Usually, people exchange wheat for what they need. This kind of transaction is described using the word *huan* (literally, "to exchange") and not the verb "to buy" (i.e., *mai* of the third tone) or "to sell" (i.e., *mai* of the fourth tone).[14] "Buying" and "selling" take place only outside the village—that is, outside one's own community. In other words, the expression "to sell" implies an action that transgresses communal boundaries. Thus, by extension, the phrase "to sell a daughter" implies that marriage should be conducted exogamously.

It is also common for people to discuss their children's marriage as a *renwu* (literally, "task"), implying that it is a responsibility rather than something they have chosen. *Renwu* was a very popular term during the Maoist era: anything assigned by the party or the collective used to be called a *renwu*. To be given such a *renwu* was thought of as an honor, because it indicated trust. My host in Dawa said to me many times: "To have your children get married is a primary and most important task (*zhongyao renwu*). To fulfill this task is a responsibility of the parents." The word "task" still assumes a third party involved in one's marriage, but it no longer presupposes a gender difference. Either a daughter's or a son's marriage can be discussed in these terms. This may suggest that a certain degree of gender equality, introduced by the Maoist revolution, has been insinuated into everyday consciousness through linguistic markers.[15] However, an important point remains unchanged: one's own marriage is still a concern of others—one's family, one's parents.

The Marriage Process

Marriage is conceived of not as a relationship between two persons but as a process of negotiation and dialogue between two families. People in the region generally recognize four stages in this process: *tanhua* (to have a word), *kanwu* (to look at your courtyard), *dinghun* (to be engaged), and *guoshi* (to celebrate the wedding). Each of these four phrases consists of two Chinese characters, a verb followed by a noun. When a marriage negotiation took place, people did not discuss the attributes or status of the potential bride or groom; rather, they focused on how each stage of the marriage process should be properly prepared and carried out. Indeed, they seldom talked about whether a particular individual was married or not; instead, they spoke of how a marriage process had been arranged or was supposed to develop. The wedding ceremony was only one part of a long process. As the wife of my host, Yin'ai, said to me: "*Guoshi* is the very last thing that you have to consider. Every person has to go through four stages of marriage. The first is *tanhua*, and without it no one could move further. And then *kanwu*—if they do not like your courtyard, you will be out. *Dinghun* needs also to be looked after carefully. The last thing is the ceremony. Every step is important and must be very carefully executed."

Tanhua *(to have a word)*

After two families reach an initial agreement, their first step is to arrange, with the help of a matchmaker, for the potential couple to meet. This is called *tanhua*. Because a mate must be chosen from a few neighboring communities, the two may have seen each other before, although in most cases they have not had a chance to speak. *Tanhua* often takes place in the house of a third person, a relative or a friend. The couple will meet and talk to each other for a few hours, though they may not be left entirely alone.

This stage of the marriage process is an invention of the revolution. According to local people, *tanhua* was initiated in the late 1950s and later became a social norm for marriage. As an old man, who married in the late 1940s, once said to me, "This is a big change. I did not have the opportunity to see my wife's face until the wedding. In the past there was no way for a bridegroom to look at his bride before the night of wedding. Everything was arranged by your parents and the matchmaker. Now, it is different. Young people may *tanhua*. If they do not like each other, they can say 'no.'" But in fact young people hardly ever say "no" to the choices made by their parents. Theoretically, a marriage process can be terminated at any stage, but in Zhaojiahe in the decade before my visit, there was not a single report of a marriage process halting after *tanhua*. It appears to be less a consultation of the couple than a demonstration of the control of the parents. The difference is that the potential couple is given this opportunity to meet, which could not have been possible before the Communist revolution. Formally, *tanhua* is an innovation in marriage that allows the young people involved to consent to or refuse the match; but the control of the process remains traditional—parents, using a matchmaker, set up this meeting.

Tanhua is not a local term but one adopted from the official language; it became popular during the Cultural Revolution. Conversation of a political kind was particularly likely to be called *tanhua*. For instance, a cadre's talking to an ordinary person about possibly joining the party would be deemed a *tanhua*. An equivalent local term is *pianhan*, which may be translated as "chat." While both terms mean "to have a word together," *tanhua* clearly has an official connotation.

What do the potential couple talk about during *tanhua*? Those young people who had married fairly recently tended to trivialize its significance. Most confessed that when they were asked to sit together for a couple of hours, they didn't find much to talk about. A young wife told me: "There was nothing to say. I did not care. It was my parents who asked me to go, so I went. I did not have anything to say. We just sat there, looked at each other, and sometimes giggled. We knew each other, though we had not talked to each other before." The parents had a very different view: they saw *tanhua* as a stage in which the marriage transaction should be finalized.[16] As one mother said, "*Tanhua* is important, since the bride-price negotiated through the matchmaker has to be confirmed. You have to make it clear whether it is fine. This is the matter that one cannot afford to be unclear about. How can one say that there is nothing to be talked about during *tanhua*?" A revolutionary innovation is thus turned into a practical concern of the traditional authority in marriage—the parents.

Kanwu *(to look at your courtyard)*

The second stage involves a visit of the potential bride and her family to the bridegroom's house. It is believed that because the bride is to move into her husband's house after marriage, she should first inspect its quality. The word *wu* here refers to the courtyard, a sign of inheritance and property. An old man explained, "To look at your *wu* is to look at your courtyard; to look at the courtyard is to look at your economic condition. As soon as one gets into a person's courtyard, one will immediately sense whether this family's condition is tolerable or not."

On a chosen day after *tanhua*, the potential bride, her parents, and a whole army of relatives will visit the bridegroom's house; the group usually includes the bride's sisters, brothers, aunts, uncles, and grandparents. The bride's mother's brothers must also be present. Since this visit is the first formal contact between the two families, no important relatives on the bride's side should be neglected. One-third of the brideprice, previously negotiated, is passed from the bridegroom's side to the bride's side at this stage. A formal meal is required to entertain the guests. Although this meal is not comparable to the engagement banquet or the wedding feast, it usually involves the hiring of cooks and is a considerable expense. On the bridegroom's side, connections outside his immediate family are not necessarily included. It is not unusual for a marriage process to break off at this stage. When this happens, the matchmaker is often to blame, for it is he or she who failed to provide correct information.

Kanwu is also an invention of the revolution, but at the same time it reinforces a traditional ideology that marriage is concerned more with material security than with romance or love. As we saw in chapter 2, the house became the sole marker of social and economic distinction and difference when the economy underwent collectivization. Within a system that was designed to eliminate economic differentiation, *kanwu* functioned as a means of maintaining social stratification.

Dinghun *(to be engaged)*

An engagement banquet must be held by the bridegroom's family in order to announce the marriage. Everyone on the bridegroom's side, *zijiawu* or relatives, is invited to this event. At this time, another third of the previously agreed bride-price must be handed over to the bride's family. After the banquet, affinity between the two families will be formally established. Once the couple is engaged, the bridegroom and his father will regularly visit the bride's house on every significant social occasion. On each visit, gifts are supposed to be presented to the bride's family, including at least one piece of cloth (though ready-made dresses are preferred these days). The potential bride will also make trips to her future husband's house. This is also the time that the young couple become acquainted. Some old people complained about these visits, alleging that the young people sometimes had sex. When asked what was wrong with sex before marriage, villagers often replied that it would make the marriage negotiation more complicated. For instance, a father of two children once said to me, "If the girl sleeps with the boy, her family will have no way to retaliate when the boy's side does not keep the promise of gifts. You sleep with them, you belong to them."

Guoshi *(to celebrate the wedding)*

A week or so before the wedding ceremony, the bridegroom and his parents must make a trip to the county's main town to purchase new clothes for the bride. Because of the market-oriented economic reforms of the 1980s and 1990s, the significance of this shopping trip has increased tremendously. An agreement about the quality and quantity of the purchases must be made in advance, but it is not always adhered to.[17] One of the major complaints I heard was that the bride often took this final chance at gaining material advantages to claim more than what the two families had initially agreed. Disputes over the last significant spending before the wedding often threaten the entire process.

Changes in this arrangement, which began in the early 1980s, make it clear that local life has increasingly been penetrated by the new market economy. In the past few years, people in Zhaojiahe began to talk about shopping in bigger cities—possibly in Xi'an, the capital of the province, where fewer than half of the adult male villagers had ever been. The demands from the bride have also grown; some have turned their eyes to gold chains, watches, or other luxury items that previously had not been included in the shopping list. These developments have inevitably introduced modern elements into everyday consciousness; nevertheless, the form in which such elements have been introduced can be seen as traditional.

Before the wedding, the final third of the bride-price has to be handed over to the bride's family. In most cases the wedding ceremony will take place in the bridegroom's house, and a temporary dining hall will be installed in his courtyard. A wedding is a feast (see chapter 6). On the following day the bride's family (her parents and close relatives) will again be invited to a family banquet at the bridegroom's house. On the third day after the wedding the bride will return to her natal family for a visit. When she is brought back to her husband's house the next day, the marriage process is complete. The time required varies from one household to another, but the entire marriage process usually takes several years. In the case of Wanbin's second son and his wife, Xincang and Zunxia, it lasted more than five years.

Gift or Transaction?

Bride-price is called *li* in this part of China.[18] In general, *li* refers to the entire payment made by the bridegroom's to the bride's family; more specifically, it indicates that part made in cash. Some portion of bride-price must be cash, and I will call this specific sense of *li* "gift money." Gift money should not be spoken of openly. When the amount does need to be discussed, people employ a local category, "share" (*fen* in Chinese). One share of the gift money was 240 yuan. Thus instead of mentioning how much was to be paid for a bride, local people talked about how many shares of the gift money should be handed over, very politely and often in hushed voices.

Bride-price varies with each family's economic condition and social expectations. In the 1980s, it was common to provide one and a half shares of the gift money, or 360 yuan. In 1984 the annual per capita income of peasants in Chengcheng county was just under 180 yuan, and the figure increased to nearly 400 yuan in 1990. Given these figures, 360 yuan is clearly a considerable amount of money.[19] In the 1990s both inflation and economic growth have made it quite usual to present two or three shares of the gift money to the bride's family. And an additional cash payment is required—*liniangfei,* which literally means "the compensation for the bride's leaving her mother."[20] This, unlike bride-price, is due to the mother of the bride, to compensate her for the years that she struggled to bring up her daughter. In the early 1990s this payment was commonly 40 yuan.

In examining bride-price, one must look at more than the amount of money transferred from one family to another; the local categories through which bride-price can be negotiated are also important. And as bride-price increased in the 1990s, these categories of negotiation also began to change. A younger generation of parents are inclined to negotiate the payment in terms of *zhengshu*—that is, the entire amount, such as "five hundred" or "eight hundred."[21] As a young father once said to his friends, "It is too much trouble to count out shares of the gift money. I would just give them a *zhengshu.* Who will bother to talk about it in terms of how many shares!? Those old people, they have nothing to do, so they have time. I won't do that!"

Moreover, as part of bride-price a certain amount of clothing has to be prepared for the bride. In the early 1990s forty pieces were required to complete the process of marriage. What mattered was not the style of these items but the material from which they were made: specifically, whether the materials were bought at markets or made at home. Every local woman could spin and weave, and was capable of producing beautiful handmade cloth, but everyone preferred materials that were purchased. Different kinds of materials were ranked solely by price: the higher the price; the better the material. Social status is defined by one's purchasing ability. When I was in Zhaojiahe, wool and leather clothing were thought of as the best to wear because they were made of the most expensive materials; cotton cloth was thought to be least valuable, since every woman could produce it at home.[22]

And although the two families are supposed to cooperate in providing the new couple with the quilts and cotton-padded mattresses used as bedding, these too should be seen as part of bride-price. Responsibilities are strictly divided between the two families. The bride's family prepares the quilts—generally ten to twelve pieces—which are filled with cotton supplied by the bridegroom's family; the groom's family prepares the mattresses. This arrangement serves a symbolic function. Mattresses, coming from one's own *zijiawu* (i.e., one's own brothers), are what one lies and relies on; quilts from one's wife's family (i.e., from relatives), are the covering that "helps" keep one warm.

In Zhaojiahe, while bride-price is a central part of marriage negotiations, there are no formal terms for "dowry"—no formal local categories in which it can be discussed. Maurice Freedman has suggested that dowry in traditional Chinese society played a largely symbolic role, demonstrating the power of the bride's family rather than transferring a substantial amount of property (1966, 55; see also Croll 1981, 113).[23] The case of Zhaojiahe supports his argument in a different way: whatever the bride brings to the wedding ceremony is supposed to be exhibited and displayed in public.[24]

From the perspective of local people, the negotiation centers on how the bride's family should be "compensated"—how much the bridegroom's family should pay to the bride's family—because the very words for marriage imply that a daughter is "sold" to another family. As we have seen, marriage is implicitly a kind of transaction. Precisely because dowry is not identified as a necessary component of such a transaction, it can be used to demonstrate the power of the bride's family. One finds a great variation in dowry in this region. Local people also believe that generally the quantity and quality of dowry has increased since the early 1980s, indicating that the greater degree of economic differentiation resulting from economic reforms has introduced a greater degree of competition among brothers. Dowry has become one means of competing.

An examination of two dowries will help us see how far a family may go in demonstrating its power. First, consider Honglu, who joined the army in the late 1980s. In the winter of 1992, a few weeks before the Chinese New Year's Day, Honglu went back to Xipo, a village near Zhaojiahe, to visit his parents; he had some expectation of marrying a local girl (his wedding will be described in chapter 6). The couple had been engaged for three and half years, though they seldom saw each other. The economic circumstances of Honglu's family were ordinary. According to Honglu's relatives in Dawa, the bride's family was eager to get their daughter married so that they could use the cash to pay the medical bills of the bride's father. The bride brought to her wedding

a desk lamp

a pair of electroplated steel chairs with red leather covers

a pair of cabinets (approximately 110 × 60 × 50 cm)
a homemade wooden dressing table with a threefold mirror
eight quilts of different colors
about twenty sheets and other pieces of cloth

All these items were publicly exhibited at her wedding, and no less public were the comments and discourse about them. This was considered a commonplace wedding. Some people pointed out that in spite of Honglu's being a soldier, the bride's parents did not have to prepare very much for their daughter, for she was far superior to Honglu in appearance.

Second, consider Hongxia, who had recently begun to work in a township clinic as a nurse. Her wedding took place on 1 May 1992. The bridegroom was a bank security guard in the town. Because Hongxia's parents thought that their daughter deserved someone better than a bank security guard, they insisted that the wedding feast be held in the town (rather than in the village, as everyone else would do). This arrangement could probably earn Hongxia's family some "face," but it also produced pressure on her parents to provide her an extensive dowry. That dowry included

a dining table with electroplated steel legs
a pair of electroplated steel chairs with red leather covers
a pair of homemade sofas, with dark leather covers
a large homemade wardrobe with golden rim
nine quilts
a huge modern thermos flask
a large mirror decorated with a cat (for Hongxia's use only)
a tea set
six pairs of handmade cloth shoes with beautifully embroidered flow-
    ers and birds on them (for Hongxia's use only)
a pair of embroidered pillowcases, one in red and the other in green
a pair of homemade aprons, one in pink and the other in blue (for
    Hongxia's use only)
a pair of quilted jackets with flowers, one in red and the other in green
    (for Hongxia's use only)

a pair of cotton-padded trousers (for Hongxia's use only)
four embroidered pillow covers
a dozen different kinds of both handmade and machine-made sheets
and cloth

A comparison of these two dowries is quite revealing. Clearly, the two differ significantly in quality and quantity. But more important is that in Hongxia's case, some items were prepared for her exclusive use; according to her mother and neighbors, her family thus indicated its wish to provide her protection and help. Although dowry can be employed to demonstrate wealth and power, people in Zhaojiahe tended to explain an unusual dowry in negative terms. The neighbors saw Hongxia's extravagant dowry as the result of her parents' insistence on having the feast in the town rather than in the bridegroom's village: the family had to provide more because they expected it to be seen by others in the town. Dowry is different from bride-price in that it always assumes publicity, given its symbolic function.

In recent years, those studying Chinese society have paid considerable attention to the question of gifts or the "art of social relationships"— a substitute for the Chinese term *guanxi*. It is hardly original to observe that people in Chinese society are bound not only by corporate relations but also by networks of personal connections.[25] Yunxiang Yan has pointed to a shift in the study of such social relationships from an earlier focus on them as a normative feature of the Chinese social or moral order to examining them as a means of pursuing individual interests (Yan 1996, 2–3). Some of the most recent scholarship on this subject seeks to link the study of Chinese social networks to the long-standing anthropological fascination with the idea of the gift (see M. M. Yang 1988, 1989, 1994; Yan 1996; Kipnis 1997). Therefore, the works of great anthropologists, including Bronislaw Malinowski, Marcel Mauss, Claude Lévi-Strauss, and Marshall Sahlins, have been revisited (see M. M. Yang 1989a, 38; Yan 1996, 4–6). The appeal to the idea of the gift is meant to lead us to the meaning of exchange. As Lévi-Strauss has insisted, a system of exchange always includes something more than what is actually exchanged. Such an orientation, which urges a more sophisticated understanding of what is going on than does a focus on the material, is no doubt valuable; but this scholarship tends wrongly to assume that the expression of social or cultural meaning is the true goal of any transaction. This is not the case with marriage negotiation in Zhaojiahe. Whatever cultural forms the marriage negotiation takes, the variations are simply means to secure an economic interest. In the process of marriage as discussed above, what we witness is a true material interest dressed up in gifts.

Matchmaking

Because material concerns, so central to the process of marriage, should not be discussed openly between the two families, a go-between is needed. Both *meiren* (matchmaker) and *zhong jianren* (go-between) are terms commonly employed in daily conversations, but the latter includes a wider range of negotiations (see chapter 5). All marriages are mediated by and through a matchmaker. Although there is no professional matchmaker in this community, certain individuals are thought of as better "go-betweens" than others. Anyone, whether a man or a woman, could become a matchmaker. Those who are fond of matchmaking are often proud of their negotiating tactics. I had the opportunity of getting to know an old man who was in his mid-sixties and was spoken of in this community as a good matchmaker. I talked to him several times about the last match he had made. The following reconstruction of its initial stage of negotiation is based on my field notes:

I am not bragging. I have made at least fourteen or fifteen matches in the past ten years, and all of them were successful. If you can't make a match, don't start it (*bucheng buweimei*). The problem is always the same: the bride's family wants more but the groom's family wishes to pay less. The last match I made was about a year ago, when my mother's sister's son asked me to look out for his daughter. I thought of Shanghe, whose son would be a good match. I went to see Shanghe one afternoon. We had chatted for a quite while before I asked, pretending that I did not know whether their son was engaged or not, "We have been here for a while; I forgot to ask you whether you've found someone for your son. Your child should be no less than eighteen, I assume?"

"Yeah, he is about eighteen. We have not yet found anyone for him. Our child is well-behaved. He listens to us."

"How could I not know *your* child? A very good child."

"I am afraid," Shanghe then said, "that you, my old brother, may have to have an eye for our child. If you know anyone suitable, please help us negotiate."

"I will have to do this for *our* child." A few minutes later: "I actually know a girl in Yangjiahe. Her family condition is quite good."

"Fine, my old brother, I am afraid that you will have to do this for us."

"I will, though only for your sake. If that girl's family agrees, I think we should first let our children meet each other and see what they have to say. And then we will talk about other things."

"That is fine."

I then went to see the girl's parents. They agreed. It was arranged that the two young people would meet in my house. After this I went to see Shanghe again.

"Our children seem to have no objection. If we carry on, how would you suggest we should do it?"

"My old brother, you know everything about us. Our family circumstances are not very good. Last year our child's grandfather died, as you know, and we had to spend a large amount of money for it. We also have to support two pupils. To support a pupil requires at least a thousand yuan a year."

"You listen to yourself! What you have said! How could I not know your condition?! I have already told this to their side. *Our* child is a good child. That is the most important thing. They understand. They do not want anything but a good child. Nevertheless, for our own sake, even if they did not ask for a cent, wouldn't we have to prepare something for the girl? They are 'selling' their daughter; we have to pay something for it."

"You are right. My old brother, we trust you. You go to talk to them."

Then I went to talk to the girl's mother.

"You know, these years, Shanghe has been pretty strapped for cash. But he has a big potential. Look at his two sons! Both are well educated and good at everything."

"To bring up a daughter is not easy. Just think about what I have done for her since she was born. Think about all the expenses and energy that I have spent on her!"

"Shanghe's boy is really good. I saw all the furniture he made for Shanghe; such an excellent carpenter he is!"

"To bring up a daughter nowadays is like burning your money. My energy is completely consumed by looking after these three girls in the family."

"Shanghe's boy is really good. He listens to his parents, whatever they tell him to do. I bet that he will listen to his wife in the future. It is really difficult to find anyone like that nowadays."

"Nowadays, everything is so expensive. Families without daughters may not feel it as we do. To bring up a daughter is such a hard task."

"How much would you like to ask for?"

"We would never ask more than what other people usually do. I will simply ask for the same amount as everybody else does. Last year when Weijun's daughter got married, they asked for four shares of gift money. That seems to be reasonable."

"Oh, give me a break! Or let me call you 'my great-grandmother'! What are you talking about? Where could we find four shares of gift money? Aren't you afraid of being laughed at by others? Don't you know that in Zhaojiahe, no one has ever demanded more than two shares?"

"Nonsense! Don't give me this shit! When Sanbao's daughter got married, hadn't they asked for more than that? Many have asked more than two shares. You won't tell me that you didn't know about them?"

"Shanghe is no Sanbao. What you want is too much. I am afraid that they will not be able to make it."

"Then, how much do you think that they could make?"

"The maximum is two and half shares, I think."

"Two and half shares are worth nothing. Nobody understands how much one has to do for a daughter. But what can I do if you say so? My heart is broken. I have to follow your suggestion, only because you are a nice person, my old brother."

I went back to talk to Shanghe.

"I came to tell you their demands. They really understand your situation and agree not to ask for too much. But *we* have to think about them, too. It is not easy to bring up a daughter nowadays. Don't you think so? If we were they, we would also want to sell our daughter for something. Don't you agree?"

"My old brother is right. We've got to prepare something for our child's marriage."

"Nowadays, inflation makes money less than half of its worth a few years ago. The value of money is not what it used to be. It is not uncommon to pay four shares of gift money for a marriage."

"That is a hell of a lot! My old brother, what are you suggesting? This is too much. I'm afraid I can't manage that. I have two pupils, you know?"

"Of course I know we can't do that. Our family condition is different. That is exactly what I told them. One should look for a good connection rather than money alone."

"That is a hell of a lot. I do not know how to manage that."

"Exactly. There is no way that we can manage that. This is what I told them. I explained to them, and they seemed to understand us."

"That is really a hell of a lot. Who could afford that?"

"That's right. That's why I told them that there is no way for us to pay this much. They then agreed to ask for three shares."

"That is still a hell of a lot. We have two pupils, you know?"

"Nowadays, money is not what it used to be, you know? One has to think about the troubles they've had in rearing a daughter, you know? Three shares is really not very much."

"That's still a hell of a lot. I have two pupils."

"I think what I'll do is argue, for your sake and only for your sake, for two and half shares. Less than that, and I'm afraid there won't be any marriage. What do you think? You can't get a daughter-in-law for free, can you?"

"I always listen to my old brother."

Thus ends the initial stage of a marriage negotiation. Throughout the whole process of marriage, such dialogues are constant, with little or no direct interaction between the two families concerned.

Negotiations of this sort display the art of social relationships, and their general characteristics are evident in the tactics employed by the matchmaker. First, anticipating what is going to be said or found acceptable is crucial to success: no response should surprise either party. Unexpected variation and genuine reluctance have no place here. A matchmaker can—and always will—tell how he or she has calculated in advance the reaction of the bride's parents, and hence knows the proper approach and response to employ. Second, exaggeration plays a key role. To allow room for compromise, the parties tend to begin by making extreme gestures or offers; exaggerated protestations and exclamations are routine, not surprising. It is all part of the performance. Third, indirection is the rule. Rather than arguing directly, one should always contradict gently, in such a way that the other is led to the point that one has anticipated. It would be shameful to argue openly about how much should be paid—although in fact the veil over these negotiations is very thin, and to an outside observer they may appear quite explicit.

Matchmaking is a practical and ethical necessity, but the reputation of matchmakers is far from respectable.[26] Very rude jokes about their character were often made in front of those known as being fond of the activity. Matchmakers were often portrayed as being gluttonous and greedy, because matchmaking allowed them to enjoy free meals in the households involved. But they themselves often complained about the difficulty of bringing two families together and denied that they derived any benefit from doing so. Wanyou, a neighbor of my host in Dawa, told me that he had many unpleasant memories of making matches. For instance, Wanyou's last match had gone very smoothly until the shopping trip. Arriving in town in the early morning, they visited every single shop there. The bride, accompanied by her parents and uncles, seemed to be overwhelmed by her desire to buy things. Eight hundred yuan, the sum that the two families had previously agreed would be spent, was gone before noon. Soon the bridegroom's father was out of money—but the bride still insisted on purchasing more. Embarrassed and humiliated, the two families began to argue in front of a supermarket. Instead of engaging in a direct fight, both sides blamed Wanyou for not preparing them well. The bride's parents threatened to terminate the marriage process—a possibility that terrified the bridegroom's family, who had paid a large amount to reach this stage. In the end, the bridegroom's father had to borrow money from a distant cousin who lived in the town so that they could continue the shopping trip. Twice the figure negotiated in the original agreement was spent. Whenever Wanyou talked about his own experience as a matchmaker, he complained and often sounded as if the process was wholly unappealing; but he never stopped acting as go-between whenever there was an opportunity to do so (see chapter 5).

Bachelorhood and Divorce

Everyone is supposed to get married. Not to marry is never seen as a choice: it is always viewed as a failure in life. To be a bachelor is not impossible, but being single never appears rational. In other words, being single may be possible, but no justification proposed for such a social status is considered acceptable.

In general, the term *shuoxiala* is employed in referring to those who are engaged in a process of marriage.[27] *Shuo* is "to talk"; *xia* literally means "down" but here should be translated as "arranged"; *la* is an auxiliary word expressing the tense of completion. Putting these three characters together indicates that a marriage has been arranged by words, though the literal translation is "having talked through (a process of marriage)." Anyone who "has talked through a marriage process" will be deemed married. In other words, marriage is not signified by one event, the wedding or the official registration; rather, it is an activity that requires communal recognition. Given this perspective, it may not be very useful to discuss the normal "age at marriage." Instead, we may ask: When is it appropriate to initiate the marriage process? The increasing difficulty in recruiting brides from neighboring communities explains the usual answer in Zhaojiahe: As early as possible. As one parent said to me, "What's the point of waiting, if sooner or later my son has to get married? As soon as my son graduates from school, I will begin to think about his marriage." It is generally believed that the parents should begin considering a child's marriage when he or she finishes primary education, which lasts between four and nine years. Because of the variation in the age at which schooling begins as well as in the length of schooling, the age of school graduates can range from fourteen to eighteen. In general, no one regards sixteen as too young to begin the process. It is only when a person might be thought old that his or her age will be mentioned. People would say, for example, "I am afraid that Junwu might be well over twenty-three, but he still has not managed to talk through a process. I am afraid that he will probably never be able to do so. He is dumb anyway. At this age he is still not in a marriage process."

In Zhaojiahe only one man in his thirties remained unmarried. His name was Zunxi, and I stayed with him for several weeks after leaving the house of my first host, Wanbin, in Dawa (see chapter 1). When Zunxi was sixteen, he went to Xi'an, the capital of the province, to join a construction team as a carpenter; he worked there for more than ten years. In 1987, after an accident at work that injured his back, he returned to Zhaojiahe to stay with his paralyzed mother. Zunxi had been introduced to many local girls while he was working in Xi'an, but he had rejected these offers. It was, and still is, a temptation for a local girl to marry someone in a city, and he could have chosen from among many possible brides. His neighbors gossiped that Zunxi had intended to marry a city girl but failed. Once he returned to the village, no one was interested any longer in making matches for Zunxi. His status as a bachelor was more or less accepted in this community, in part because he was thought of as an outsider, since he was not engaged in farming. He relied on a pension from the government.

Once I went with Zunxi to tour the county town, where we met a young woman who was distantly related to one of Zunxi's uncles. To my surprise, I heard him introducing himself as having two children and a wife in Xi'an. He told her that he lived in Zhaojiahe alone, looking after his mother. While conversing with the young woman, Zunxi winked at me; he later invited her to visit his mother a few days later. The night before she arrived, Zunxi came to my room; and looking serious, he asked me to help him keep his fiction of married life alive. The following day, the woman arrived; and even before she had said a word, Zunxi began retelling his story about his wife and two children in Xi'an, so convincingly that few could have doubted it.

I do not believe that Zunxi's performance can be explained simply in terms of his personality. Rather, his effort of creating a fiction of married life indicates the impossibility of narrating the truth of his being single: such a narrative is impossible because it is socially unaccept-able. The social norms place constraints not on what people actually do—an individual bachelor may be accepted—but on what they are *supposed* to do, which is in turn regulated by a socially determined for-mal set of language.

Wanyou was an old man in his sixties, and his first wife had died when he was twenty-seven. He later married a widow whose name was Min-fang, but they did not live together. Minfang was from another section of Zhaojiahe. When Minfang's first husband died in 1986, her children were still little. Wanyou helped Minfang with her agricultural work; in return Minfang helped Wanyou with his household chores, such as washing and sewing. This domestic cooperation brought some ethical problems. Their neighbors gossiped behind their backs, wondering how they were related, because the woman who washes a man's clothes must be his wife. Under such circumstances, they decided to get married. They therefore registered with the local government as a legal couple in 1990. But after marriage they continued to live separately, because one of Minfang's sons, Jinwu, had not yet entered into the marriage process. Minfang had to stay in her house in order to look after her son—that is, cooking for him and maintaining the house. Wanyou never challenged the assumption that Jinwu, who was in his mid-twenties, needed his mother's care. "When the boy comes back from the field, he has to have something to eat," Wanyou once told me, talking about his marriage. "His mother therefore has to stay with him. But he is stu-pid and may never find a bride. He is too old to find anyone now. Nowa-days, as early as fifteen or sixteen, boys have already begun talking through their marriage processes. Jinwu is already twenty-four but still a bachelor. What can you say about this? I myself tried to fix him up with a bride several times, but it never worked."

Remarrying is hardly a moral problem nowadays, but it is often a practical one, as Wanyou's case illustrates. At the same time, there is a very practical reason for remarriage: the necessity of a man and a woman to cooperate in daily life. Men were believed to be incapable of managing a house on their own, as Wanyou explained: "A man sim-ply cannot live by himself. How can he do those little jobs? I'm an ex-ception because I know how to cook. Household chores have to be done by women. Women can live by themselves. They know how to do every-thing." The women differed, for they believed that a woman could not survive without a man: even carrying water home from a well needed men's physical strength. The two views coincided in their agreement that men and women must live together in order to deal with the tasks of everyday life.

In this social context, one may understand why divorce is perceived as unreasonable and morally wrong: it destroys the material foundation of the cooperation on which a couple has come to rely. In the past ten years, there was only one such case in Zhaojiahe—Rongcai's divorce. Rongcai's father used to be a village doctor, and his mother had been the party secretary. Rongcai had been married for more than eight years, and his wife, Jinhua, came from a neighboring community, Yangjiahe. The couple had two small children. According to Rongcai's mother, Xiulian, the couple's relationship had been very good, and she blamed her daughter-in-law's parents for this family tragedy. Xiulian said that Jinhua's parents wanted her to remarry into another family, so that they could demand another bride-price. Encouraged by her parents, Jinhua began to create trouble within the family. Rongcai's mother and father had tried to help every way they could, but to no positive effect. Later, the conflict took such a terrible turn that Jinhua attempted to commit suicide by drowning herself in a well. But Xiulian was skeptical: "It was a fake suicide. She did not try to drown herself in that well. It must have been other people who helped her go down that well. When we took her out of it, her clothes were dry. How could anyone be drowned in a well without getting her shoes wet?"

Other people told a different story. Some said that the true reason for the discord was that Rongcai's mother treated her daughter-in-law very badly and always criticized Jinhua even when she was not feeling very well. Once when Jinhua was ill Xiulian did not believe it and claimed that her daughter-in-law was pretending to be sick to get a whole day of rest. Therefore, she asked not a doctor but an old woman, notorious for being "superstitious,"[28] to judge Jinhua's mental status. The old woman told Rongcai's mother that her daughter-in-law had no physical ailment; instead, her body was possessed by an evil spirit. In order to discharge the evil spirit, Jinhua should be beaten up. Xiulian followed this advice and whipped Jinhua. Some even said that she did so not to expel the spirit but to give her daughter-in-law a good lesson.

After several beatings, Jinhua left Rongcai for her natal family. Rongcai's mother and father immediately set off for Yangjiahe to inquire about their daughter-in-law. They were greeted with fists and feet at Yangjiahe. The face of Rongcai's mother was covered with blood when she returned, according to some witnesses. Rongcai's brother, Wangcai, who was said to be a hothead, saw his mother bleeding and immediately assembled a group of brothers and relatives. They marched to Yangjiahe the following day and beat up Jinhua's whole family. Violence between the two families continued for a few weeks, and finally Jinhua's parents proposed that the couple agree to divorce. Rongcai, supported by his parents, refused.

Jinhua filed a lawsuit against Rongcai, and the court, located in Leijiawai township, ruled in her favor. Rongcai's mother insisted that this decision was the result of Jinhua's parents' having bribed officials in the local government. While the case was in progress, Wangcai went to the court with his mother several times, and each time he insulted and fought with the judge. Indeed, Wangcai tried to beat up everyone in the court, and because of his abusive behavior he was held for two days by the local police. However, Wangcai believed that by his going to court his family was able to avoid further financial losses or even to reap some financial gains. For example, Jinhua's parents were required by the court to pay for the medical treatment of Xiulian's back pain, a pain with a history of some twenty years that she successfully argued was part of her injuries during the fight with Jinhua's parents.

Such cases further demonstrate that marriage does not concern only the husband and wife: it remains central to a group of kin and is constituted in a set of material relations of life. This may not seem to be a new observation in the study of Chinese society. But I am arguing two points. First, this group of kin, which in Zhaojiahe is defined by the *wu*, is no longer bound by any corporate qualities or ideological principles, such as Maurice Freedman ascribed to property relations in his analysis of lineage organization in southeastern China. Zhaojiahe is a community only in a demographic or a geographic sense; its ethical and genealogical content has disappeared, largely as a result of the Maoist revolution. In a sense, it is a community without communal sentiments and obligations. Or as people in Zhaojiahe often commented: "We are now a plate of sand." Second, the past two decades of economic reforms have legitimated the emergence of an implicitly materialistic conception of society—a conception that may have always been rooted in the minds of the poor but has become so dominant that no other forms of ideology can take hold.

More generally, I am using the process of marriage to argue that different elements of everyday practice informed by and derived from the macro sources of historical influence—that is, the traditional, the revolutionary, and the modern—are so combining as to form a unique moment of social existence. Although analysis can identify the major historical forces that determine the shape of rural life, the combinations of these influences are specific to local or regional conditions. In the case of northern rural Shaanxi we find that traditional elements, such as those embedded in the patriarchal language of marriage, continue to shape how revolutionary or modern sentiments can be expressed. That young people were allowed to meet before their weddings was supposed to create a revolution in marriage, but the innovation had to be wrapped in traditional authority and rhetoric.[29] This pattern may not have held everywhere in China, but it illustrates one way that the macro sources of historical influence combine to shape everyday practice. Here the Maoist revolution removed the content of tradition, such as ancestor worship or family temples, much more thoroughly than the form of tradition, which, as we have clearly seen, is embedded in the everyday language in ways both conscious and unconscious.

We have also noted that the language of the revolution, including terms such as *tanhua* and *renwu*, began to be necessary to communication. As the discussion of the four stages of marriage shows, it was mixed with the traditional vocabulary; but this mixture of revolutionary and traditional linguistic codes and units did not develop fully until the economic reforms were instituted, when another set of vocabulary—the modern—came into daily life. Two decades of these reforms, which have advanced the process of modernization, made it possible for these historical influences to combine more freely. That freedom has allowed local people in some regions to return to practices that are more conventional, both in linguistic and nonlinguistic terms, particularly in areas where economic or industrial development is relatively weak. The part of rural Shaanxi where I worked is one such "weak" area, and residents have a strong sense of returning to pre-Maoist practices. However, their sense—as well as the term "returning" itself—is misleading: what appears to be "traditional" has taken on revolutionary and modern features.

To an outsider, what people do in Zhaojiahe may appear to be traditional, but in fact these traditions are often relatively new inventions that incorporate many different social and cultural elements. Anyone seriously attempting to understand twentieth-century China, it seems to me, must grasp a particular moment of history by analyzing a particular combination of traditional, revolutionary, and modern elements. And as I write, the relations among these three sources of historical influence are less stable than ever before in the history of the People's Republic.

4

Meaning and Eating

The previous two chapters have dealt with practices of kinship and marriage in everyday life as shaped by historical influences. In other words, we have examined how macrosocial transformation is incorporated and absorbed into everyday practice to form a unique moment of existence in northern rural Shaanxi. This chapter will turn to the internal structure of cultural life, as exemplified in the meaning of eating, from which the logic of social action and its explanation are derived.

Echoing an anthropologist's earlier assertion that "kinship is to anthropology what . . . the nude is to art," one may say that the nude is to art what food is to the local people in this region.[1] Food, as well as its preparation and consumption, serves as a system of signification in and through which meanings of social action are construed and fields of social relations constituted.[2] I use the term "a system of signification" to indicate that food in this part of rural China is at once a social institution and a system of values.[3] In viewing food as a social institution, I mean to stress that it constitutes a form of collective representation: that is, something beyond the domain of individual choice. Day by day, occasion by occasion, individuals must learn rules and conventions of preparing and presenting food in order to communicate with others and to become full members of the community. As a social institution, food—like language—is a kind of collective contract that one must accept in its entirety if one wishes to survive in the community it dominates. As a system of values, food is made of a certain number of units or elements: on different social occasions, we find different types of food or different codes of behavior associated with food and eating. Each of these elements is equivalent to either a cultural event, an agricultural activity, or a category of social relationships. In this chapter I provide a systematic account of this system of values in food, with particular reference to the conceptualization of time.

The Circle of Livelihood

Has life changed in Zhaojiahe? This simple question cannot be answered without considering from whose perspective it is raised, and under what circumstances. Women were more inclined than men to say that there has been a great change in their life. As Wanbin's mother, who was in her late sixties, once said, "Nowadays, everything is very different from the past. When I was married and came here, few households could afford to have brick houses, but look at everyone's house today: all of them are made of bricks. Nowadays, everyone is a god (*shen*)."[4] In the past, their houses were simply dug into hills; today, these cave dwellings have brick vaults to support them. Women frequently referred to the difficulties they used to have when they cooked: mud, dropping from the ceiling, often fell directly into the soup that they were preparing. When men did speak about improvements introduced by the Maoist revolution, they most often talked of changes in how wheat flour was processed. Up to the mid-1960s, flour processing had required either animal or human labor. They had primarily used a specially designed millstone, which was extremely heavy; the work was very strenuous. Most old men had done it, and they often said, "That was not a piece of work for humans!" Water mills were introduced soon after the Great Leap Forward (1958), but it was not until 1989, when electricity was made available to this community, that wheat processing became easy and simple.[5]

Thus the local people conceive of and talk about change in ways always linked to food and cooking. This is not to say that no other kind of social and cultural activity was taken as essential or necessary; but food and its metaphors lay out the very foundation of a cosmos, according to which other activities and relations are understood. Indeed, much of social life in this part of rural Shaanxi is organized around the production of wheat and the consumption of steamed bread.

Figure 6, which outlines the circle of livelihood, shows three main flows of activities that are at once productive and consumptive. The first and most important is the planting of wheat, whose different parts

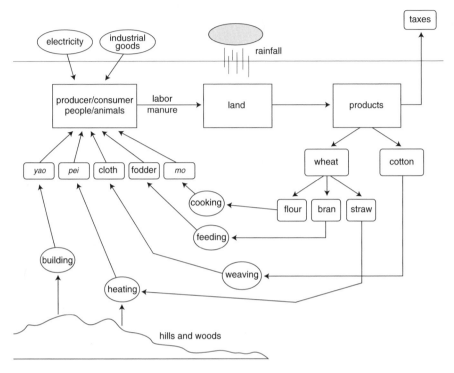

Figure 6. The circle of livelihood.

are used for different purposes in daily life. Besides making steamed bread from wheat flour, the villagers use bran—often together with other kinds of fodder—to feed draft animals such as cows, mules, donkeys, and so on. Wheat straw is the main source of energy for heating; it is burned to keep the family's bed warm in winter. Steamed bread, called *mo* in the local dialect, occupies a central place in the local system of signification. Contrary to the image of the Chinese meal as always characterized by variety in dishes and excess of amount (see Chang 1977, 6),[6] the types of food consumed in this area are very limited and simple. Most people in Zhaojiahe had never tasted any kind of fish in their life. Meat is reserved for festivals or for special occasions such as weddings and funerals.[7] However, simplicity in what is consumed does not mean that what food signifies must also be simple.

The second locus of activity is around cotton, which is the main economic crop. Women in this area were able to spin and weave, although the younger generation prefers clothes purchased from markets. For most people, the experience of buying ready-made clothes from the town was recent. In the early 1990s, women continued to weave and spin, producing cloth and making various kinds of sheets and coverings. Everyone's house contained a loom, often placed opposite the oven.

Third is the building of a house, the major activity of production least evident in the figure. The materials required are taken from the hills that surround the village, and everyone makes their own bricks. A visitor to the area, particularly in winter when there is little agricultural work, would see many kilns in operation and piles of bricks here and there. The 1990s was a decade of mass construction of new houses.

Figure 6 gives little indication of how this community is connected with the outside world. Indeed, to the local people that outside world seemed very distant, even after two decades of economic reforms. Though the flow of goods and of people in and out of the community has increased, travel is not easy. Methods of transportation have remained very primitive: the most popular, even in the 1990s, were the bicycle and the donkey cart. The bicycle, which is the only essential of daily life that could not be produced locally, became common during the years of the Cultural Revolution.[8] Each household has at least one (some have two or even three), and it has facilitated frequent travel to the county town, where the most important local market was located. No one in this community owned a motorcycle, but some had bought small tractors in recent years, to be used in place of draft animals.

What is missing in this sketch of livelihood is the increasing significance of "money" as a general social category in daily life, which has been greatly affected by expanding markets and the growth of the market economy since the late 1970s. Industrial goods must be purchased with money, not gained through barter. Although a younger generation has begun to consider other ways to earn money, most people in this part of rural Shaanxi continue to rely solely on agriculture for their livelihood; their only way of making money is to sell their agricultural products, whether wheat or cotton. In their lives, agriculture seems to bear the most fundamental meaning. From their perspective, figure 6 captures not what is desired but what is necessary for a particular form of life.[9]

That form of life has several essential characteristics. First, those in it remain predominantly subsistence farmers; about 90 percent of their wheat production is consumed by the growers themselves. Second, in this community communication is still face-to-face; there is no telephone or other modern device. Third, the mode of production is essentially circular. Men and animals both consume the wheat that they produce and nurture it with the waste from that wheat, their feces. Chemical fertilizers were rarely used before the 1980s. Fourth, land (the soil) is important not only in that it provides the fundamental means of production but also in that it supplies materials for constructing their housing.

Three Calendars

The flows of agricultural and social activities register in time on three calendars: the traditional lunar calendar (TLC), the traditional solar calendar (TSC), and the Western solar calendar (WSC). That several frameworks of reference of time or several modes of temporality coexist in rural Chinese communities is not a new discovery. For example, when Fei Xiaotong studied the rural community of Kaixiangong (Kaihsienkung) half a century ago, he found these three calendars already in use. As Fei demonstrated, the traditional lunar calendar "has its widest use in such situations as remembering sentimental events and making practical engagement. It serves as a system of names for the dates in the traditional social activities" (Fei 1939, 148). The traditional solar calendar, which is also called the section system (*jieqi*), was used for organizing agricultural activities. The Western solar calendar was mainly employed to schedule activities and events in such newly introduced institutions as the community school and factory.[10]

To a large extent, such an analysis remains valid for rural Shaanxi: that is, three flows of activities and events are supposed to be coordinated according to three modes of "time." Yet simply correlating a certain set of events with a mode of time does not demonstrate how these different calendrical systems or modes of time are *articulated* into a meaningful whole in practice. Table 3 provides a full view of a complete circle, or one year. Although the activities or events organized may differ greatly from one year to another, the internal structure of this multiple temporality is rather stable. The table lays out the particular year 1992. The middle of the table lists the three calendars, whose correspondence with one another will change annually to some extent. On the left side is a list of important agricultural activities typical of this area of rural Shaanxi in the 1990s; on the right side is a list of social events.

The crops grown vary little from one household to another.[11] In the early 1990s most households were not engaged in productive activities other than agriculture. Therefore, there is clearly a communal consensus in dividing an agricultural year into two parts: the busy versus the slack season. From Chunfen to Qiufen—that is, roughly from March/April to September/October—is the busy period of the agricultural year (*nongmang*). To mark out the summer harvest, two moments before and after the harvest are called Mangqian and Mangpa. Winter is a long holiday, the time for all social activities and events.

Such events may be classified into three main categories: family celebrations, festivals, and market days. Of family celebrations, weddings and funerals are the most significant, both in their scale and social importance. Most weddings take place in the first month of the lunar calendar, which is the Chinese New Year period. Even funerals tend to be organized during this time of the year. If a person dies in summer when everyone is busy, he or she is usually buried in a very simple manner; the formal funeral, a series of related activities in remembrance of the deceased, is prepared only later, during the New Year period. That most important time in social life lasts more than four weeks; it begins on the fifth of the twelfth month of the previous lunar year and continues until at least the fifteenth of the first month of the new lunar year.

Except for the Chinese New Year, the boundary between a festival and a market day is not clear. In his classic study of "marketing and social structure in rural China," W. G. Skinner (1964–65) has shown that rural residents are members not only of their own communities but also of a larger circle of local and regional markets. In this part of rural Shaanxi, there are two kinds of "markets," which may parallel what Skinner has called "the economic and social aspect of marketing." The first involves exchange within the boundary of a rural community. As mentioned in chapter 3, daily needs such as cooking oil, sugar, salt, plastic utensils, and so forth are usually obtained from traveling traders who carry their goods from one community to another. This sense of market is economic in nature, and the goods are most commonly acquired by exchange—for instance, wheat for sugar—rather than purchased

TABLE 3. Three Calendars

Agriculture			TSC	WSC
Fruit and veg.	Cotton	Wheat	Date	(Feb. 1992–Jan. 1993)
corn, sweet potatoes, hp		° ° ° °	Lichun: 4/2 Yushui: 19/2	February (0.4C°, dry)
wm, soybeans	cultivation	° ° °	Jingze: 5/3 Chunfen: 20/3	March (6.9C°, windy)
sowing ° ° ° ° ° ° ° °	sowing ° ° ° ° ° ° ° °	weeding ° ° ° ° ° ° ° °	Qingming: 4/4 Guyu: 20/4 Lixia: 5/5 Xiaoman: 21/5	April (13.2C°, windy and sunny) May (18.9C°, sunny)
° ° ° ° (reaping wm and hp) ° ° °	° ° ° ° blossoming ° ° °	reaping, husking, sun drying storing	Mangzhong: 5/6 Xiazhi: 21/6 Xiaoshu: 7/7 Dashu: 22/7	June (24.3C°, sunny) July (25.4C°, rainy)
° ° ° ° °	° ° ° ° °	deep cultivation	Liqiu: 7/8 Chushu: 23/8	August (24.6C°, rainy)
° ° reaping (corn and sweet potatoes) °	° ° ° ° ° reaping	shallow cultivation, sowing ° ° °	Bailu: 7/9 Qiufen: 23/9 Hanlu: 8/10 Shuangjiang: 23/10	September (18.2C°, sunny) October (12.8C°, cool)
		° ° ° ° °	Lidong: 7/11 Xiaoxue: 22/11	November (5.3C°, cool)
		° ° ° ° °	Daxue: 7/12 Dongzhi: 21/12	December (-1.2C°, dry)
		° ° ° ° °	Xiaohan: 5/1 Dahan: 20/1	January (-2.3C°, dry)

NOTES: TSC = Traditional Solar Calendar.
WSC = Western Solar Calendar.
TLC = Traditional Lunar Calendar.
wm = watermelon.

TABLE 3. Three Calendars

TLC	Social Activities
(the Western solar equivalents)	
I (4/2–3/3) II (4/3–2/4)	The first—Chinese New Year's Day; the New Year period: family gatherings and activities that concern the rememberance of ancestors; visiting neighbors; visits to relatives and the entertaining of guests; the fifth—Powu: dumplings are eaten; the fifteenth—Shiwu.
III (3/4–2/5)	The first: the community market day in Zhaojiahe; visits to relatives; Qingming: remembrance of ancestors; a series of market celebrations in the neighboring area.
IV (3/5–31/5)	Mangqian (literally, "before getting busy"): mothers visit and send steamed bread to daughters and vice versa.
V (1/6–29/6)	Mangpa (literally, "after being busy"): mothers visit and send steamed bread to daughters and vice versa; the fifth—Duanwu: *zongzi* is eaten.
VI (30/6–29/7)	
VII (30/7–27/8)	The ninth: Qincheng market days ("Qincheng Hui").
VII (28/8–25/9)	The fifteenth—the Full Moon Festival: mothers and daughters visit each other.
IX (26/9–25/10)	The ninth: family gathering.
X (26/10–23/11)	The first: a family meal of *hunton* and the burning of paper before the dawn for those who have died.
XI (24/11–23/12)	Dongzhi: a family dinner, including dumplings.
XII (24/12–22/1)	The fifth: a kind of soup made of five kinds of beans is eaten; the eighth—Laba: a special kind of noodles are eaten; the twenty-third: mothers and daughters visit each other; the kitchen god is served, and then sent to heaven; the thirtieth: they receive the kitchen god

hp = hot pepper.
Following the TSC and TLC dates, the equivalent in WSC is given.
According to TSC, each section which is divided by every fifteen days has a changing time.

with cash. Transactions taking place in this kind of market are called *huan* (literally, "to exchange").[12]

The second refers to markets held at particular places, often outside one's community, where purchases commonly involve cash. But these places are not called "markets"; instead, they are "meetings," or *hui*. The core meaning of this term is "gathering."[13] For local people, to go to a market is "to go to play at *hui* (*dao hui shang shua shua*)." Although transactions at *hui* require cash, one can visit a market without purchasing anything. In fact, most people go to *hui* simply for entertainment and relaxation, such as visiting their relatives or friends. At a local *hui*, people gather in small groups, enjoying tea or cigarettes together. As one old woman told me, "Going to a *hui* is just going to enjoy. There are more people there. To buy things needs money. Who has money? My son never gives me money. I just go there to have fun."

Hui are social rather than purely economic in their orientation, and they fall into two categories: annual and regular. Each community usually organizes its own annual *hui*. In Zhaojiahe, for instance, the annual *hui* takes place on the first day of the third month of the lunar year. Communal *hui* are often more like a social gathering or festival than a market. In particular, mothers and married-out daughters customarily visit each other on these occasions. In contrast, regular *hui* are more often used for economic transactions, and are set up according to the lunar calendar.[14] For people in Zhaojiahe, two regular *hui* are especially important. First, in Qincheng, a major neighboring community, there is a "9 *hui*": that is, a gathering on every 9th, 19th, and 29th of the lunar month. Second, in the county town a "3–6–9 *hui*" meets on the 3rd, 6th, 9th, 13th, 16th, 19th, 23rd, 26th, and 29th of the lunar month.[15]

What table 3 does not show clearly are activities and events that are supposed to be regulated by the Western calendar. These include schedules for the community school, which are determined by the township government. For instance, school vacations are arranged in accordance with national holidays. For those whose family members work outside Zhaojiahe, the Western calendar is also useful in calculating when their relatives are expected to return. But for those who have no relatives in towns or cities, national holidays such as National Day (1 October) mean very little. As we were talking about these holidays, one old man told me: "No, we do not celebrate National Day. What is the point of celebrating that? Every day is a holiday if we don't have to work. Who bothers to celebrate National Day? Nobody gives us anything for that. We don't celebrate it either!"

We may roughly generalize as follows: the Western calendar indicates a flow of time that connects a specific locale with society more broadly, the lunar calendar regulates the social world, and the section system represents the agricultural world.

Food as a System of Signification

Anne Murcott (1988) has provided a useful summary of various sociological and anthropological approaches to food, categorizing these studies as falling into two main schools: "structural" and "materialist." At the risk of oversimplification, one may follow Murcott in arguing that recent studies of food reflect two main sources of theoretical influence: one derives its energy from French structuralism and the other does not. The former school is primarily under the theoretical shadow of Claude Lévi-Strauss, Roland Barthes, and Mary Douglas;[16] the latter draws on a wide range of anthropological authors, such as Marvin Harris, Jack Goody, and Sidney Mintz, and a number of sociologists, such as Pierre Bourdieu, Stephen Mennell, and Joanne Finkelstein.[17] One fundamental battle between these two schools concerns the nature of meaning. The nonstructuralist scholars may not agree on what explanatory factors are most important—the historical or the cultural or the economic or the political or some combination of these elements—but they all agree that food and eating are social phenomena that cannot be analyzed without reference to their social essence. In other words, their meaning is socially determined. This theoretical stance differs fundamentally from the structuralist proposition that meaning is determined by the relationship between semiological units within a system of signification. The structuralist authors do not deny the social nature of food relations, but they believe that there should be another level of analysis—the semiological—besides and not reducible to the sociological.

Mary Douglas has pointed out an often-overlooked innovation of French structuralism, using Barthes's *Fashion System* (1983) to demonstrate how a complex analysis can be achieved that is neither primarily "social" nor "historical" (Douglas 1984, 18–25). Barthes identifies two systems of signification in the fashion magazine, one represented as photographed or drawn and the other as written; both are in contrast to the fashion as worn. His analysis, which is essentially metalinguistic, may or may not be criticized; however, as Douglas observes, Barthes's method is a striking innovation that makes it possible to distinguish the semiological from the sociological so that another kind of analysis can be produced.

Methodologically, my analysis in this chapter may be seen as following a structural approach. Rather than focusing on how meaning is generated in or as a social process, I outline how food represents a meaningful system, through which flows of social and economic activities are organized in several temporal modes. I thereby emphasize the structural relations between different elements or units of food relations taken as a system of signification.[18]

Classification of Food

The first and the most important distinction in food is that between the steamed bread (*mo*) and the other types of food. In structuralist terms, this distinction may be appropriately called an "opposition," for the social or agricultural events marked out by different types of food are seen as *contrasted* to one another.[19] Steamed bread should be viewed as the core food, and other types are supplementary in two senses: as something not necessary for daily life and as something extraordinary.

On everyday occasions, steamed bread is the only food prepared and consumed; it is generally eaten much like a Western sandwich—but with no filling except hot chili inside the bread. Boiled water most commonly serves the function of a soup; occasionally millet soup is prepared. The growing economic differentiation resulting from the reforms that began in the 1970s has allowed some people to enjoy a better meal; however, for most local people, a very simple kind of meal that has long signified an ordinary day remained the norm in the 1990s.

Every special day, whether festivals or market days, is marked out by a different type of food (see table 3). The supplementary food can be summarized as follows:[20]

Days *(according to TLC and TSC)*	Special food
Powu (the fifth of the first month)	dumplings (*jiaozi*)
Shiwu (the fifteenth of the first month)	dumplings (*jiaozi*)
Duanwu (the fifth of the fifth month)	*zongzi*[21]
The first of the tenth month	*hunton*[22]
Dongzhi (the day of the twenty-second section)	dumplings (*jiaozi*)
The fifth of the twelfth month	a special soup made of five kinds of beans
Laba (the eighth of the twelfth month)	noodles

No significant day, whether on the lunar calendar or in the section system, can be conceived of or talked about without invoking a particular type of food. As the list makes clear, some days are specially named and others are not. It would not be surprising to find local variations in the particular food consumed; but replacing a given element—for example, substituting noodles for dumplings—will not affect my analysis of structural relations.

Another important distinction is that between two types of the steamed bread, *mo* and *huamo*. The former, which as we have seen is the daily staple, is made in a shape very similar to that of a scone, though the method of its preparation is completely different.[23] *Huamo,* which can be literally translated as "flowery steamed bread," is prepared for festivals and ceremonial occasions. *Huamo* is often shaped like a small animal such as bat, cat, pigeon, or *hundun,*[24] though one can hardly tell which looks like what after it has been steamed. It also may differ from ordinary bread in color, for some edible colors are always added into the dough before steaming. Before it is cooked, the *huamo* looks astonishingly beautiful: vividly colored and imaginatively shaped. Each mother is responsible for teaching her daughter how to make *huamo,* and for a housewife to be told that she is good at making it is a much-desired compliment.

Huamo itself is further divided into two categories: those prepared for calendrical (i.e., annual) events and those made for events related to the life cycle (i.e., to the celebration of birth, marriage, and death). Both kinds can be referred to as *huamo,* but the latter often have a particular name that varies according to the occasion.

The "normal" *huamo,* commonly in the shape of small animals as described above, is made primarily during the Chinese New Year period. A large amount is both consumed by one's own family and exchanged with one's relatives, who are normally visited at that time. Exchanging *huamo* is an expected feature of such visits.

The wedding *huamo*, which is the most colorful and imaginative type of all, is called "tiger bread" (*laohumo*). In most cases one cannot tell whether it indeed imitates a tiger or simply presents a raging monster. Tiger bread is frequently as large as a real tiger's head. Usually two eggs, dyed black, represent the eyes of the "tiger." Its mouth, which is often forced open by another egg, and nose, which is sometimes decorated by a carrot, are specially colored. Commonly decorated (in a rather untigerlike way) with a pair of horns in green or red, the animal sometimes looks more like an enlarged cricket, because it is never given a body beyond a number of short and skinny legs. The combination of colors is always fantastic.

There is no particular name for the steamed bread prepared for the funeral. It is often as large as a tiger bread, but its shape—usually just a simple circle, so that paper flowers may be stuck on it more easily—is less imaginative. Those paper flowers are symbols of blessing. Amazingly, the colors of the *huamo* made for the funeral are no less eye-catching than those of the wedding *huamo*. Without prior knowledge, it is very hard, if not completely impossible, to tell which type of *huamo* has been prepared for which occasion.

To the mother who has given birth, *ganmo* is prepared and presented. *Ganmo* is the only type of bread that is not steamed; instead, the dough is baked on heated crushed stones. Because it is thin and crispy, this type of bread is believed to be good for the digestion; no artificial color is added to it. In contrast to *huamo* prepared for weddings or funerals, *ganmo* is supposed to be presented informally. A final kind of special *huamo* is also informally presented. On the fifteenth of the first month of the lunar year, those under three years old are supposed to receive some *jianjianmo* from their neighbors. The shape of *jianjianmo* is similar to that of the normal *huamo,* and no color is added.

Eating and Being

There are gender distinctions in food and eating.[25] Women and men are supposed to eat differently. Most men do not and cannot cook; it is the duty of a woman (usually the wife) to prepare and serve food on everyday occasions.[26] As we saw in chapter 2, women and men take up different parts of the domestic space, as evidenced most clearly by the seating arrangement of daily meals. The woman is the guardian of the oven, which is connected to the bed. She looks after both food and men in the house. In contrast, the man is supposed to be looked after during a meal. He sits down at a table and does not move until he finishes his meal.

The presentation of food also marks out the relationship between host and guest. Though the formal aspects of the encounter do not vary, the quality of food prepared for the guest is determined by the guest's relationship to the family, as well as by his or her social significance (as judged at that moment by the host). Suppose that a certain poor relative comes to visit a family; even though the family may not provide him any other food than what they would have on a normal day, they must still arrange the plates on the dining table in such a way as to signify the visit of a guest. Ordinarily, a family would not eat more than bread and water, together with hot chili and perhaps some pickles. I have observed many times that while an insignificant guest is given the same fare, four plates are set on the dining table: the chili and the pickles, which would otherwise have been in a small bowl, are placed on separate plates; and the other two plates hold, respectively, salt and a tiny bit of sugar. The use of four plates is a signifier of the presence of a guest. For a guest of great social importance, they would have to be filled with vegetables or fried eggs or meats.

As mentioned above, food—the exchange of steamed bread—helps structure as well the relationship between a mother and her (married-out) daughters.[27] The importance of such an exchange is that it metaphorizes the relationship between the mother and her daughters. The explicit emphasis on exchange between two categories in this social relationship suggests that mother-daughter relations are viewed in terms of reciprocity rather than obligation. Steamed bread alone can serve this reciprocal function. In other words, in this region exchange, sometimes in the form of gift (see, e.g., Yan 1996; Kipnis 1997), is carried out through a particular medium—the steamed bread. On many occasions, exchanges of steamed bread between the mother and her daughters are customary, but they are compulsory on two occasions: Mangqian and Mangpa.[28]

Mangqian (literally, "before getting busy") and Mangpa (literally, "after being busy") are not festivals, strictly speaking; they indicate two significant periods of time, one before and the other after the summer harvest. For those engaged in agriculture, the summer harvest is the busiest time of year; it is also the most important period in terms of economic production. The harvest lasts about ten days, and before and after it the mother and her married-out daughters are supposed to visit each other to exchange steamed bread. On these two occasions, both the old flour from the previous year and the new flour from the harvest year are shared among relatives. These exchanges have a practical as well as a sentimental rationale. The harvest of each rural community may be slightly earlier or later than that of its neighboring communities, and the members of any given community are unlikely to be able to help one another since they are busy reaping their own wheat. If help is needed, it is more likely to be obtained from one's relatives—that is, married-out daughters or those linked through affinal ties and residing in another community, whether near or far.

In a sense, the steamed bread "travels" between different households or between different rural communities to create and reiterate social relations of various kinds. It is meant to be exchanged. Thus it is not difficult to understand why inhabitants of this region do not speak of "visiting a relative." Instead, local people say that "it is time *to send some bread to a relative.*"[29] More generally, one finds that many aspects of social life are metaphorized through food or eating. For instance, although weddings and funerals can be referred to as *guoshi* (literally, "to pass through something"), local people also talked about these events in terms of "having the feast" (*chixi* in Chinese). When there was a wedding in a nearby community, people would ask "Are you going to eat the feast?" or "Did you eat the feast?" instead of "Are you planning to participate?" or "Did you participate?" The implication is that not just social relationships but indeed social actions are envisioned through metaphors of food and eating. The use of this semantic register has a series of significant consequences. In the case of a poor family, for example, the parents may not be able to build a new house for the son when he marries; but they must fulfill the minimum responsibility of preparing—no matter how symbolic such preparation may be—the oven and a set of cooking utensils for the son. Otherwise, the wedding cannot take place.

The above sketch of the elementary forms of food classification and its social functions enables us to move to another level of analysis. We will look next at a number of signifying oppositions and equivalences embedded in food but beyond everyday consciousness.

Opposition and Equivalence

The Ordinary versus the Extraordinary   As we have seen, there are two material frames of reference that are registered in the calendar: the agricultural and the social. What is signified in the sphere of the social is "extraordinariness," that which is set in contrast to the ordinariness of the everyday.[30] The signifier of the extraordinariness can take several forms. First, holidays or festivals are signified by particular types of food, such as noodles or dumplings, that are distinguished from the steamed bread eaten every day. Second, events related to the life cycle of an individual are marked by the presence of *huamo*, a fancy steamed bread, rather than plain steamed bread. Third, the receiving of guests is signified as extraordinary by the formal arrangement of plates on the table, ordered quite unlike the ordinary way of the family's daily meals.

The feast, prepared either for the wedding or for the funeral, combines these three forms of signification at once. A wedding, for example, is a special occasion where there are many guests; it requires the preparation of a special kind of steamed bread, the tiger bread; and it requires other types of food than the steamed bread, in part because the celebration often takes place during the New Year period, a time for festivals and feasts. Thus on any particular occasion more than one signifier may be employed, but in such cases there is only one signified—the extraordinariness, registered either as a temporal difference (as in the case of annual festivals) or a spatial difference (as in the case of receiving a guest).[31]

The Busy versus the Slack   Because of the agrarian nature of the local people's life, closely intertwined with the natural environment, one should not find it surprising that qualities of days or months of the year vary according to the season.[32] In this part of rural Shaanxi, the agricultural year is divided into two periods: the busy and the slack season. However, since the meaning of this difference in agriculture is secured by the change of season, what needs to be marked out is not the qualities of these periods themselves but the moments at which they begin and end—the moments at which each season is recognized *as* a season. The busy period of the agricultural year ends when the anticipation of the New Year begins, before the last month of the lunar calendar. In the third and fourth months of the lunar calendar, the period roughly corresponding to March, there are a series of market celebrations. Most communities in this area have their own annual market days, which indicate that the slack period is almost over and the busy time in the agricultural year will soon begin. These two annual turning points are marked out by a series of feasts and exchanges of food. The series of market days involves more exchange of food across community boundaries than does the New Year period. When local people visit their relatives on these days they always prepare some steamed bread as a gift, and they always receive some steamed bread from those relatives as well.

Equivalence   The meaningful units in the food system, which is always defined broadly to include eating and associated behaviors, pertain to a variety of occasions in life; but if we analyze a series of equivalences among these units, we will see how they are governed by a set of unconscious rules. First, consider the social and the agricultural frames of reference: we may say that the agricultural is more essential to the life of local people, but in the order of signification, the social is the more obviously marked category. Like plain steamed bread, the agricultural is *necessary* but not *central*. What is central to them is the social, at least in a calendrical sense. Thus the relationship between the agricultural and the social is equivalent to the relationship between steamed bread and other types of food. The very meaning of the necessary category has to be defined by the variation from it. Second, as we have noted above, a number of elements in the food system are used to signify extraordinariness in the sphere of the social. Because these elements are always construed in oppositional terms, we can set out a basic set of equivalences:

steamed bread : other types of food :: plain steamed bread : fancy steamed bread :: ordinary meal : feast

Underlying and corresponding to these oppositional equivalences are three elementary dimensions of local life:

the circular : the continuous : the reciprocal

It is quite clear that the first pair is associated with the events defined by the annual circle. The second pair, which corresponds to the events of the life cycle, implies a continuity, both collective and individual. The third pair refers to a dimension of social relations that are neither circular nor continuous but spatially distributed and reciprocal in nature.

Articulation of Temporal Flows

Another question we need to raise is how these different units of signification, dependent on different material frames of reference, are *articulated* into a temporal whole. Such articulation need not be deliberate. Following the view of Lévi-Strauss (1963, 1–27), I am suggesting that although the local people are conscious of the content of their cultural practice, they are not always conscious of its form.

To answer this question we must draw on anthropological discussions of time, for the "glue" that combines different elements of food and eating into a cosmos relies on a conception of multiple times or temporalities. The term "time" itself may be confusing, because it can mean a number of different things, as Edmund Leach has reminded us (1961, 124). "Temporality" is hardly better, since it may be confused with "the temporal" as a quality of practice that is simply part of the actor's intention (e.g., see Bourdieu 1990, 103–11). Instead, I will use the term "mode of time" to distinguish the analysis here from the philosophical discussion of time as a pure category of thought, on the one hand, and the sociological treatment of time as often part of an intentional act, on the other.[33]

In an influential essay, Leach has suggested that there are three basic modes of time. The first two are quite obvious:

Firstly, there is the notion of repetition. Whenever we think about measuring time we concern ourselves with some kind of metronome; it may be the ticking of a clock or a pulse beat or the recurrence of days or moons or annual seasons, but always there is something which repeats.

Secondly, there is the notion of non-repetition. We are aware that all living things are born, grow old and die, and that this is an irreversible process.

I am inclined to think that all other aspects of time, duration for example or historical sequence, are fairly simple derivatives from these two basic experiences:
(a) that certain phenomena of nature repeat themselves
(b) that life change is irreversible. (1961, 125)

In order to explain the third mode of time, which is somewhat more difficult to understand, Leach provides an example from "one of the most puzzling characters in the classic Greek mythology, that of Cronus, father of Zeus." He argues that "Cronus's time is an oscillation, a time that flows back and forth, that is born and swallowed and vomited up, an oscillation from father to mother, mother to father and back again" (1961, 129). Leach describes this as "a pendulum view": "With a pendulum view of time, the sequence of things is discontinuous; time is a succession of alternations and full stops. Intervals are distinguished, not as the sequential markings on a tape measure, but as repeated opposites, tick-tock tick-tock" (134–35).

My concern here is not with associating these three modes of time with different types of societies. Indeed, such attempts have been convincingly criticized, particularly by Alfred Gell (1992; see also Bloch 1977). However, I am contending that in northern rural Shaanxi, there exists a cosmological complex that articulates these three modes of time in food.

First, each year is experienced as an annual repetition, marked by the return of each season. This mode of time is circular; harvests vary from year to year, but the sunshine and rainfall necessary for agriculture will come back in an annual circle. Therefore, each year is experienced as one repetition of the circle of seasons. Second, nonrepetitive time is exemplified in and actualized through the idea of the life cycle. Three main events—birth, marriage, and death—are the significant markers of this mode of time. It extends beyond one's own life, linking one's ancestors and descendants in a chain of being to constitute what Hugh Baker calls "the Continuum of Descent." Baker uses the phrase to emphasize that "descent is a unity, a rope which began somewhere back in the remote past, and which stretches on to the infinite future" (1979, 26); in that rope or chain, each individual is only a link. I am instead pointing out here a sense of time that is nonrepeatable or continuous and that crosses the boundary between the individual and the collective. In other words, a certain linearity is in fact expressed in the events defined by the life cycle.

Third, within each year there is always a mode of "pendulum time," which oscillates back and forth between the agricultural and the social frames of reference. It is fundamentally dependent on a series of "binary oppositions" (to use the term made notorious by structuralists). For local people of this region, temporal units smaller than a year are always experienced in terms of a series of oppositional contrasts. As mentioned earlier, even funerals have to wait until the New Year's period so that the dead person can be buried properly. If asked, they always give a practical explanation for this delay: one may not have time for a proper funeral in summer or any other season. But perhaps there is a more significant though less conscious reason: because the funeral is a signifier of the social, it must be done in winter in order to mark out the extraordinariness of the period of time. In other words, the social nature of the funeral determines its temporal location in the lunar year.

Furthermore, the section system itself is binary: it contains twenty-four sections in twelve pairs, such as Lichun, Yushui, and so forth. These pairs, which do not exactly correspond to the lunar month, are organized in oppositional relationships. The division is emphasized by the special meanings frequently given to the lunar month's first and fifteenth days, which are called in Chinese Chuyi and Shiwu (see table 3). Special events, such as annual festivals, are often arranged to fall on either Chuyi or Shiwu.

It may not be surprising to find that it is customary in this part of China to have meals twice rather than three times a day. The first meal is often served between nine and ten. The second meal, called "the afternoon meal" (*shangwufan*), is generally served around three. These times of course vary from one household to another, but the pattern in time remains constant. It can be broken only on special occasions, such as when festivals are celebrated or guests entertained. The two meals provide the temporal points by which local people recognize "hours"—not in the sense of units measured on a clock but as coordinates on which a collective rhythm is founded. To ask someone "Have you eaten?" is as much a way of knowing "time" as of adjusting one's rhythm to the collective hour. These two points of reference divide a day into three parts: *dazao* (before the first meal), *shangwufan toushang* (before the second meal), and *shangwufan houshang* (after the second meal). These terms of time make it possible to talk about and organize everyday life. The quality and duration of the three parts of the day are determined by the season.

How should we understand the internal coherence of this calendar system and what it implies about the question of cultural continuity and social change posed at the beginning of chapter 3? As we have seen, there are three interrelated but different temporal flows in this system of food and time. Within each annual circle, there is a mode that I have called "pendulum time." Its most evident marker is the division of a year into two distinct spheres: the social and the agricultural. That is, time within a year shifts from the social to the agricultural and from the agricultural to the social. Underlying this contrast is a cultural opposition: the celebrative versus the productive. Although the material base of the calendar is its agricultural mode of production, in actually experiencing this multiple temporality one is compelled to feel instead the centrality of the social in a cosmos of food and time. The relationship between social and agricultural activities, two poles of a pendulum oscillating through the year, is defined from the perspective of the social: that is, s (social) and $-s$ (nonsocial) determine what is a (agricultural) and $-a$ (nonagricultural). Hence, we have

$$s : a :: -a : -s = s : -s :: a : -a$$

The negative sign marks a simple negation of a positive quality. This equation indicates that the relationship of $s : a :: -a : -s$ is analogous to that of $s : -s :: a : -a$. In other words, production itself necessarily contains a negation of its social significance; and the significance attributed to the family celebration already implies its being "leisure" or perhaps even "idle" time (see figure 7).

In this calendrical system, pendulum time serves a crucial function in organizing temporal units, such as days, months, and so on, into spatial ones; the series of contrasts or oppositions likewise allows social categories of a spatial kind, such as gender or kin relations, to be organ-

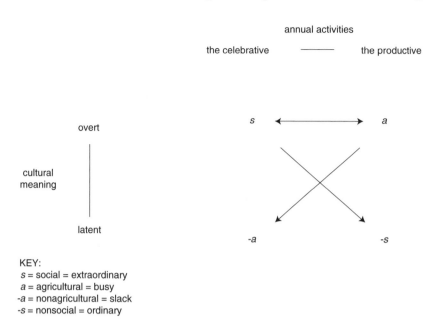

Figure 7. The celebrative versus the productive.

ized in accordance with the flow of time. In other words, the cultural signified—the extraordinariness—is at once a spatial and a temporal concept, as such occasions as receiving guests or organizing feasts exemplify. The prescribed exchanges of food between a mother and her married-out daughters provide another example of how social relations, spatially distributed, are also temporally recorded and registered.

This pendulum mode of time is stable insofar as it is repeated annually. The circular mode of time reinforces the oppositional arrangement of the social and the agricultural events. But at the same time, it also introduces a new element: the continuation of descent. Each new annual circle is at once different from and the same as the previous one; it is a repetition in a structural sense, as change occurs without modifying the structural relations between constituent units within a structure. This circular mode of time can be expressed as follows:

$A_1(s_1, a_1), A_2(s_2, a_2), \ldots, A_p(s_p, a_p), \ldots,$
    where A_p = Annual Circle (the present year)

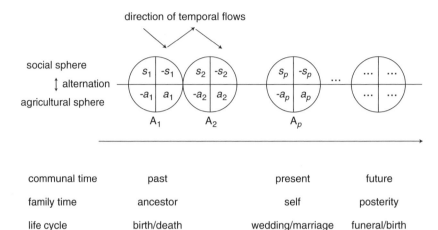

Figure 8. The temporal flows.

One sees clearly that a new element of continuous, nonrepeatable time is here introduced. This new element is not reducible to any spatial categorization, but it can be organized into discrete temporal categories, in such sequences as past–present–future or ancestor–self–descendant or birth/death–wedding/marriage–funeral/birth. It is impossible to represent as an oppositional system because its material reference has become the environment or the physical world. That external reference makes the experience of nonrepetition or linearity in time inevitable, even within the annual circles that are themselves experienced as repetition. In other words, the "continuum of descent" is in fact embedded in the (re)turning of the seasons (see figure 8).

The idea of family plays a central role in how the local people conceptualize temporal continuation. It is through the organization of family celebrations that nonrepeatable time, both collective and individual, is actualized as a chain of ancestors and descendants is built. For birth signifies both an individual's past and the community's future, just as death signifies a community's past and an individual's future. This may explain, at least partially, why Chinese villagers cannot be "individuals" in a strict sense: their experience is so temporally constructed that it is impossible for them to separate themselves, in a social or a cultural sense, from their family.

A crucial characteristic of this calendrical system is the structural stability that it derives from its internal organization. First, there is an effective articulation between temporal flows and spatial distributions of social relations, as already noted, through a series of contrasts and oppositions. This link allows the more abstract categories of time to be realized in experience as spatial relations; conversely, the social relations provide an experiential basis for conceptualizing duration and continuity in life.[34] Second, as a cosmological system, the calendar gains much internal stability from the multiplicity of its frames of reference and cultural contents. As we have seen, the three modes of time are interwoven into a complex whole; unless the structural relations between them are shaken, changes of individual elements in each of these modes of time may not force any radical modification of the system itself. Finally, several levels of signifying practices are intertwined in such a way as to form a total web of meaning. It is food—in particular, steamed bread—that anchors this web of meaning in a set of material practices of exchange and reciprocity. Thus the dynamic between the material and the symbolic aspects of this calendrical system contributes to its internal stability.

With respect to the larger theoretical issue of cultural continuity and social change, two further points may be made. First, food is central to the organization of social life in this part of rural Shaanxi. In comparison to other parts of rural China (southern or southeastern China in particular), the food system of rural Shaanxi may appear rather simple, as only a small number of staples are commonly consumed. But complexity in meaning depends not on elements or units in isolation but on the relationships they constitute within a system of signification. The key characteristic of the system in northern rural Shaanxi is its power to synthesize, a power that allows different aspects of social life to be combined in such a way as to form a complex system of meaning. I am arguing that these different aspects of social life cannot and should not be treated separately; they must be treated in their entirety—that is, as simultaneously a social institution and a system of values. Relationship rather than function, or relationality rather than functionality, should be the focus of ethnographic research of this kind.

Second, the calendrical system as a cosmos in practice sets cultural categories of time and space in action. Its central characteristic is its structural arrangement between food elements, temporal flows, and spatial distributions of social relations. Essentially, such a system constitutes a multiple frame of reference, cutting across the material and the symbolic dimensions of social life to integrate the celebrative and the productive into a coherent system of meaning. Each single element or unit in the current system of signification may be replaced, but the structure of relations continues to function and to ensure the stability of the system. One crucial implication is that such a cultural system may have a greater capacity than usually thought to accommodate social and cultural change introduced from outside while maintaining a certain stability—not at the level of actual practice but at the level of collective unconsciousness. This insight may well shed some light on the mechanism of cultural continuity in the context of dramatic social change in contemporary Chinese society.

1. A view of the village.

2. The wheat fields in summer.

3. Spring plowing.

4. Weaving in the courtyard.

5. The wedding bread.

6. The courtyard door.

7. Sacrifice to the sedan chair.

8. Burning paper (money) at the grave.

Part Two

The Logic of Practice

5

The Practice of Everyday Life

In the first part of this book, I have shown how a particular form of life in a specific local setting was shaped in the larger context of rural China's unique experience of revolution and development. By tracing several areas of social life central to the logic of cultural practice in northern rural Shaanxi, I have provided an analytical framework of the social environment in which individual actions and behaviors can be understood. In the second part of the book, I will turn to describing the modes of behavior or patterns of practice from the perspective of the actors. Here I focus on a set of historically situated everyday practices central to the life of this group of people in rural Shaanxi in the 1990s: I make some general observations in this chapter, and turn specifically to weddings and funeral celebrations in chapter 6 and political life in chapter 7. My contention is that in the very way they behave and perform, these people reveal the nature of the modernizing process in Chinese society at large.

Differential Hospitality

The constant winds in this area of rural Shaanxi make it a very dusty place. At times, I found myself unable to see anything more than a few feet away, as the whole sky was covered by yellow-gray grains of dust, whirling and tossing in a horrifying wind. I had naively assumed that in such living conditions, it would be better for me to wear clothes that were casual and perhaps not too clean; in an old jacket and a pair of gray, loose trousers, I might sit down anywhere and work with the people whenever necessary. The idea of washing my trousers had never occurred to me until my host, Wanbin, came to talk to me about it.

The formal manner in which he entered my room escaped my notice at first. Wanbin began his prepared conversation by commenting on my belongings, such as my notebooks and pens—with compliments. After this long, incomprehensible preamble, he mentioned that wherever one was, one should pay attention to one's own trousers. Finally, Wanbin made his point: "There is a lot of dust on your trousers." "I thought that it was very dusty, and I had better not change or wash them too often since I wanted to follow you everywhere in the field," I replied. "But that is not hygienic (*weisheng*)," Wanbin protested. He continued, "You are a person from a big city. You therefore should be paying more attention to what you wear. If you do not care about it, *people will laugh at you.* To let people laugh at you does no good to my family, because you are my guest."

This seemed a matter less of hygiene than of prestige and control. What underlies this conversation is Wanbin's concern about how he might be perceived by others. In such cases, the phrase *renjia xiaohua* (other people will laugh at you) is always invoked to explain the need for action. This mode of explanation focuses not on how other people react but on what they *would* or *might* do. That anticipation is what induces one to act in a certain way. Here, an individual's action is governed by the rule of not "being laughed at."

Let us take another example. All men and some older women had the habit of smoking, which is called *chiyan* (to eat smoke). Traditionally, local people smoked a kind of water pipe (*shuiyandai*). The bent pipe is about a foot long; fixed on one end is a box, slightly bigger than a large match box, made of iron and containing water. The tobacco is put into a small pit on the box. Each household usually has only one water pipe, which the host will share when a guest is present. Since the early 1980s cigarettes have become more popular, particularly among the younger generation.

A few days after my arrival, Wanyou, Wanbin's father's brother's son and a neighbor, came for a visit. With his hands wrapped in his sleeves, Wanyou moved very slowly to sit at the edge of the bed. Wanbin, still at lunch, raised his head and said, "Eat a cigarette. This is Teacher Liu's cigarette."[1] "No, I just had one," Wanyou replied. Ignoring Wanyou's response, Wanbin nodded to his daughter-in-law to show where a box of matches was and again urged, "Eat smoke!" While saying this, Wanbin stood up and passed a pack of cigarettes to Wanyou. Wanyou put it aside without saying anything. A few minutes later, Wanbin made his offer again: "Eat a cigarette." "No, I just had my water pipe and don't want it now," Wanyou replied. "That is different. This is a cigarette," Wanbin insisted. Wanyou seemed to be very reluctant, explaining, "Nowadays, I am too lazy even to smoke. People say smoking does no good for one's health." But before he finished his sentence, Wanyou picked up one cigarette and smoked it. He continued to smoke for about two hours while he was there.

Persuasion is the duty of a host, just as the duty of a guest is to initially refuse any favor offered. Otherwise, one will be laughed at by others. Although such performances may have a long history, they seem to be viewed more positively now as a strategy for coping with the changing conditions of life. Economic stratification, brought about by the economic reforms, has made local people sharply aware of the differences in wealth. This awareness has resulted in a series of transformed traditional practices in the field of guest-host relations. What I call "differential hospitality," as a practical ideology, is the essence of such practices. As Wanyou later explained, "Different people have to be treated with different kinds of cigarettes. When we offer them cigarettes, we have to think about who they are. In different pockets, we usually have different kinds of cigarettes, ranging from the very best to the ordinary. If it is just a neighbor, you will offer him an ordinary cigarette, or even the water pipe will do. If it is someone from a town or city, you will have to offer him at least a filter; otherwise, you will be laughed at." Some people with more experience, according to Wanyou, prepared different brands of cigarettes in one pack; they were able to pick out the right choice for the right person with their tactical fingers.

In order for such a strategy to work, one must know the roles of other people and how they are related. The accuracy of the information that one man possesses about his neighbors in this community can be quite amazing. One day I was trying to talk to my host, who was cleaning his tools and was not very interested in explaining kinship terms. Wanbin concentrated on his work and did not answer my questions properly. Just before I was about to leave, he suddenly began to talk—but not to me. Someone whom I had not noticed came toward us, from the direction behind Wanbin. Wanbin turned around just in time, when this person was about three or four meters away. He carried a bicycle and did not look like a farmer. Wanbin said to him: "Have just got off the train." No pronoun was used in this utterance, nor was the sentence a question. The man nodded and passed by. I was unsure what this was supposed to mean—a greeting? I did not know who the passer-by was; however, it seemed to me a little peculiar that Wanbin talked about getting off the train to someone carrying a bicycle. Later on I found out that this person was Gencai, who was from Dawa but was temporarily working for the township government. Gencai had recently gone on an official trip to Xi'an, the capital of the province. When we saw Gencai, he was returning to Dawa for the first time.

The above examples suggest that the social status of a person is seen as closely linked to where he belongs or from what place he comes. Someone from a big city should be offered better cigarettes. Someone who has moved to the township and was working for the local government should be properly addressed. In rural China, social differentiation is increasingly represented in spatial terms, and it has thus shaped—and yet been shaped by—a hierarchy of places. Whoever failed to meet the expected quality of the place from which he or she came would be "laughed at" by those in Zhaojiahe.

A Chinese friend of mine who was living in Australia surprised me with a visit to Dawa just after the Chinese New Year's Day (4 February 1992). Her long, beautiful overcoat, which distinguished her from all others in this community, made me a little nervous, because I was afraid that it might jeopardize my relationship with my host and his neighbors. I was uneasy about its fashionable design; it was orange-yellow with an elegant designer's label on the back. Soon after she left, my host commented on her appearance: "Your friend is a very 'simple' (*pusu*) person. This kind of person is seldom seen nowadays. Although she lives abroad, she has dressed in such a simple manner!" "Why do you think so?" I asked in amazement. He replied, "Look at what she wore, a cotton dress with even a patch on her back! Nowadays, who wears clothes with patches? Not even children!" I realized that my host had mistaken the designer's label on the back of my friend's overcoat for a patch.

My host and his neighbors often used the term *pusu* in discussing my friend's appearance. No literal translation can do justice to this word, which refers to one's attitude toward a lifestyle. If one prefers to wear plain clothes and to live simply, particularly if one has the means to live differently, one will be called a *pusu* person. In this sense, the term bears a positive connotation. During the Maoist period, being *pusu* had been made a revolutionary virtue: the Communist heroes were always represented as having a *pusu* lifestyle as well as a set of *pusu* proletarian emotions. In contemporary China, this quality is no longer taken as completely positive and good: being *pusu* may also indicate that one is poor, implying one's incompetence and inability to achieve a better life. My host and his neighbors used the term in this second sense.

Any of the inhabitants paying attention to the material of the overcoat would have agreed with my host's observation. What was significant in their eyes was *what* clothing was made of rather than *how* it was made. As noted in chapter 3, local people did not particularly value cotton, because it marked nothing but a local product that any woman could produce—though their handmade cloth was often beautiful. If I had asked which kind of cloth was preferred, anyone would have bluntly answered: "The homemade cloth can never be as good as the machine-made one." Until the late 1970s, most people, especially children, often wore clothes that had either holes or patches. This is no longer true, and the change was driven by a desire to possess greater purchasing power. Such power is demonstrated in the material. Cotton, a product that everyone was able to produce, therefore lost its significance. When I asked an old man what was supposed to be the best thing to wear, he replied simply, "The most expensive materials!"

Forms of Everyday Practice

Action is carried out in everyday life through certain social and cultural forms. I use the term "form" for a number of reasons. First, I am dealing not with actions that can be reduced to individual intentions or motives but with certain cultural forms according to which those individual actions are rendered significant to the agents. These forms are *transindividual* in nature. Second, I see particular cultural forms as historical products: that is, subject to change by larger historical forces and contingent rather than inherent to a certain social group. Third, as I observed in chapter 4, a given cultural form may not be consciously known to the agents who act in accordance with it. They cannot satisfactorily explain their own behaviors. We must thus examine certain ideal situations in order to make sense of the minutiae of daily life.

Bargaining

The observation that there has been enormous development of market systems in rural China since the late 1970s is a commonplace.[2] My concern here is not with how these market systems have affected local life, but with what bargaining as a cultural form implies about how social relationships are conceptualized in the context of economic development. Certainly bargaining, which in the past took forms such as marriage negotiation, is not a new phenomenon. But it is fair to say that at the end of the twentieth century its degree and intensity in northern rural Shaanxi are unprecedented. Everyone—male or female, old or young—has to some extent engaged in this form of practice, affecting how they conceive of their neighbors, community, and society.

Qincheng is a large nearby village, and its regular market attracts people from the neighboring areas. Many people from Zhaojiahe frequent this market. The Qincheng vegetable market is arranged along a main T-shaped intersection. On both sides of the road, traders lay out on the ground their vegetables—carrots, cabbages, potatoes, hot peppers, Chinese chives, and so on. These traders, mostly men, carry their own scales. On a normal market day, there are fifty to sixty traders, and each of them usually sells only one or two kinds of vegetables. As buyers come to the market, they first walk around to inspect the quality and price of the desired vegetables at several stalls. The bargaining begins after the tour of the market is over.

The following example of bargaining is reconstructed from one of my tape recordings. The buyer was a woman in her late twenties or perhaps early thirties. She had twice passed the stall where I was recording various interchanges, and finally she stopped and started to ask the price. The primary monetary unit employed in the conversation is yuan.[3] In most cases, the customer did not ask how much a particular amount of vegetable cost; instead, he or she would ask how much of it one yuan could purchase, usually without mentioning the yuan directly. The weight unit they use is *jin* (0.5 kg).

The woman inquired about the price in the usual manner: "How much are they, your chives?" None of the traders provided price labels, and thus such inquiry was a necessary first step in bargaining. While asking, she bent over to check the quality. "Six *jin*," the trader replied. "Ya, ya, what kind of a precious thing are you selling?" the woman cried out, "How could you dare sell this so expensively? Even in town it is much cheaper!" "Oh, my elder sister," said the trader, showing his respect in addressing her even though he was older than she, "it is impossible! Impossible, you know. You know how much these chives cost me? I bet you don't. I have been selling at a price lower than what I bought them for." "What about seven *jin*?" the woman bargained. "My elder sister, let me call you my aunt, please don't make me suffer," the trader replied, but added, "If I say I'll give you seven *jin* and then play tricks with my scale, won't it be the same?" The woman changed her strategy: "How much if I want only one *jin* then?" "*Yimaoqi* (0.17 yuan)," replied the trader. She did not say anything more but picked up a bunch of chives, "Try this amount." The trader weighed the chives and said: "Two and half *jin*. Add a little bit more, you will make it three *jin*." After saying this, the trader tried to pick up some more for her. "Stop it! if I want, I will pick up some more myself," she yelled at him. "Don't you think I'll pick the best for you!?" the trader yelled back. "Don't you dare cheat!" she shouted as she moved closer to check the steelyard. "If you don't trust me, you may go to any other place to weigh it a second time," the trader said, but without anger. "If it is less than what I told you, I will pay you compensation—all my chives." "You dare to cheat!" the woman said, "Why don't you put a little bit more on top of that. Nobody is like you, you stingy man!" While saying this, she tried to grab some more chives from the ground and add it to the scale. "We can't do that. It is already much more than three *jin*," said the trader, attempting to avoid her arms. "Who knows about your steelyard? Put in a little more, won't you?" "Why don't you take more in that case?" "No, we can't eat that much. We have only two people in the house. Here is the money." "Oh, my elder sister, I have given you much more than three *jin*, but you gave me less than half a yuan. You cannot and should not do this to me." "Just a difference of three cents (*fen*). Why are you so fussy? You are such a fussy man. I will never come back to you again." "My elder sister, I beg you, we cannot do this. I will be broke if everyone does this to me." "You never will; trust me!" The woman went away.

Such bargaining illustrates the general fear of being cheated. One had to be very careful when buying things from the market. During the Chinese New Year, I went to town and bought some beef for my host family. But it turned out that the "beef" could not be consumed, because it was actually a big chunk of cow bowels dyed with artificial color to fool the unwary. I was very ashamed. The wife of my host told me, "Whenever you go to buy things like roast pork or beef, you have to ask them to cut it into tiny pieces; otherwise they will always cheat you." "What will happen if I go back to find the trader?" I asked. "They will never admit it unless you know somebody in town." Strangers are assumed to be liars: one should not believe those who are not related to oneself. Two months later, I bought a thermos bottle from a state-owned shop in town. Soon I found out that it was defective. I expressed my hope of exchanging it, but my host, Famin, told me: "Don't bother. They will give you another one exactly the same as this, because they have already tried every one, and all the good ones were sold or will be sold to those whom they know."

This kind of experience demonstrates the significance of the network of personal relations (cf. M. M. Yang 1994). Children were taught to be careful with money at an early age. One day, when I was chatting with an old man, his daughter-in-law's sister came in. She told the man how much she had spent on a wooden bar for her loom. The old man immediately frowned at her, asking her how much she had initially handed over to the carpenter from whom the bar was purchased. The girl said that she had brought only a ten-yuan note, and the carpenter did not give back any change. The old man then said, "Whenever you go to buy things, never bring big notes. You should only bring small notes. I know someone who bought a similar bar for only nine yuan. If you had small notes, you could have given him eight yuan first and seen what he would say. If he had considered the fact that we were relatives, he should have charged you only eight yuan. But if he had asked for more, then you could have given him another yuan. He would feel embarrassed to ask twice for more. Because you had only a big note, you were at a disadvantage. The carpenter charged you more than he should have."

Even within one's own community, there was a clear sense that a man must try to avoid being cheated by his own brothers. The difference was that any negotiation between two brothers had to be carried out with the help of a go-between. Wanbin, my host in Dawa, owned a cow that consumed a large amount of wheat straw. Straw was often piled up in the threshing yard after harvest. There was little reason to keep the straw for another year except to provide forage, and not every family had draft animals. Those families without these animals often sold their straw to those who owned them. Wanbin hoped to buy some from his father's brother's son, Jinkai. Wanbin did not directly go to see Jinkai; instead, he went to ask Wanyou for help.

Early one evening when I was visiting Wanyou, Wanbin came in. After several rounds of cigarettes were exchanged, Wanbin began to comment—without mentioning Jinkai's name—on the quantity and quality of Jinkai's straw. They spoke as if they were talking about something completely inconsequential. Short words and phrases were repeated, with long pauses between exchanges. Then Wanyou left. When he returned shortly thereafter, he told Wanbin that Jinkai would like to know who the buyer was. Wanbin and Wanyou started to smoke again, without talking much. After a long pause, Wanbin said, "Don't let him know." And Wanyou left again. He soon returned, bringing back the same message as the previous one. Wanbin showed little surprise and began to ask why Jinkai should keep his straw, since he had no cow. Wanyou sat down comfortably in a chair, mumbling words from time to time as if he had nothing to do with what was going on. On Wanbin's insistence, Wanyou went out one more time. Before he left, Wanbin told him to tell Jinkai that it was an "acquaintance" (*shuren*) who wanted to buy his straw. When Wanyou came back the third time, he told Wanbin that Jinkai had agreed—only if the straw was needed by an "acquaintance." Wanbin then repeated his previous comments on the quality of Jinkai's straw while Wanyou kept silent. After a long while, Wanbin asked Wanyou to go to ask Jinkai how much he wanted for his straw. When Wanyou returned, he did not state any possible price but started indirectly to contradict Wanbin's view. While Wanbin was focusing on the straw's quality, Wanyou talked about its quantity and about the decreasing value of money. About a half hour later, Wanyou went out again; when he came back, another round of discussion about the quality and quantity of Jinkai's straw began. Wanbin never suggested an amount; instead, he insisted on knowing how much Jinkai would like to sell it for. Finally, after seven rounds of negotiation, Wanyou said that 40 yuan was his best offer. Wanbin jumped off the chair and reacted negatively: "No, no way!" I was sure that Wanbin would refuse to buy the straw because he thought the price was too high. But in fact, the deal was done.

Several days later, I talked to Wanyou about this transaction. He said, "Let me tell you something, because you are so ignorant of our complex life. There are things that cannot be discussed openly and directly. We are brothers. How can you talk about such things if you are brothers? As a go-between, you have to work out something for both sides.

I know from the very beginning what Wanbin wants. I know him too well. Every time he lifts his butt I know what his fart will smell like.[4] I am an old man with enough experience that I can tell what everyone wants. But I did not have to keep Wanbin's secret, and I told Jinkai who wanted to buy it the first time I went to see him anyway." Wanbin later admitted, "Well, no matter how expensive it would be, I had to buy it; otherwise there was nothing for my cow. But I have to be careful. It is a most difficult thing to negotiate with one's own brother. I will never let Jinkai cheat me."

Individuals in today's rural China, having left behind the collective protection of the people's commune, find themselves forced to bargain with everyone and for everything. Everyday negotiation should not be considered an invention of the past two decades, but the economic reforms have given it a specific character. As local people talked about how others were always trying to cheat them, they clearly demonstrated their sense of uncertainty. One implication of this constant exercise of bargaining by those in various social relationships is that social groupings of any kind have become more and more unstable; it seems as if all boundaries of social groups or subject positions are always negotiable, and thus always dependent on the skills of the individual. From the perspective of the local people, they live in a world of bargains and bargaining. The boundaries between the self and various kinds of others have become further blurred.

"The Content of the Form"

I have borrowed the phrase "the content of the form" from Hayden White (1987), who argues that narrative is not simply an empty form through which real events are represented. Instead, the narrative itself, as a form of historical representation, has its own ideological and epistemological contents. I use it here to stress that the contents of certain forms of cultural practice need to be considered very seriously. An ethnographic example will illustrate what I mean by this.

A regular entertainment was offered by "the traveling cinema" (*fangyingdui*), which would come to a rural community to show movies on a temporary screen. On special occasions, the traveling cinema might be invited by the village committee to provide public entertainment. But more often, they were invited by individual families for events such as weddings or funerals. Whenever there was a movie, people would pass on the good news, but what movie was being shown was seldom part of the information—and few would bother to ask. Even after seeing it, hardly anyone remembered the movie's name or plot. If one asked, the likely answer would be something like, "Oh, who knows, some men and some women. They were doing things in it." Here the movie itself is the content of this activity, but how its viewing is organized and talked about is its form. What is important is to tell each other the news, to go to the viewing, to share with others a moment of happiness. What is actually watched is of only secondary importance. The political implications of such a split is obvious. Ideological doctrines imposed on local people from outside may be easily transformed into an empty form that has no effect on actual practice.

Consider another example. In most cases, in this region the bare, gray bricks of interior walls of rooms are left exposed. Old newspapers in the past had been the best material to cover some areas and provide both decoration and some protection. In the 1990s, the old newspapers were replaced by pages of the calendars of previous years, usually decorated with photographs of female actresses. In one old woman's room, where she kept the remembrance altar for her recently deceased husband, I found a number of large prints of female actresses on the walls, smiling and staring at the steamed bread that the old woman had prepared as an offering for her late husband. Another old woman put a calendar of Hong Kong scenery on her wall, and one of the pictures showed a big sign of a night club. When I asked her what that sign meant, she smiled at me and said, "How could I know anything about that?" She did not even know that it was Hong Kong, since she was one of a few elderly women in the community who remained illiterate. Even more interesting was the choice of an old woman in the main village. On her window was placed a postcard—a blonde with extraordinarily huge breasts sticking out of her bikini, and with a seductive smile on her face. The picture was removed immediately after I inquired about it to the old woman's son. He told me that he did not know where his mother had gotten it, but she just felt it was *pretty*. The son also told me that there had been a campaign in the last summer against "yellow pictures" (*huangse huapian*). In China, the term "yellow" is associated with pornography. He explained, "Schoolboys and -girls were told by their teachers that these calendar pictures were poisonous. They were told to burn these pictures. My son came home, asking me to burn these pictures." At this point I thought he meant that these pictures of women were "spiritually polluting," a favorite expression of the government. But it became clear that he had something else in mind, as he continued: "Some of these pictures were covered in plastic that was not good for children. When little babies eat them, they get sick." To me, this was a very surprising explanation of "poisonous." If local people could conceive of half-naked actresses above the "ancestral altar" or the naked blonde on their windows in these terms, I may easily imagine that written party doctrines could have no effect on their thinking.

Yet the emphasis on maintaining certain forms of cultural practice may place a great pressure on individuals who do not wish to comply with common rules. During the Chinese New Year's period, I went with Zuncang, the youngest son of my host in Dawa, to visit his friends and one of his aunts in a nearby village. We left Dawa in the early afternoon. On our way, we came across a middle-aged man on a bicycle that was carrying his daughter as well. Even from a great distance, the man immediately recognized Zuncang, and they warmly greeted each other. He was Zuncang's elementary school teacher, who asked his former pupil many questions about his college life. Their conversation was full of warmth and mutual respect. When we parted, Zuncang's teacher insisted that on our way back to Dawa, we must visit his family. Zuncang promised him a visit that afternoon.

When we reached the main village, Zuncang began to knock on the doors of his friends. We tried two doors; unfortunately, neither friend was home. They were probably doing the same thing—visiting others in other communities. I felt sorry for Zuncang but he did not look disappointed or unhappy about it. When we turned to the house of another friend of his, he uttered, "I actually hope he won't be home either." I thought he was joking, but he explained to me that, in fact, he did not want to visit any of these friends at all. Nevertheless, he had to; otherwise, people would think ill of him. He did not wish to be thought of as arrogant because he was able to go to college. It is a communal rule that people should visit each other during the New Year period. This time, however, his friend was home. Just as we were preparing to leave his friend's house half an hour later, the village head, a young man in his early thirties, came by. He invited Zuncang to his place for dinner, and Zuncang accepted immediately.

When we arrived in Zuncang's aunt's house in Dangjiahe, it was already about four o'clock in the afternoon. We had a formal meal with four cold dishes and four hot dishes. Time went quickly. It was not until I found that it had already become dark outside that Zuncang, while sipping his tea carefully, suggested that we move on. I was a little worried about our plan to visit the families of Zuncang's teacher and the village head. When we actually left his aunt's, it was completely dark outside. It must have been about seven o'clock. I followed Zuncang but soon found out that we were not making any more visits: we were heading home. I asked Zuncang whether he had forgotten his promises to visit the other two families. Zuncang smiled, "Oh, they did not mean it. We were simply being polite."

How can one tell whether a person means something or not? Not by what is said but by *how* it is said. The meaning of a statement is often determined by the way in which it is expressed. This point has been made very well by Maurice Bloch (1975a), and other anthropologists continue to argue for it in different contexts.[5] What I am emphasizing here is that in fact an outsider cannot possibly understand the meaning of an utterance or the significance of an action without learning those cultural forms through which these utterances or actions are performed. These cultural forms can be learned, but they cannot be taught.

Arthur Smith, a sinologist notorious for his very negative—at least to the eyes of some native scholars—portraits of "Chinese characteristics" (1894), might view my ethnographic examples as congruent with his depiction. Some incidents may appear to be similar, but my mode of explanation differs sharply from Smith's. While Smith used his examples to determine the inherent attributes of the Chinese, I have employed mine to investigate a particular historical moment. The ability to manipulate these forms of cultural practice is partly a consequence of the constantly changing political and economic realities in rural China. The local people have developed the ability to accommodate abrupt changes within an old framework of cultural forms so that they might maintain a certain stability and continuity in life. At the same time, today's rural China has no single dominant local authority, such as the traditional authority held by the gentry class or the revolutionary authority held by the rural cadres, that imposes on others a symbolic system for interpreting social action, whether collective or individual. Thus, a certain sense of collectivity or commonality can be maintained only through the often unconscious manipulation of cultural forms. Because there is now more room for individual maneuvers, one should expect to find a greater discrepancy between the form of a particular type of practice and its content; this argument is developed in the following chapter.

The Indocile Body

Foucault made his argument that in the classical age, the body was discovered as a site of power (1977). In this section, I invert his notion of "the docile body" not to suggest the historical emergence of "biopower" (see, e.g., Dreyfus and Rabinow 1982) but to stress that the local people use their bodies to convey a variety of meanings and feelings, both collective and individual. These bodies are "indocile" because they communicate via physical contact—contact that is often violent. Even on happy occasions such as weddings, such contact might physically harm whoever is on the receiving end, though the intent of the other person involved is usually to celebrate.

Wanbin and I went to a funeral in Yangjiahe, a neighboring rural community, in February 1992. Wanbin had told me that the son of the dead man was his friend, but we were not invited to the feast because Wanbin was not related to the family. The funeral had started before we arrived. Wanbin tried to explain what was happening as the funeral proceeded. Invited guests took turns in joining the funeral feast. About one o'clock in the afternoon, two men approached Wanbin to invite him and me to join the feast. Wanbin refused to go with them. But they insisted, raising their voices and becoming so loud that everyone nearby could hear. While Wanbin tried to explain why we should not join the feast, the two men began to pull his arms. Wanbin tried to get rid of them by moving in the opposite direction. They soon became excited, yelling: "Why not? Why should you? If you don't come to eat, my brother won't be happy!" One of the two men suddenly grabbed Wanbin by his waist, while the other firmly caught his collar. The first man lifted Wanbin and dragged him toward the courtyard where the feast was being held. After Wanbin was pulled about five meters toward the courtyard, he managed to cling to a tree, wrapping both his arms around it like a drowning man who had suddenly found a piece of wood floating in the sea. The two men could not move him any further, no matter how hard they tried, and they finally gave up. Later on, on our way back to Dawa, I discovered that they had torn one of Wanbin's pockets. According to Wanbin, we should not have joined the feast because we had not been formally invited. If we had gone, we would have been "laughed at" by others.

Happy occasions also give rise to excitement and violent physical contacts. A more elaborate treatment of violence as an expression of celebration will be given in the following chapter. Here I simply wish to point out that the meaning of violence is not necessarily tied to conflict or hatred.

There are other uses of physical force that perhaps fit the notion of violence better. For example, teachers in the village school quite commonly hit pupils. To celebrate Children's Day (1 June), each village school was supposed to prepare some performance, such as dancing or singing. In Zhaojiahe a team of four girls and four boys, whose ages were between nine and ten, were chosen to represent their school with a dance devised by one of its female teachers. These girls and boys rehearsed every afternoon under the instruction of the young schoolteacher, whose name was Caiyun. I had met all the teachers in the school, and Caiyun impressed me as being quiet and shy. She seldom spoke. One afternoon, I went to watch the students practicing their performance. At a certain point, the boys needed to bend their heads and raise their arms in a quite complicated way, while swirling at the same time. One boy, whom I knew very well because he was from Dawa, could not raise his arm properly; he was a little slower than the others. As she watched from about five meters away, Caiyun sang for them. After she saw that the boy could not get his movements right, she went straight to him and slapped his head hard several times, shouting, "How can you be so stupid?" When the boy screamed and tried to run away, Caiyun followed him and hit his shoulder. The boy fell on the ground—but he smiled back at his teacher.

Is this physical punishment? In my presence, one parent said to the teachers: "I have given my child to you and want him to learn something. If he does not listen to what you tell him to do, beat him. My child is yours." And a teacher once remarked, "The village boys are not like pupils in the cities. They do not listen to you. You have to slap them; otherwise there is no way to educate them." The local government had issued several directives prohibiting physical punishment in schools; according to the rules guiding the behavior of schoolteachers, it was strictly forbidden. These rules were on the wall of each teacher's dormitory, including Caiyun's. This example shows that the use of violence is not confined to a particular social group defined by generation, age, or sex. In this part of rural Shaanxi, violence is a widely employed means of communication available to everyone—male or female, old or young, senior or junior.

Indeed, fights were common in daily life. One afternoon in April, when everyone was in the fields, looking after their newly cultivated cotton, they suddenly began to hear two women's voices; what at first sounded like a loud argument quickly developed into a mixture of screaming and swearing. Next to Wanbin's field, just one step up on the terrace, Xicai squatted, calmly chatting with Wanbin about the weather. The quarreling became louder and louder, with obscenities launched at full force. The two voices, like the terraced fields, rose higher and higher. Those standing high enough could see the two women standing in the middle of a little road on the other side of the hill. Although the two women's voices increased dramatically and everyone could hear, no one showed any interest in intervening. No one even bothered to try to find out what was going on. Xincai, the party secretary of this community, stood on another road nearby, watching the fight.

My host later told me that the two women were Maixiang, Xincai's wife, and Wenfang, Xicai's wife; they were fighting because Wenfang had deliberately blocked the road used by Xincai and his wife to reach their field. Friction between these two families had begun several years earlier. At that time, when Xicai quarreled with a clerk from the local government over an agricultural tax, Xincai was in charge of resolving such disputes. Xicai was justly punished for his misconduct, according to Xincai; but Xicai believed that Xincai had unfairly favored those from the local government.

As usual, endless comments were offered afterward. Wanbin said, "Xincai, as the party secretary, lost face this time. He is by no means a good person to hold such an important position. If he had said anything provocative, Xicai would have beaten him to death. Maixiang is a master of obscenity." Wanyou also had an opinion: "If they had fought, I am afraid that Xincai would have probably been beaten. There is nothing wrong with beating someone up. Nobody would have cared. Wenfang and Maixiang are relatives, though." There is more to this story: when Wenfang and Maixiang met again the following day, they immediately got into a fight. As a result, Xincai sought help from the local government. Two policemen came to Zhaojiahe and took Xicai away for a couple of days for interrogation. After he was released, Xicai gathered a group of friends, discussing how to take revenge. But the proposed revenge had not occurred by the time I left.

Fights occur for various reasons. One man had beaten his brother's wife, causing her brain damage, just because she had dropped some garbage in front of his house. As in many other cases, different interpretations were offered for this fight, all referring to some series of prior events. I witnessed another fight between two sisters-in-law who were at odds because one had gossiped about the other. One day, they threw themselves at each other and fell to the ground, twisting and punching. People came out to watch, but no one tried to stop them. These fights can be dangerous. Two or three years before my visit, Yangkai's wife, Fenglan, fought with Jinchang's wife, Huanfang, because Fenglan was believed to have stolen several eggs from Huanfang. Although Yangkai and Jinchang were brothers by birth, their wives fought with each other violently. Both women's faces were covered by blood after the fight, and each tried to bite the other—indeed, Fenglan bit off the tip of Huanfang's finger.

These fights, which often grew out of some economic disagreement, were supposed to be settled within the community. If there was a serious dispute between two families—one that involved property redistribution—people would abide by a solution mediated by the court located in Leijiawa township. The conflicts and quarrels between Zhaojiahe and its neighboring communities also had to be mediated by the local court. People in this area constantly complained about the procedural change introduced in the early 1980s, which required the parties involved to pay a settlement fee in advance. Local people believed that no fee should be charged in advance, and no fee at all should be paid by the one who won the case.

Craftsmanship

In order to account for the cultural differences between Western and
Chinese social worlds, some scholars have pointed to their different
ways of understanding the function of emotions. In the West, the individual's emotional experience is assumed to legitimate social action
and the formation of social relations; for instance, it is taken for granted
that marriage should be based on love. But in China, people tend to
believe that there should be no such connection between individual
emotional experiences and the larger forces of society (see S. Potter
and J. Potter 1990, 180–95): instead, the legitimizing basis is provided
by work.[6] Sulamith and Jack Potter argue that for people in rural China,
"work is the symbolic medium for the expression of social connection,
and work affirms relationship in the most fundamental terms the villagers know" (1990, 195). Stressing the centrality of work in constituting
social relations in rural China, though correct, is not enough: the nature of that work must be explained. For the people in Shaanxi, "work"
does not usually mean a productive process, as commonly conceived
in the West—that is, the manufacture of a certain material product under a rational plan of organization based on a certain division of labor.
It is more often taken as a flow of mediating experience, perhaps oriented less toward the completion of a product than toward the work
itself as an opportunity for new experience. An ethnographic example
will help illustrate this point.

When the wooden lid used to cover the heating tunnel of the bed
in my room (see figure 4) was damaged, a carpenter came to repair it.
The lid was about thirty centimeters long and twenty centimeters wide.
The carpenter raised his right hand to me when he came into our room,
showing a piece of plank that he intended to use to carve a new lid. I
noticed that he had already nailed a piece of wood on the plank to act
as a handle. The plank looked like this:

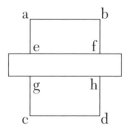

After the carpenter came into the room, he took out his ruler but—contrary to my expectation—he did not measure the flue; instead, he put the ruler down and tested the fit of the plank directly on the flue. It took a while for him to do so. And then he returned to his chair and began to measure the plank. He turned the plank around several times and measured it from one angle to another. He then stopped to focus on the length of "a–c" *and* "b–d," taking each measurement several times. When he picked up his saw, I thought he would cut either along "a–b" or "c–d"; instead, he took a pencil that had been resting on his left ear and drew some marks on "b–f" and "h–d." To my puzzlement, he actually moved to saw at "g–c." The wooden crossbar made the operation a little difficult. The carpenter went out to find a plane and an ax. On returning, he first employed the ax to cut the "b" corner and then used the plane on "a–c." He then went to try the fit again. As earlier, he used his ruler not on the flue but rather on the plank. He repeated the process until he came to "a–b," changing from one tool to another in complicated patterns. After he finished cutting "a–b" and "c–d," he checked again. It was still bigger than it should be. He went outside, applying the ax and plane on "a–b" and "c–d." Every few seconds he came back to fit the plane to the flue. Throughout the whole operation he neither spoke nor smoked.

I observed all this and found his approach puzzling. For instance, if it makes the piece more difficult to saw, why does he have to fix the handle before he starts working? why not measure the flue first? why draw some lines on one side and begin to saw another? While working on the lid, he demonstrated amazing skill with different kinds of tools and an amazing degree of proficiency. That is my point here: it is the technique, the tactics, the experience—in short, the craftsmanship itself—that defines work, rather than simply the results. What constitutes the fundamental sense of work is process, not product: "work" means a new experience. If work, even routine work, is considered as fresh experience, then it is perhaps not surprising for one to find that even when dealing with the agricultural work that they have been doing for generations, people in this community sometimes hesitate and seek advice from others on how to carry it out.

Draft animals were used for both transportation and agricultural production. Most households had an animal cart for such uses, and every male adult was supposed to know how to harness it. One day, while

getting ready to attend a wedding in Baocheng, Famin, my host in Nan-
jian, tried to prepare his donkey cart so that he could bring his mother
to the ceremony. Harnessing the donkey to a small wooden cart was a
chore that Famin did all the time. Famin said that he had to use the
cart at least every few days.

Zunxi, my previous host, and I, leaning on our bikes, were talking
to each other and watching Famin prepare the cart. Famin first took
the donkey from a pole to which it had been tied, and led it to the
wooden cart. Famin began to put on the reins, which were two long
ropes. The donkey was completely passive and moved slowly but without resistance to whichever position it was dragged. However, after
moving the donkey into several different positions, Famin hesitated
and looked perplexed, mumbling words as if they were directed to
himself; in fact, he was speaking to Zunxi. "This rope must be going
this way, mustn't it? No, no, it could not be going this way. It should
be going the other way." Famin first tried to make the rope go underneath the belly of the donkey, and then tried to make the rope go
over the animal's back. It looked as if he did not know how to harness
a donkey. Though Zunxi was not a farmer and he was not supposed to
know much about this task, he nevertheless made some suggestions.
Famin nodded his "yes" and tried it again. "No, it was not this way; it
could be the other way around." Famin turned the donkey to another
position and tried the rope as he had done the first time. He seemed
to forget whether the rope should first go underneath the donkey's
belly or above its neck. Finally, he got it: underneath the belly was the
right way.

I need to stress that this was not an isolated case. On many similar
occasions, I observed local farmers hesitate in doing what they had been
doing for many years. It seems that no matter how many times the same
piece of work had been done, one would always approach it as a new
experience. This is the technology of craftsmanship—that is, the meaning of work for people in this area. It may seem appropriate to apply
Lévi-Strauss's notion of "bricolage" to understand such situations as
these.[7] But his discussion of "the savage mind"—as well as the discussions of "primitive mentality" by Lévy-Bruhl, Mauss, and Durkheim—
is limited by its too-exclusive focus on systems of classification, which
fosters a high degree of conceptual abstraction in analyzing types of

society. We are concerned here very little with "how natives think" but a great deal with "how natives work." In using the term "work," I am alluding to something close to the notion of practice as a form of embodied knowledge.[8]

Judith Farquhar's study of Chinese medical practice provides a very good example to illustrate my point. Focusing on how Chinese doctors, particularly those who practice Chinese traditional medicine, diagnose and treat patients in clinical situations, Farquhar contrasts two modes of knowledge, one scientific and the other "practical." With Chinese medical practice as an ethnographic example, Farquhar provides an epistemological critique of so-called scientific knowledge. She argues:

The practical form and methodological capabilities of the clinical encounter in Chinese medicine have been shown here to depend neither on a fixed base of essences instantiated in material forms (the single "real world" of positivism) nor on an abstract body of scientific standards by means of which the truth or falsity, adequacy or inadequacy of statements can be evaluated. Knowledge, method, theory, even the medical archive itself, have been shown to derive their value from practical processes in which the virtuosity of the doctor and his mastery both of his own clinical experience and that recorded in medical history are highly valued. Practical, artistry, and seasoned wisdom are not, of course, confined to the world of Chinese medicine. But Chinese medicine appears to have developed unique means of acknowledging, understanding, and refining the skills of its practitioners. Skill, specificity, and contingency are in its discourse central to the practice of knowing. (1994, 220)

As Farquhar has shown, in the Chinese clinic a certain symptom cannot be reduced to or predicted by an analysis of its individual elements, because such elements are never analyzed separately; they are always treated as part of a whole system of function in process. Furthermore, no one prescription follows a given symptom, because each symptom is taken as situational evidence that is always related to some other bodily or spiritual reactions. Therefore, the clinical experience of Chinese doctors is characterized not by a mode of scientific knowledge but by a knowing practice. There may be a danger of exaggerating this difference in modes of knowledge, but it provides a useful model for us as we consider the meaning of work for the rural Chinese. I am tempted to suggest that the nature of work in rural Shaanxi is similar to what

Farquhar calls "knowing practice"—in the sense that "work" is not seen as derived from a set of standards of effectiveness and efficiency but is rather oriented toward itself as a form of experience. The significance of these forms of cultural practice is even clearer on ceremonial occasions, when their performance and expression are intensified: we turn to next to examine such ritual celebrations.

6

The Pliable Emotions

In the previous chapter, I suggested that a certain form of cultural practice may continue to function even though its content no longer
matched its original purpose. I also suggested that the body, often used
in violence, was crucial for local people in exchanging feelings and emotions, both collective and individual. In this chapter, I will develop these
arguments with particular reference to wedding and funeral celebrations: that is, examining not everyday but "ritual" occasions.[1] Ceremonial celebrations are intensified moments of social life that can be
taken as a kind of "ideal type" of experience, to use a Weberian term.
This chapter will introduce two extensive ethnographic examples that
I will draw on in developing my argument about the significance of certain cultural forms in the age of economic reforms.

Any ethnographer of northern rural Shaanxi in the 1990s would note
that after decollectivization, there was very little activity of any kind
sponsored or organized by the community as a whole. Wedding and
funeral celebrations, prepared by each family relying on its own network of relations and connections, became the only form of collective
activity.[2] During the radical years of the Maoist revolution, elaborate
forms of celebrating were prohibited by the government as "feudal remnants," but since the 1980s government policy controlling such events
has been less strict. The scale of weddings and funerals in the 1990s
grew so fast that a community regulation had to be issued in order to
try to limit extravagant spending on these occasions.[3]

The two "celebrations" were viewed by local people as being very
similar in their social functions. They were treated the same, both lin-
guistically and practically. In Chinese, weddings and funerals are of-

ten put together under the single description *hongbai xishi. Hong* and *bai* are color terms, meaning "red" and "white." The character *xi* is "happy," while *shi* means "thing" (or "event"). Therefore, the four characters together mean "red and white happy things": the wedding is a "red happy thing," which can be shortened to "red thing" (*hongshi*); while the funeral is a "white happy thing," which is often abbreviated to "white thing" (*baishi*).[4] People in this part of rural Shaanxi tended to simplify the expressions even further, referring to weddings and funerals as just *shi* (something). When talking about either a wedding or a funeral, they would simply say, "The X family today *guoshi*"— literally, "passes through something" (the dictionary definition of *guo* is "to pass through," or "to live").

"The Rites of Passage"

Honglu's Wedding: 11 February 1992

Soon after breakfast, Wanbin, my host in Dawa, came to see me in a new Mao-style blue suit and urged me to get ready.[5] I had been told several days previously that we would be going to join a wedding in Xipo, a neighboring rural community two or three miles away. The bridegroom was one of Wanbin's nephews: Wanbin's father's brother's son's sister's son,[6] whose name was Honglu. He had joined the army a few years earlier and was living in Shijiazhuang, a city in Hebei province. Having returned to Xipo in the winter of 1992, Honglu was going to marry a girl from another nearby rural community.

Soon a horde of bicycles was on the road. Men were wearing brand-new blue Mao suits; women, especially young women, were dressed in beautiful colors. The young people were all on bicycles, followed slowly by a donkey cart carrying the elderly. On the back seat of each bicycle was a pair of hanging baskets, covered with colorful homemade handkerchiefs, which held wedding presents.

It took about half an hour to reach Xipo. Honglu's house, where the wedding was supposed to take place, was at the end of the village. It was an ordinary courtyard. Three red posters were placed on the door, and Chinese characters of blessing were written on them in golden letters. On walls inside the courtyard were similar posters, with blessings such as "newly wedded auspiciousness," "newly wedded happiness," and so on. To the right of the door, there was a table set up for receiv-

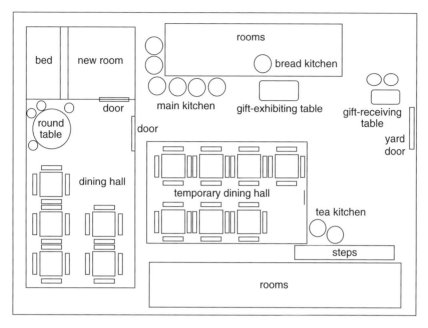

Figure 9. A wedding courtyard.

ing gifts (see figure 9). Two middle-aged men sat behind the table as gift accountants, making records in a notebook. If the gift was cash, they wrote down the exact amount. No single item, no matter how small, was left unrecognized.[7] No person would come to a wedding without presenting a gift; some neighbors contributed only a few cents, but their offerings were recorded as accurately as any others. Next to the receiving table was another table on which all the presents were piled up, so that they might be shown to the public audience. Leaning against the window next to the exhibition table were placed, together with several bottles of spirits, two pictures: Honglu's late grandfather and father.

On the wall above the exhibition table, all the names of those who had been invited to help with the ceremony were written on a red paper called the *zhishibu* (list of managers). They were divided into twelve categories: "receiving gifts," "greeting guests," "scooping gifts,"[8] "serving the meal," "carrying bread," "bread chefs," "tea chefs," "serving tea," "assisting in the kitchen," "carrying water," "looking after ovens," and "washing up." Under each of these titles were two or three names.

The inner part of the courtyard was divided into two halves, one for cooking and the other serving as a temporary dining hall; the latter was shaded by a plastic roof supported by wooden poles. Paintings of figures from traditional operas hang from the roof. Seven square tables were set up in the temporary dining hall. At the end of the yard, a "new room" (*xinfang*) was prepared in a larger room for Honglu and his bride. Five square tables and a round table were also arranged in the large room as part of the dining space. There were twelve tables in all, each seating eight people.

No sooner had we come into the courtyard than our basket was taken away. The present, a "tiger bread" that Wanbin had brought with him, had been placed, together with other gifts received, on the exhibition table; it stayed there for quite a while before being brought into the kitchen. Having been seated in the large room, we were offered tea and cigarettes. People walked around, making compliments to the host family and exchanging words with those whom they knew. About ten o'clock in the morning, a huge empty truck arrived. I was told that the truck belonged to the local government, and one of Honglu's uncles had managed to request it to bring the bride and her family to Xipo. A small group of people were called on after the truck had arrived. This was a "greeting team" (*yingqinde*) that would follow the truck to the village of the bride. The greeting team was supposed to include the bridegroom's father, his mother's elder brother, and the "best man" (*banlang*). Honglu's father had died some years ago, and his mother had remarried; his stepfather did not join the greeting team. Wankai, Honglu's mother's elder brother, represented the family. A special meal was prepared for the truck driver and the best man.

No sooner had the truck left Xipo than the feast started. Guests were invited to sit down, either in the large room or in the temporary dining hall. We were seated at a corner table in the large room. At that table were Wanbin and Wanyou from Dawa; two young men and two young women, one with a small child, were strangers to us. The men had paid their respects to each other and exchanged a few words before the first course arrived—nine cold dishes. Not very much was on each tiny plate; in two of them there was only sugar—brown and white—though all the dishes were arranged neatly on the table. The meal was accompanied by either tea or wine, and each table was attended by a man.

Table manners were quite graceful (except for the wild behavior of the child, who must have been five or six). Guests took a little at a time from the nearest plates; they drank no more than two or three cups of wine, and they were not persuaded to take more. The second course arrived sooner than we had expected. Pork, tofu, and vegetables were brought on the table in turn, together with steamed bread. A bowl of soup was to end the meal. Only one spoon was provided for the eight people at each table, and each had the soup in turn. We finished our meal in about half an hour. Our table was immediately taken by other guests after we had left it. The feast went on.

About two o'clock in the afternoon, the truck returned, this time with an enormous Chinese character—*Xi*, "happiness"—on its front window. The bride and bridegroom were squeezed onto the front seat, next to the driver in his cab. Behind them the best man and two brides-maids sat in the back seat. Dowry was piled up on the truckbed. The bride's family and relatives were brought to Xipo by a big bus. When the truck parked right in front of Honglu's house, the best man and Honglu both got out; but the bride and her attendants, one slightly older than the other, refused to move. The driver went away, and a crowd gathered in front of the truck. Honglu and the best man stood very close to the truck door, negotiating with the women inside. According to a local custom, a bridesmaid was supposed to be paid before setting her feet on the ground. Without the bridesmaids, the bride should not be allowed to move. Most people also believed that the amount of money presented to the bridesmaids should be symbolic rather than substantial—a few yuan, perhaps. But in this case, the bridesmaids de-manded fifty yuan each, according to the best man.

The negotiation, which was a job for the best man, took longer than usual: that is, long enough to make those in the crowd lose their pa-tience. Honglu had little to do except giggle at the bride, who had hid-den inside the driver's cab. Onto the truck children began to throw peas and pieces of millet straw, which were supposed to be tossed over the bride's head as a sort of blessing. Some young people were even throw-ing small stones at the truck, trying to hit the bride and her maids. One of the bridesmaids tried to close the door but she failed, and they shrank even further inside. Although disturbed by such attacks, they seemed determined to succeed in their demands. Someone passed a baby only a few months old to Honglu, a daughter of one of the bridesmaids. "Tell your mother to get off the truck," Honglu said to the baby. The baby began to cry but her mother was unmoved. At one point, after observing the hopeless situation and the exhaustion of the best man, Honglu's stepfather came to talk to the bride. Nothing was achieved by his pleading. Cash, wrapped in red paper, was handed over for the second time, though far less than the amount demanded by the bridesmaids, and they still refused to surrender.

The crowd became irritated. The bride smiled at everyone but stuck to her seat as if she were a piece of iron attached to a magnet. Some in the crowd shouted, "Force her out!" Having heard this, the bride moved her body even further inside, very close to the door on the other side of the truck. The best man in desperation suddenly opened that door and caught the bride's left arm. He then pulled her off the seat— she was forced out of the truck. The unusual scene drew loud applause. The bride tried to run away, but every possible direction was blocked by the crowd. She was welcomed by a rain of peas and pieces of millet straw over her head. Resistance by the bridesmaids now meant little and they got off the truck, though reluctantly. Firecrackers were set off very close to their faces, as the crowd enjoyed seeing how such threats frightened them. Everyone died laughing when a little boy tried to burn the bottom of a maid's trousers with a cigarette butt. It took no less than an hour for the bride and her maids to make it from the truck to the ground.

The bride, for the first time in full view, looked beautiful. She was wearing a loose red cashmere jacket and a pair of tight blue trousers. With her shining dark hair combed back neatly, she was wearing an orange silk scarf. Her leather shoes were of a modern design. Her appearance made the bridegroom's look plain. He was in his army uniform, all in green apart from a pair of black leather shoes, and wore his army hat, like a soldier in battle.

At this time, the courtyard door, through which the bride and bridegroom were supposed to pass, was blocked by a group of young people. The door was narrow and small, and two persons could barely pass through at once. Now there were more than twenty young people standing in front of it, waiting for the new couple to come. With her hand in his, the new couple launched their first attempt, running as fast as they could toward the door and throwing themselves heavily on a wall of bodies. They failed. They were forced to retreat and catch their breath. A few minutes later, all of a sudden, they collected themselves and dashed toward the door again, with such energy and strength that a number of people fell to the ground. They fought, both literally and metaphorically, with those who were in their way. In the middle of this struggle, a voice was heard: "We have forgotten to burn a bunch of millet straw!" According to a local custom, the bride must step over a bunch of burning millet straw when she crosses the groom's threshold. The fire on the ground helped the new couple break through the blockage. As people were forced to give way to the flame, the couple was able to run into the courtyard. The bride's jacket was left with smears from sweaty hands and her beautiful scarf was on the ground, torn almost to pieces.

After the bride and bridegroom moved into the courtyard, they first went to the pictures of the bridegroom's late grandfather and father. They bowed together three times. Then they went into the large room. The "new room"—that is, the *xinfang*—prepared for the new couple was located in its right corner. The new room had been open to everyone before the bride arrived, but now it was locked in a peculiar manner. One end of a big rope was tied to the door handle and the other end of the rope was firmly fastened to a window frame in the large room. The rope was knotted in several places, and on each of these knots a big lock was placed. In order to open the door, one had to unlock all the locks on the rope. Two bridesmaids and the bride, facing out, were seated at the round table in the large room; the best man, next to Honglu, was standing on the other side of the table, ready for another round of negotiations. They were surrounded by a crowd of young people.

Those who had locked the door and knotted the rope would be willing to open it only if they were given some gifts or money. This time, it was supposed to be at least in part the bridesmaids' duty to present some kind of gift.[9] The negotiation, which was mainly conducted between the bridesmaids and the best man, centered on how much should be paid for each lock; the bride and bridegroom were almost silent. None of the senior family members of either side was present. The bridesmaids were showered, from time to time, by cigarette butts and small pieces of foodstuffs. The crowd greatly enjoyed watching them become irritated. The best man now turned to talk to those who had locked the door—to argue, to persuade, to beg, to threaten them to give in.

Two yuan for each lock seemed to have been finally agreed on. Without success in persuading the bridesmaids to pay for it, the best man took out some money from his pocket. No sooner did he pull it out than a young man leaped on him, grabbed his hand, took the money, and ran away. Then everyone learned that the young man did not have any of the keys. The demand now was more directed toward the bridesmaids, who had the duty to present some gifts. It was settled that the compensation for each lock would be two handkerchiefs. The older of the two went out to get the handkerchiefs; as soon as she walked back into the room, a few men jumped on her shoulders. Seeing this, everyone went crazy. They all threw themselves on her so suddenly that she fell down on the floor. There she was crushed under a dozen people, as everyone tried desperately to grab the handkerchiefs. Arms and legs intertwined wildly as they wrestled. It looked as if she was going to be torn apart, and she had to give away the handkerchiefs that she had been holding firmly. The bridesmaid stood up, looking very angry, and left the room. The other attendant also wanted to leave but she was stopped by the best man. He asked her to give some money to the crowd, and she did so.

When the door of the new room was finally opened, small children ran into it first. Nuts and dates had been left everywhere, and after the children had picked them all up the couple entered the room. This "rite of passage" ended when the couple succeeded in sitting on the bed.

The feast continued for the rest of the day. A much better banquet was prepared for the bride's relatives, who left in the late afternoon.

The Yang Funeral: 20 February 1992

When we arrived in Yangjiahe, a small rural community not far from Zhaojiahe, the funeral had already begun. In front of Yang Mancang's house, a reception area was set up (see figure 10). A picture of Mancang's deceased father was placed on a table outside his courtyard. Six desks, which were borrowed from the village school, were arranged in a row in front of his house. These desks were prepared for receiving gifts. There is a specific term for the gift presentation

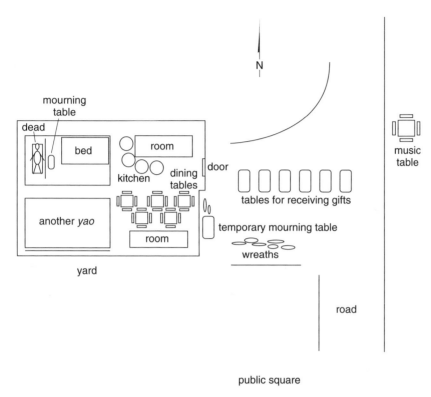

Figure 10. The spatial arrangement of a funeral.

at funerals: *xingmenhe*, which means at once "receiving" and "exhibiting" gifts. On the first table, the one closest to the house, was a large wreath on which were hung two elegiac couplets: "Great virtuous man when you were alive" and "Remembered forever when you are dead."

Most guests arrived in animal carts of some sort on which *menhe*— a set of gifts, often placed in baskets and chests—were carried. Guests began to line up in front of the desks as soon as they arrived. They were helped by those from Mancang's family to move their gifts from their carts onto the exhibition desks. A complete set of *menhe* was supposed to include a number of items, both symbolic and material. A pig's head, sometimes a cloth one, was customarily presented on the very first table; on each of its ears should be clipped a five-yuan note. Also expected on the first table were a bunch of incense and a box of candles.

On the rest of the tables, a whole banquet was usually displayed. Just as on any formal occasion, the cold dishes, hot dishes, cigarettes, wines, and spirits must be carried out as if they were in the procession for a banquet. Fried bread was quite popular. Most of the food was home-made, but it was not unusual for guests to bring fruits or meat pur-chased at a market.

The food brought by guests was displayed for about ten minutes be-fore being moved into the kitchen. Every time a new set of gifts was shown, the musicians, who were sitting on the other side of the road, would play a piece of music. Firecrackers were also fired each time. Mancang and his son, both in white, knelt down in front of the gifts, touching their heads on the ground, for each new set. After being helped with their gifts, guests would go to bow to the picture of the deceased. And then they would join the feast.

A temporary dining hall was set up inside Mancang's courtyard. There were two *yao* in Mancang's courtyard; one was used as a mourn-ing hall (see figure 10). Mancang's father's body was placed on a bench in the inner part of the mourning hall, hidden behind a curtain. In front of the curtain there was a small table, on which were placed four pieces of steamed bread, four bowls of noodles, and an incense holder.

The funeral feast was no different from any other in its organization and management. With much noise, guests took their turns in joining the feast. After the reception was completed at noon, the musicians were invited into the house for their meal. Meanwhile, an order was given by a tall man, Mancang's uncle on his mother's side, requesting that everyone concerned move into the mourning hall. It was time for all to put on mourning garb. The mourning hall was packed with people, and some of them were on their knees. Mancang and his son, who had been in white suits and trousers, were now asked to change into white gowns that were long enough to cover their feet. Their shoes were also covered by white cloth, and they wore hats that had a long white strip of cloth hanging down. Their faces were covered with gauze kerchiefs. Mancang was told to wear two ribbons, one white and one brown, across his chest. Mancang's son, the grandson of the deceased, wore a gray ribbon. Each was given a willow twig to hold, on which red and yellow strips of paper had been placed. In their final act of preparation, Man-cang and his son placed a linen rope around their waists. The rope had to be knotted at several places, and the number of these knots was determined by their relationship to the deceased.[10]

Those closely related to the family were also supposed to change, a process that was quite simple for men but rather complicated for women. Most men simply added a white armband to whatever they had been wearing, and some tied a linen rope around their waists. Women changed completely into white and covered their faces with gauze kerchiefs. I was surprised to observe mothers helping their daughters to arrange colorful scarves.

As soon as everyone had dressed up, some paper was burned on the mourning table. With everyone on his or her knees, women began to wail. A few minutes later, the wailing was stopped by the tall man, who said: "My children, that is enough for the moment!" Then, several men went together with Mancang to move the deceased into a coffin that had been placed behind the curtain. The dead body was covered by a red gown. They carefully lined the coffin with two mattresses, one from Mancang and the other from his son, and then the body was put in. On the body were placed a dozen quilts presented by the dead man's relatives: from his daughters' families, from his wife's family, and from his own mother's family. All these quilts had been exhibited in public before they were taken inside. The cover of the coffin was closed without being nailed shut.

The coffin was left for a time in the mourning hall, where the women stayed; the men, following the musicians, went out of the hall, moving slowly toward the other end of the village. Mancang and his son, supported by their cousins and uncles, walked in the front row. They passed through the whole village on their way to place an obituary notice on a wall, stopping in the middle of the road several times to burn some paper. Traditionally, one was supposed to burn "paper money" (*zhiqian*), which was made in a particular shape and usually had to be purchased, symbolizing the cash that could be used in the other world. People in this area simply said "to burn paper" (*shaozhi*) rather than "to burn paper money" (*shaozhiqian*); they often burned any kind of paper that they could find rather than buying "paper money," which became available to them again in the mid-1980s.

The obituary, which gave the location of the grave, was placed on a wall where public announcements were displayed. It was such a windy day that the notice was blown off immediately after being posted. When the men returned, it was time to move the coffin out of the mourning hall. The task was carried out by a group of young men, followed by the women who had been wailing without stop. A sedan chair, or *jiao* as local people called it, was set up where the gift receiving desks had been. The sedan chair was made of an iron frame that could be taken apart when it was not in use. It was decorated with a combination of beautiful colors: red, orange, blue, yellow, green, black, all startling and eye-catching. A small table had been placed in front of the sedan chair, and on it was a large steamed bread decorated with various paper flowers. At this time, all the women surrounded the chair, crying and wailing; men took turns drinking a drop of wine in front of the table. No one was supposed to finish his glass; half had to be sprinkled on the ground. This act was called *dianjiao*, or sacrificing to the sedan chair.

Before the coffin could move further, another performance was carried out. A woman, one of the musicians, stood on the table and began to sing a song from a local opera. Women stopped weeping and together with men became an earnest audience. Fathers carried their sons on their shoulders; people applauded and screamed when the opera singer reached a seemingly impossible note. Even after several songs, the singer was not allowed to stop. Finally, a young drummer replaced her on the table, and with great talent he began to play a huge drum.

After everyone had been fully entertained by the opera and the drum, the coffin in the sedan chair was ready to go on its way. Mancang walked behind the musicians and ahead of the coffin; Mancang's son was behind the coffin. The grave, which had been chosen by a geomancer three days earlier, was located on a hill behind the village. Ten or so young people carried the sedan chair on their shoulders, almost running on the narrow, hilly roads.

The grave was very deep, and it took a while for the coffin to be lowered into it. After the burial was over, most of the wreaths brought to the funeral were burned at the grave. On the way back to the village, only one musician still had any energy for performing. Other people were quiet. The funeral was over. As we returned to Zhaojiahe, my host asked me: "Did you notice what music they played?" "No, I'm afraid not." "They played 'Nothing on Earth Is Better Than My Mom'": a pop song from a Taiwanese TV soap opera recently released on Chinese television—even though the dead person was a man.

Weddings and Violence

At either a wedding or a funeral, each person attending is put into a so-cial category that determines how he or she should behave. At wed-dings, the principle of classification primarily concerns how a person is supposed to be entertained—particularly how he or she is supposed to be fed. At funerals, which I will discuss in the following section, social categories are clearly marked out by one's relationship to the deceased.

At a wedding, four major groups of people interact at three levels. First, at the level of kinship, people are divided into two main social categories: *huoke* and *xinke*. *Huoke* are those who are related to the bridegroom's family, either as his *zijiawu* or as his relatives;[11] *xinke* are those who are affiliated with the bride's family, either her *zijiawu* or her relatives. The Chinese character *ke* means "guest"; *xin* means "new" and *huo* in this context may be translated as "old," though its literal meaning is "goods." These two groups of kin are treated differently at the wedding. *Huoke* are supposed to come to the wedding by them-selves, whereas *xinke* will be transported in some manner by the bride-groom's family. In this part of rural China, in the 1990s trucks and buses were the most popular means of transportation. Any *huoke* must pre-pare a gift—two loaves of tiger bread at minimum—in order to join the wedding feast; *xinke* are not supposed to bring anything for the wedding except the dowry prepared by the bride's family. *Huoke* cus-tomarily do not have their meals with *xinke*, who always receive a bet-ter and larger meal.

Second, at the level of practical management, a group of "managers" (*zhishi*), who are supposed to be in charge of the ceremony, constitutes a distinctive category of participants. They are usually not directly re-lated to the bridegroom's family, whose members do not engage in any jobs of a practical kind. Friends and neighbors are likely to be invited to help at the wedding, particularly those who have particular skills (such as cooking). The most important management task is to organ-ize the feast, which includes borrowing cooking implements from many households in one's own local community and sometimes beyond. Plates and chopsticks are borrowed from every possible source. In this sense, a wedding is always a communal event.

Third, at the level of performance, there must be an audience for a wedding. Any celebration of this kind must also be a spectacle. A wedding has to be performed in public: that is, it has to be watched. Local people have a practical explanation: the spectacle serves as a means of demonstrating one's economic condition and social power. The emerging economic differentiation that began in the 1980s seems to be a reason for, as well as a consequence of, the increasingly elaborate wedding celebration. From their perspective, such economic differences demand, on the one hand, to be acknowledged; on the other hand, the acknowledgment itself is believed to be a significant means to gain economic power.

The wedding celebration involves a series of symbolic encounters that are designed to "prevent" the bride from reaching her "new room"; three are particularly significant. First, the bride, in the company of her groom, must try to cross the threshold of the courtyard of her future husband's family. They should be blocked at the yard door by violence, symbolical as well as literal, just as we have seen in the case of Honglu's wedding. The encounter is most appropriately described as "a fight." Second, her attempts to unlock the locks on the door of the new room provoke another vehement battle. Everyone has the right to lock the door at a wedding ceremony, and then to demand whatever he or she wishes from the bride. Finally, the bride must struggle in order to reach the bed in her new room, which is supposed to be taken over by others as soon as the door is opened. To be able to sit on the bed represents the end of this journey: the marriage of the new couple.

Indeed, any moment of a wedding seems to be suitable for an act of performance whose logic is that of blockage, making the desired journey of the bride more difficult. The bride must be transported from her natal family to her new room in a vehicle provided by the bridegroom's family, but as soon as that vehicle is set on the road, anyone can block any part of the journey with rope. The distribution of *xiyan* (happy cigarettes) and *xitang* (happy candies) is expected at these moments of unexpected stops. In a sense, "the rites of passage" might be better called "the rites of blockage."

Observing the marriage ceremony, Maurice Freedman once wrote that "the Chinese rites of marriage are lengthy, elaborate, and dense with esoteric meaning" (1979a, 261). He intended to find out what each act at the Chinese wedding signified and how these elements of signification functioned as parts of a whole system, as a cosmos in action. His sources were largely literary, which means that the ceremony was recorded by those who knew how to interpret the existing symbols or performances and thus each symbol or performed act was given a definite interpretation in writing. Although the focus of Freedman's discussion is clearly to articulate a symbolic system tied to the Chinese worldview, an underlying assumption is less obvious: that this view, through the hands of an interpretive authority—that is, the gentry class in the past—informed the actual practices of the wedding celebration. My question is this: From the perspective of the participants, in this part of rural China is there still a recognizable correlation between each act (or each symbol) and its literary meaning? If not, then why not?

To an outside observer, Freedman's statement may appear to still hold true. That is, one may explain what was going on at a Shaanxi wedding in terms of a meaningful system that reflected a cosmological view of the local people's world. However, my focus here is not on a system of meaning viewed from the outside; rather, I mean to stress two points important to the participants. First, they no longer have a sense of a consistent or master version of this view as a system of meaning; and second, there is not, at this moment of historic transition, any structure of local authority that can impose such a system of interpretation for the symbols or acts performed at the wedding.

For those who were involved in such celebrations in northern rural Shaanxi, what was crucial was not what particular acts were supposed to mean, but what effects such performances might achieve. In other words, each performance at the wedding was practical in its orientation and largely detached from the literary meaning that had originally been given to it in custom and the annals of local history. No person in this community could have provided a systematic account of what should be done at the wedding. People did not even wish to talk about why there must be fire when the bride was crossing the threshold of her future husband's door. Rather than the performance being imprisoned—determined—by having to convey a particular meaning, the meaning of the action had to rely on the performance itself. From the perspective of the participants, what took place seemed to be a spontaneous physical interaction. That is, the rites of blockage were "lengthy" and "elaborate" but not informed by a system of "esoteric meaning." The significance of these performances appeared to have been completely lost to them.

This experience may not be unique to the people in northern rural Shaanxi. In studying the funeral rites in South China, James Watson found that local people knew how to do them but often could not provide any systematic explanation for their practices (1988, 4–6). When asked about the meaning of an act or a symbol, Cantonese villagers often said to him: "I'm not clear about that. We do it this way because that's how it has always been done" (6). Watson develops this ethnographic insight into an argument that relies on a distinction between "orthopraxy" and "orthodoxy." He explains, "By enforcing orthopraxy (correct practice) rather than orthodoxy (correct belief) state officials made it possible to incorporate people from many different ethnic or regional backgrounds, with varying beliefs and attitudes, into an overarching social system we now call China" (10–11).[12] I agree with Watson that there was a double structure of authority, represented by two distinguishable social groups, the gentry class and the ordinary villagers. The former was concerned with the meaning of cultural symbols, the latter more with practice. I am not concerned here with how this double structure of authority functioned but wish simply to point out a fact: in the People's Republic of China in the 1990s, there was no longer any social group that could authorize the meaning of ceremonial acts or symbols for local people. Under these conditions, what we must understand is not what is said about what they commonly do but, to quote Bourdieu, their "logic of practice." As far as northern rural Shaanxi is concerned, this logic of practice seems to be embodied in the very uses of violence on ceremonial occasions that I have described. Before further general discussion of this topic, let us first look at another ethnographic example.

The Baocheng Wedding: 1 May 1992

Zunxi, my second host, told me that his sister's husband's sister's son was going to get married in a couple of days. He wished to help me "expand my knowledge by participating in a wedding of a better-off family," and so I went with him to Baocheng. On our arrival, I noticed that a chain of cars, rather than a truck, was employed to transport the bride. A crowd of three or four hundred people had gathered in front of the bridegroom's house before these cars arrived.

As soon as the bride came out of the car, firecrackers were set off and a bunch of millet straw was burned at the threshold. The best man tossed several handfuls of sweets and cigarettes over his head, which made the crowd applaud with joy. People jumped as high as possible, trying to catch the items in midair. Those who failed threw themselves to the ground, searching for what had not been caught. They pounced on one another, trying to grab a piece of sweet from whoever was holding it. Many of those who had got something were lying on the ground with their faces downward, eager to consume what they had seized.

When the crowd finally began to resume its order, suddenly a scream rent the air. As I turned my head around, I saw an amazing scene: one old woman had tightly grabbed another by her waist, and was madly kissing her all over her face. They were both over sixty and looked quite healthy. The aggressor had bound feet, very small, like some other old women in this region. What was going on? Then I realized what had happened: after the woman with bound feet had successfully grabbed a piece of candy, she was attacked from behind by another woman, who had managed to put a great deal of red lipstick on her cheeks. The crowd stopped fighting for sweets or cigarettes, roaring with laughter to see an old woman with her face so smeared with red. The woman with the misplaced lipstick immediately sought to retaliate: running after the woman who did this, she grabbed her tightly and kissed her violently, trying to remove the lipstick from her own face by rubbing it on the other woman's face. The other woman was desperately trying to get away, but she could not. Pushing and pulling each other fiercely, the two women stumbled, and both fell on the ground. Lipstick and dirt were all over their faces and clothes. They were both wearing traditional black suits, and they rolled quickly from one side to another; once they stopped at the bride's feet, just beside a pair of shining high heels. The crowd went crazy, and no one seemed to be paying any attention to the beautiful, gold-covered bride any longer. The applause from the crowd made the sound of firecrackers seem remote. Getting more excited, these two old women then tried to tear off each other's clothes. The woman with bound feet pulled off two of the other's buttons, but unfortunately her own trousers were ripped by a tree branch beside the road. Through a triangular tear, the surrounding people glimpsed her underpants! The women ran away after this.

The crowd's attention then turned to the door, as they were ready to watch the bride and groom's attempt to get into the house. A number of young men, all in their early twenties, stood in front of the door, pretending to look angry and ferocious. One with a scar on his right cheek rested his hands on his waist and shouted to the new couple: "You fucking bastards, you want to get through this door today? Fuck your mother! I have been your friend all the time but not fucking today! You fucking try to go through here, idiots!" While yelling at the couple, the young man was also throwing beans and small pieces of millet straw onto their faces so violently that the bride could hardly keep from covering her face. When the couple tried to pass through the door, they were stopped and forced back. The pushing and pulling were so intense that it looked like a real fight. After several failures, the couple's efforts became more vigorous. Once the bride almost succeeded in crossing the threshold, but she was pulled back by several hands on her collar. A flower that the bride was wearing fell from her red jacket. It was very hard to pass this door. . . .

Why does a wedding have to be celebrated in such a violent way? The English term "violence" may not be entirely appropriate here, because two basic senses of the term are not implied. First, my usage does not entail a violation of other people's rights; and second, there is no negative connotation of conflict or hatred.[13] I am simply indicating the degree of physical contact at the wedding celebrations, without suggesting that it is somehow negative. By calling the interaction "violence," I am suggesting that it is possible to understand the wedding performance as the embodiment of a particular type of experience.

Stevan Harrell introduces a collection of essays investigating the nature of violence in Chinese society with the following question: "Why does a culture that condemns violence, that plays down the glory of military exploits, awards its highest prestige to literary, rather than martial, figures, and seeks harmony over all other values, in fact display such frequency and variety of violent behaviour, that is, of the use of physical force against persons?" (1990, xi). He grounds his discussion of violence on two propositions. First, violence is associated with conflict or antagonism. Second, for violent action to take place, people must have some motivation to settle the conflict by force (xi). From these, two further assumptions follow: that violence is naturally related to feelings such as anger and hatred and that conflicts or confrontations derived from such feelings are embedded in the structure of society. Harrell therefore argues that although the high culture of Chinese society condemns violence, the popular culture persistently encourages its use.

I agree with Harrell only in part. I believe he is correct in arguing that we must distinguish between high and popular culture if we are to understand the problem of violence in Chinese society, but I am suspicious of his assumptions about the nature of violence. My observations suggest that for the rural residents in northern Shaanxi, who may be seen as part of the popular culture, violence can be used to communicate both positive and negative feelings. The messages conveyed by this means are dependent on situations rather than determined by a certain mode of emotion or a certain type of behavior. Therefore, the interesting question is not about the meaning of violence but about the channel through which such a mode of communication is made possible. This channel of contact, in our case, is the body. By shifting our attention from the meaning of violence to the practice of the body, we may be able to understand a certain structural rearrangement taking place in contemporary Chinese society.

Before the Maoist revolution, there had been frequent fights in Zhaojiahe between members of different villager groups.[14] However, as local people recalled, there was always a certain authority within their own community—the gentry class in general—who determined whether collective violence was being properly used. Ceremonial celebrations such as weddings and funerals were also arranged according to the patterns laid down by this group. As local people recalled, violence on ceremonial occasions had not been common. Particularly at funerals, proper address and behavior were demanded by the strict rules internalized within the agnatic hierarchy (see, e.g., Hsu 1949).

But the Maoist revolution changed the structure of local authority and control considerably. After the land reform (1950–52), individuals were categorized by class background. Poor and lower-middle-class peasants were supposed to unite regardless of their kin and territorial networks. Rich peasants and landlords, labeled as class enemies, were under constant surveillance; they would not dare participate in any village fights or collective gatherings. The establishment of the community militia allowed collective violence to be employed in class struggles (see Perry 1985). During the radical Maoist years, collective violence came in a sense to be "administered" by the state. Landlords, rich peasants, and other "bad categories" were criticized or sometimes beaten by masses of people. Yet though the meaning of collective violence changed during this time, its management remained in the hands of local authority—now the Communist cadres.

In its turn, decollectivization has changed the structure of local control by removing any effective group wielding local authority, at least in this part of rural Shaanxi. At a time when the expanding of the market economy demanded better communication, collective activities were reduced to a minimum. In such a historical context, I believe that the body has become more violent as a vehicle of expression. In other words, the body, which had been imprisoned by the meanings imposed upon it, now grounds the language of these people. Ceremonial celebrations have become their "rituals" of collective expressions. Because there is no longer any interpretive authority within each community to legitimize the meaning of such ceremonies, the body has taken over the task of celebration. Punishment as well as happiness must be conveyed by means of physical interaction.

As local people now look back, even fights in the past are not remembered as expressions of anger or hatred. Instead, they were often equated with "having fun." Zunxi once explained, "You see that big ditch? That is the place where we used to fight. Before the collectivization, everyone kept a heavy club behind his own door. Whenever there was a small quarrel between any two of us, other people would quickly join in and make it a big fight. There was not really any reason for a fight. *It was simply for fun. We enjoyed it very much. No matter how trivial an argument was, we would like to make it a bloody fight. At that time, whenever there was a fight, everyone would join it. It was so much fun*" (emphasis added). My point is not that the fights in the past occurred simply for entertainment, but that at present violence is not viewed simply in terms of negative feelings.

Freedman has observed that the use of firecrackers and other kinds of noisemakers at weddings was meant to purify: "Noise is used as marker. . . . The marker is, so to say, neutral. But noise, as a symbol, can be linked to light and fire; crackers are all three. Noise and fire are purifiers. Noise and bright light are signs of joy" (1979a, 266–67). In the case of northern rural Shaanxi, it seems that purification has given way to the defilement of the body. Instead of purifying, noise and bright light have become signs of violence.

Death and Entertainment

There is a great deal of similarity between the celebrations at weddings and at funerals, but a significant difference is that the funeral was believed to be the more important social event because it offered greater scope for elaboration and expansion of scale. One old man explained, "The funeral is always bigger in scale than the wedding, because at a funeral you have musicians; you can even have two groups of musicians. You can also invite the local opera to perform at a funeral, but these things are not done at weddings. At a funeral, one can even show a film; but at weddings, what you can do is very limited. The wedding is for the new couple who will have a nice time together, but the funeral is a big thing for the family."

There are a number of reasons for the difference in emphasis. First of all, the funeral was believed to be the most appropriate occasion for presenting gifts, enabling brothers to compete in demonstrating their economic status and social connections. A wedding might also provide an arena for such competition but to a much lesser degree, partly because it was seen as being concerned mainly with the transfer of the bride from her natal family to the new house. The wedding was therefore viewed as a gradual process through which the symbolic meanings of the transfer could be acted out. The clear sense of temporality in the rites of passage at the wedding also differentiates the wedding from the funeral. Of course, at a funeral, activities are also carried out in time, but their meaning is essentially spatial: that is, all the activities are meant to be shown at the same time, once and for all. At the funeral, time simply serves as an external reference; at the wedding, in contrast, the temporal dimension is a constituent part of the action itself.

A wedding is rather like a drama, unfolding its plot in a series of symbolic encounters: each leads to another in a chain of actions. As soon as the truck for transporting the bride begins to move, a series of later events is implied. The new couple should and must break through a connected series of obstacles. But a funeral is more like an exhibition—a tableau vivant in which everything must be on the display all the time, made to be observed and to be commented on. Unlike the wedding, each act at the funeral is not a prelude to the next but is complete in itself. For instance, gifts presented at a wedding will be taken away from the presentation table after having displayed for a few minutes; whereas at a funeral, anything received from the guests except food must be publicly exhibited outside one's house and exposed to everyone until the very end. All close relatives are supposed to bring to a funeral at least one quilt for the deceased, and all the quilts—sometimes more than one hundred—would be arranged on ropes outside the dead person's house, so that everyone present might look at them. This points to another key difference between the two ceremonies: at a wedding important acts such as the occupation of the new house by the bride are supposed to take place inside the house, but at a funeral nothing important can be done that is not watched outside the dead person's house.

Local people explained that the increasing economic differentiation that began in the late 1970s led to more elaborate funeral celebrations, in order to display that new status and economic power. Thus one's emotional attachment to the deceased is by no means central to determining such arrangements; indeed, little consideration is given to the dead at all. It may be correct to argue that in traditional Chinese society, people were living "under the ancestor's shadow" (Hsu 1971), and that an individual was seen only as a link in a chain of family relationships connecting one's ancestors in the past to one's descendants in the future (Baker 1979, 27). From this perspective, death must be taken as an important social event that bridges the two worlds of the dead and the living. Moreover, ancestor worship becomes fundamental to organizing everyday experience (Freedman 1958, 81–91) and seniority becomes important in the hierarchy of family lineage (Baker 1979, 15).[15] In mainland China, the traditional ideology of kinship was attacked by the Communist government, particularly in the early years of its control (C. K. Yang 1959); consequently, respect given to the elderly dramatically lessened during the radical years of the Maoist revolution (Davis-Friedman 1991).

In this part of rural Shaanxi at present, the term employed in describing death is *die*.[16] According to the dictionary, *die* is "to fall down" or "to fall out." It is important to note that *die* is a verb. Local people would seldom call someone "dead"; instead, they would say that "someone died," thereby always conveying a sense that an action has occurred; someone has been removed from the world of the living. The dead person's relationship with those who are living lies not in any supernatural power that may influence their fortune but simply in the fact of being dead and how he or she is then to be treated. There is no sense, as in the traditional ideology of kinship, that it is crucial for the living to seek the protection and blessing of the dead (see Freedman 1958; Hsu 1971; Baker 1979). What has to be done for the dead reflects only the relationships among the living themselves.

A funeral is therefore intended as a show for the neighbors and others. The members of a family perform by engaging in exchanges of gifts and social relations, which can be meaningful only when they are watched by others. Visibility is therefore a central concern. When people in this region talked about funerals, they tended to say little about the person who was dead; instead, they would extensively comment on what had been done (or what should have been done) at their relative's or neighbor's ceremony, gossiping endlessly about how the funeral was carried out. They would focus on the details: how many people had joined a particular funeral feast, how many individual gifts had been received, and so on.

Under such circumstances, growing old in this part of rural Shaanxi may not be a pleasant experience—or so it appears to an outside observer. There was considerable variation from one household to another in Zhaojiahe, but old women—who could always be of some practical use to the family—generally were treated better than old men. In 1992 Yusheng, Tiancai's father and Zunxi's father's brother, was the oldest man in this community, at eighty-five. He could not move properly and spent most of his time sitting in the sun in front of his door. One day when I was talking with Zunxi and his mother, I saw Yusheng coming into Zunxi's house very slowly, walking with a cane. As soon as he entered, he said: "Why have I not yet died? What is wrong with me?"

"You're right, why don't you die?" replied Zunxi's mother (Yusheng's brother's wife), who was herself paralyzed. "You're suffering at this age! You also make other people suffer."

"Don't you believe it," Yusheng answered. "I can't move well but I still have a great appetite. This morning I had three pieces of steamed bread but still felt hungry. I eat a lot but do nothing."

"What a waste! Why do you still eat so much?"

"I don't know. I always want to die, but I cannot choose my death. I'm always hungry, too."

"Why do you live this long, when you're useless? Everybody hates you, you know?"

"I know," Yusheng replied, "but what else can I do? I can do nothing about my own death."

Perhaps in part because of this attitude toward old age, the funeral celebration was often joyful. It was common to hear jokes and laughter burst out at funerals. As an outsider, I found it quite difficult to tell a funeral from a wedding just by the emotions of those attending: both seemed to be happy occasions. At funerals, the decorations were often even more colorful than at weddings. The emotional detachment required by the funeral as a social occasion is evident in the performances, particularly the music and the wailing.

Musicians must be invited to funerals, but no one type of music is prescribed; in fact, there was no such thing as "funeral music." It is not a particular kind of sound but noise itself that signifies the funeral. In recent years, under television's influence, local musicians sometimes adapt cheerful pop music to play at a funeral (as at the Yang funeral, discussed above). The music is important not because it expresses certain feelings associated with death but because it announces a social event—just as exploding firecrackers do. As people in this area often commented, being able to invite a group of musicians indicated a well-off family. Much more important than the choice of music was the number of musicians invited. At funerals, people would go to the musicians' table and make requests; here, too, what mattered most was their performance in asking for music—made possible by the presence of a group of musicians—rather than the music itself performed.

Once music is understood as an announcement, a declaration, it is easier to make sense of the curiously emotionless performance of wailing. At funerals, women are supposed to wail; they can begin or stop at any moment of a funeral, as if on cue.

Wancheng was a brother of one of my hosts in Dawa, and his father had died a few weeks before I arrived. I joined a ceremony to burn paper for Wancheng's late father at his graveside. As soon as Wancheng's relatives came and changed their clothes into white in his house, all the women started to wail, though they had been joking with one another a few seconds earlier. They began as soon as they covered their faces; their sudden wailing indicated that people were ready to leave for the graveyard. The men kept talking as people began to walk toward the graveyard, which was behind Dawa. The further they went from Dawa, the lower women's voices fell. The wailing had almost completely disappeared by the time we arrived at the grave. After a couple of cups of wine were splashed onto the grave by Wancheng, the women again wailed briefly; the paper was then burned. The men kept laughing and talking to one another as they left, just as they had done on their way to the grave. The women did not resume wailing until they reached the outskirts of Dawa—where they might be heard by people in the village. The closer they came, the louder their voices.

As the procession made its way through Dawa, one woman, who was sitting in front of her own house and watching, called out to Wancheng's wife: "Look at you; you weren't crying, in fact you were laughing! Don't pretend any more! You wanted your father-in-law to die, didn't you?" Wancheng's wife, still among the wailing women, then began to exchange obscene jokes with her. The two kept laughing and joking, until finally Wancheng's wife simply sat down and joined the other woman, whereupon they began chatting happily. The others did not seem to be disturbed by this at all and continued to march into Wancheng's house, with the women still wailing.

Wailing at a funeral without tears may not be unique to this area. To a greater or lesser extent, such performances may occur in different parts of rural China, past or present (see Watson 1988, 12). For instance, Martin C. Yang once observed similar wailing in a Shandong village, Taitou (1945, 87). However, I contend that this kind of performance—which was done much more obviously in Dawa than in Taitou, and with those involved fully aware of their actions—suggests a significant shift in the constitution of everyday strategies, allowing the agents of practice to *manipulate* cultural forms in a way not possible before. I do not mean simply that local people were capable of putting a modern element into a traditional cultural form, such as singing a pop song at a funeral; rather, in so doing, they have already assumed that the form and content of a cultural practice are separable and, therefore, can be rearranged to benefit their own interests and needs. There is no longer anything sacred about the relationship between a cultural form and its content: for example, between what is played by the musicians and what that music is supposed to mean. To put it in structuralist language, one can no longer presuppose any fixed relation between the signifier and the signified—between the actual performance of a cultural practice and its meaning.

More important, those who engage in the action recognize that the relationship between an action and its signification is arbitrary. A formal structure of meaning, a system of signification, that used to guide action when interpreted by a local authority has collapsed: the meaning of an action is now reduced solely to its effectiveness. This is a condition of everyday life that has emerged only after the Maoist revolution. It enabled Wancheng's wife to leave the other women wailing in the funeral procession and join her friend for a casual conversation. I doubt very much that this could have occurred in Taitou in the 1940s, although in other ways the stereotyped wailing recounted by Yang was quite similar. What Wancheng and other people might have thought about his wife's behavior would be determined not by meaningful rules of family behavior after visiting a grave but by their judgment of its effect on this particular occasion. Obviously, it was not taken as a violation of the practical game of this ritual on that particular day.

In this chapter I have dealt with ceremonial celebrations that involve emotional reactions, collective or individual; and if we define emotion in terms of a physiological reaction—that is, a certain feeling as a reaction to a given situation[17]—then the emotions of the people in this part of rural Shaanxi are highly "pliable." By that term, I mean two things. First, on given social occasions individuals may display emotions that do not correspond to any collectively required mode of feeling; and second, individuals may show very different emotional reactions to those social occasions. To an outsider, individuals appear to react not with spontaneous emotions but with a performance, always with an eye toward its effects on the audience.

In northern rural Shaanxi, such reorganization of these cultural forms directly resulted from the structural arrangement of contemporary Chinese society at large, which removed any dominant local authority that could secure their meaning and significance. Ordinary villagers have taken over these cultural forms, whose meaning used to be controlled by a particular group of interpretive authority (the gentry class in the pre-Communist era and the local cadres in the years of the Maoist revolution), into their own hands. In their hands, those forms have become purely means of producing effects in action, regardless of the original meanings attached to them—and have become more flexible and context-dependent. Such a fundamental change in the conditions of everyday life surely has political consequences as well—and I turn to that subject next.

7

Immoral Politics

In this chapter, I sketch the changes that took place in the political life of northern rural Shaanxi in the 1990s. Unlike most studies of politics in Chinese society, which generally take an outsider's perspective, I discuss these changes from an insider's view.[1] In particular, I focus on politics as a moral discourse through which a certain type of subject is made.[2] Community politics has always borne certain moral contents (see, e.g., Madsen 1984). But as the state's direct involvement in and control of local affairs in China has weakened from the late 1970s on, politics has become intrinsically moral in character—reversing the emphasis of the Maoist years, when morality was completely politicized.

The Maoist society has been often portrayed as a "political culture" (see Pye 1988), and studies of it have tended to focus on its ideology and official organization.[3] Scholarly discussions of the post-Mao society have mainly paid attention to the political economy of the reform (see Perry and Wong 1985) and the resulting modification of the relationship between the state and the peasantry, perhaps best viewed in terms of a relationship between patron and clients (e.g., see Oi 1985, 1989a). Rather than examining the structural relations of Chinese politics, I will show how the changes in the sphere of political life in this part of rural Shaanxi were *experienced* as they unfolded in the micro process of everyday life and how the elements of these changes were articulated in a particular form of (im)moral politics.

Land and Luck

Land was a popular subject of gossip in daily life in the 1990s, but there was very little complaint about the way in which the collective land was redistributed to each household in 1981.[4] In order to understand "the past and the present in the present," to borrow a phrase from Maurice Bloch (1977), we need to look carefully at how local people talked about this redistribution.

When they recalled that time, everyone seemed happy about the process; many people even referred to it as "democratic" (*minzhu*). The redistribution rested on three major principles. First, each person was entitled to the same amount of land, and an effort was also made to give exactly the same share of good and bad land to each family, in proportion to the size of each household. Second, all the representatives from each household had to agree at every stage before taking the next step in redistribution. Finally, the assignment of particular pieces of land was determined by lot, which was called *zhuazidan* (drawing the bullet).[5]

Because of the very complex topography of this area, it was impossible for everyone to have exactly the same kind of land. Even if two pieces of land were considered equally good, one piece would usually be closer to the village than the other. Therefore, some people were unhappy with the land they were given, but they never complained about the procedure. Instead, they blamed themselves for having bad luck, for not being able to draw a "good bullet." As one old man said, "Yes, it was so; whatever you got, you got it by yourself. No complaints. You cannot complain about your own bad luck! You got it yourself."

This linkage between the past and luck is significant because, as we will see in the following section, there is no place for luck in interpreting what is going on now. If anyone in this community happens to be a little better off than others, he will be seen either as corrupt (particularly in the case of the community cadres) or as the beneficiary of a superior network of social relations. The kind of explanation embedded in the statement "You got it yourself" no longer applies to the current economic differentiation and social stratification. We might also keep in mind that the past, remote or not so remote, is likely to be remembered as happy simply because everyone feels the burden of the present (see Croll 1994).

With respect to land holdings, the problem was not in the past but in the ongoing adjustments that had to be made. According to the regulations laid out by the local government, each family's holdings had to be adjusted every five years to reflect the demographic changes in each rural community. Thus if someone died in one family, then a portion of its land should be returned to the community, to be allocated to the families with newborn babies. This process caused much conflict between families.

One morning, when I was having breakfast with my host family, my host's wife, Yin'ai, burst into a rage. As it seemed to come out of nowhere, I could not understand much of what she was complaining about, except for a sense of her fury against Xincai, the party secretary of the community. The grandmother of the house joined Yin'ai in cursing Xincai, accusing him of being corrupt. I had known that Wanbin was not on good terms with Xincai, but I had not witnessed any performance like this in the house before. I had always thought that Wanbin disliked Xincai in part because he himself had been a cadre during the years of the people's commune, and the local government selected a younger generation of cadres to replace him in the 1980s. It was also true that there was tension between Wanbin's brothers and Xincai's, who constituted the two main sets of *zijiawu* in Dawa. Wanbin's father was the third of four brothers, who themselves produced eight sons. Wannong and Wanyou were sons of the first of the four brothers; Wanbin the (adopted) son of the second; Wankai, Yangkai, Jinkai, and Jinchang the sons of the third; and Wancheng the son of the fourth. Their political attitudes differed. Wanbin, who had a clear interest in community politics, was the most active; but Yangkai and his brothers were not interested in politics at all. Yangkai once told me, "I had also been a cadre in the 1970s, and I chose to become one not for myself but for my younger brothers. They were both in high school at that time. I thought that if I took the job, they would have a better chance to join the army or get a job somewhere else. Now, I don't want to be an official at all. How much can a cadre make nowadays? Not very much, I'm afraid. I'd rather do something else. I have rented a stone mill and I can make a good fortune out of it." In contrast, Lucai, Xincai, Mencai, and Gencai, who were all sons of Genwu, were more involved in local politics. Xincai himself was serving as the party secretary of the community, and two of his brothers held positions in the local government. However, among each group of these brothers, there were also conflicts and dislikes. For example, Gencai was said to be on bad terms with his other brothers due to some problems generated by the division of family property. Wanyou, though very close to Wanbin, also complained that Wanbin was stingy.

Wanbin's fresh anger, as later I found out, was caused by Xincai's decision that Wanbin should return some of his land to the community because two of Wanbin's sons had left Zhaojiahe. Xincai's request was passed to Wanbin's family by Wancheng, who was the group head at the time. "I want to see who dares take my land away, fuck your motherfucking bastard," said Yin'ai, who now regularly began her day in this fashion. "Look at yourself! How much have you stolen from the collective?! Look at your own brothers! Their whole family has moved into the town but they still refuse to return any of their land, don't they? What else do you want to say, you motherfucker? You want to take my land? I dare you! Your asshole is full of shit!" The grandmother was always willing to join in the cursing—with a better command of obscene language. One who heard all this might feel that Wanbin was not afraid of Xincai. However, some neighbors said, to the contrary, that Wanbin's family was indeed in a panic and that Wanbin feared that further action might be taken against him.

In order to avoid being put at a disadvantage, Wanbin decided to turn the best piece of his land into an orchard. This maneuver was seen as a precautionary action by his neighbors, an attempt to keep this land. Wanyou commented, "They are clever. They have planted fruit trees. Even in the future when they are all dead, you will have no way of asking them to return their good land, because you simply can't cut down their fruit trees. So, if they are asked to return extra land, they will give you the worst part of what they have. You can't take their fruit trees, can you?" Turning one's best land into an orchard was a popular strategy in this community. Lucai, Xincai's brother, whose family had migrated to the town but who continued to own land in the village, had done the same thing. Ironically, the local government had earlier encouraged farmers in the area to grow apple trees to increase their income, but local farmers had refused, claiming that they knew little about growing anything except wheat and cotton. This attitude toward fruit trees changed only when a large number of people began to realize that to own an orchard was the best way to claim a piece of land forever.

No one was interested in taking sides in the conflict between Wanbin and Xincai. Wanyou criticized Wanbin behind his back, but to his face Wanyou was always obliged to support his brother. Yangkai and his brothers seemed indifferent. Gencai was close to almost everyone.

Wancheng passed messages from Xincai to Wanbin, but he was forced into the position very reluctantly; he saw no reason to be involved in this. Other people in Dawa seemed to be angry at Wancheng because he was not fulfilling his duty properly. If extra land was not collected from people like Wanbin, those families who had new babies could not obtain more land for themselves. Some accused Wancheng himself of being corrupt, though no one was willing to speak about it in public.[6] Even the principals avoided direct confrontation, for the circumstances that gave rise to comments, complaints, criticism, and accusations—and that also determined the social relations between people—were constantly changing. For example, although Xincai was in charge of community affairs, he never made any attempt to confront Wanbin. And despite making threats, Wanbin never tried to challenge Xincai in public.

The above discussion has two important implications. First, actors are finding it increasingly difficult to identify with a given subject position, because social relations have become so dependent on particular situations that are constantly changed and modified. For instance, being the party secretary does not automatically guarantee one's authority, which will depend on the specific situation in which that position is tested. Second, the result of a conflict between two parties is almost impossible to predict; actors thus put a great deal of emphasis on the process of negotiation. Because of this unprecedented indeterminacy of social action, all have begun to pay extremely close attention to the tactics of everyday politics.

The Significance of Social Connections

Although less striking than that in the coastal areas of southern or southeastern China, a certain degree of economic differentiation was also felt in this part of rural Shaanxi. As I have already mentioned, no one pointed to luck or chance in explaining these distinctions. Many people continued to believe that the state constituted the ultimate source for producing and distributing wealth.[7] If a specific instance required an explanation, they would always turn to an external factor. For example, if one of their brothers became a little better off than others, they would say he possessed a superior network of social relations. Furthermore, any sense of superiority in social connections was always represented through a spatial hierarchy. More generally, spatial images and metaphors have come to dominate everyday experience in post-reform rural China.

Of all the houses I had visited, Xicai's house was most impressive in that his interior walls were painted white, which made the room look bright and clean. When I mentioned this to Wanyou later, he gave me an unexpected answer: "Do you know why his house can be better than others? You don't know why, I'm sure. Xicai's brother-in-law, working in Xi'an, is in charge of a big construction project. Xicai is certainly better off than others because his brother-in-law will give him everything he needs. Otherwise, Xicai couldn't paint his walls. How would he be able to paint them without his brother-in-law's help? Who is going to give him the chunk of white clay and other materials? It's his brother-in-law who has done it, not him, I assure you." Such explanations were very common when somebody seemed to be slightly better off; no one assumed that chance or hard work could be responsible. A particular "lucky" person must have powerful connections behind him.

An ethnographer cannot help feeling that there is a contradiction here. On the one hand, everyone seems to view society as stratified, both economically and socially; but on the other hand, they refuse to accept any explanation that ascribes this stratification, even in part, to differences between individual capabilities. Good fortune must be explained by factors external to that fortune itself. To be sure, some people in this community are seen as better farmers than others, and some people are described as hard workers. But such differences affect only one's reputation in an ethical sense; they do not explain how economic differentiation emerges.

There is a gap, therefore, between the local people's abstract view of society and their concrete conception of their neighbors. They are "rational" as long as society is discussed in general terms; but when a specific instance is brought up, they are conceptually imprisoned by what George Foster once called "the image of limited good,"[8] in that they cannot imagine how they themselves might produce good fortune. Clearly, they have a worm's-eye view, a vision fundamentally limited to the inside of their own immediate environment. From this perspective, there is no need to explain the creation of wealth; what needs to be explained is simply its distribution, which is seen as wholly independent of the organization or reorganization of social and economic production within one's own community. Their view of society and community resulted in their overemphasis on making social connections outside their own community in the 1990s, when the state allowed a greater flow of goods and people across local and regional boundaries than ever before in the history of the People's Republic.

Famin was in his mid-thirties, and he had four brothers and six sisters (born to the same parents). Famin saw his family as powerless in both economic and political terms, because all but one of his siblings remained in the area as farmers. One "lucky" sister went to work in Urumqi, the capital of the Xinjiang Autonomous District, in northwestern China. In order to earn some cash, in the winter of 1987 Famin went to Urumqi to look for work, hoping that his sister and brother-in-law might help. Famin stayed in Urumqi for about half a year, working for a construction team and taking various small jobs as a laborer, which could not bring him a fortune. But Famin could not find anything else, so he decided to return to Zhaojiahe. There, in another effort to become prosperous, he managed to get a contract from the village committee to operate a stone mine for a year. The work involved collecting and milling stones for local construction sites; the contractor, who was responsible for the management of the mine, paid a small license fee. Again, Famin failed to make a profit. He blamed his lack of success on who he did (and did not) know:

I thought of going to Urumqi because my sister was there. She and my brother-in-law might help me, I thought. So I went. I had a hard time there. The work was so hard that I could hardly manage. I worked at a construction site as a laborer. My sister and my brother-in-law didn't know many people; they didn't know any officials, therefore they couldn't have found me anything better than a job like that. The work was too hard to bear, so I ran away. I didn't make any money. When I came back to Zhaojiahe, I saw other people making a good fortune by milling stones. I managed to sign a contract with our leaders to operate a stone mine. In the beginning, they were reluctant to give me the contract. But I have so many brothers here. They helped me. Then I got the mine. But I couldn't run it, because I didn't know the right people. Nobody wanted my stones when I was operating it. In order to sell your stones, you have to bribe those who are in charge of construction projects. I worked hard myself and my stones were of better quality, but still, no one wanted them. *People do not want your products if they don't know you.* All my brothers are ordinary peasants and we don't know people outside the village, so we can't make it work. Even if I wanted to give gifts to the powerful people, I wouldn't have known how to find their doors! I don't even know where they live!

Such a way of conceiving society and community leaves very little room for individual innovation and capability; instead, success and fortune are seen as qualities intrinsic to social networks and connections. Yet people who hold such a view, such as Famin, intensely engage in social activities in the hopes of bettering their positions. In other words, local people acted as aggressively as any other social groups in the 1990s, despite their belief in how little the individual can accomplish. In order to understand the effect of such views on their political strategy, let us consider how people in this community react to the government policy of birth control.

Stratification and Strategies

Enforcing the birth control policy was said to be the only task left for the local cadres in the 1990s. Wanyou once said, "Nowadays, there is no policy, so everyone does whatever he wants. Nobody intervenes. All policies are 'soft' (*ruan*) except for the birth control policy, which is the only 'hard' policy. The cadres have been told that they should employ whatever means are needed to keep the number of births under control. Any kind of local measures should be allowed as long as they can control population growth. That is the only government policy that exists today."

As understood by local people in the early 1990s, that policy included several components. First, one couple *should* have only one child. Second, if the baby was a girl, the couple would be allowed to try for a son with the following conditions: an interval of five years must separate the first and the second birth, the mother must agree to be sterilized after the second birth, and the couple must pay a fine of 400 yuan for the second birth. And third, under no circumstances would a third birth be allowed.[9]

In order to ensure effective contraception and sterilization, women were provided with free or low-cost health care by the local government. Sterilization was viewed as the most effective means of birth control, and doctors at the Hospital for Maternal and Child Health in town provided the operation throughout the year. Twice a year, usually in spring and autumn, local officials from the township would be sent down to inspect each rural community. Women who had two children were supposed to be taken away and sterilized. Those who refused to comply with the birth control policy of the government could have their property confiscated. Such confiscation was a measure invented by the local cadres to provide more effective control; the local people called it *pochan*, which literally means "bankruptcy." The term has been widely used in mainland China since the late 1980s, when there was a great deal of official discussion about whether the state enterprises should be allowed to declare bankruptcy. Local people borrowed it to mean "confiscation" of property only in connection with the birth control policy.

In 1992 in a nearby community, a man named Jiancai and his wife decided to try for another child despite already having two daughters. Besides farming, Jiancai was also operating a small retail shop, selling sundries such as cigarettes, wines and spirits, sweets, soap powder, stationary, and so on. Jiancai knew that there could be trouble ahead, but he wanted a son. Hoping for better luck this time, Jiancai arranged for his wife, together with his two little daughters, to move elsewhere to avoid being caught by local cadres. During his wife's pregnancy, Jiancai himself closed his shop, locked his door, and hid.

Having failed to trace the couple but certain that they were preparing to have another child, the cadres invited a group of thugs to confiscate Jiancai's property.[10] They broke into Jiancai's house and shop and then took away everything that could be removed, both his personal belongings and his retail goods. Under threat of destitution, Jiancai had to appear and agree that his wife undergo an abortion followed by sterilization. What was confiscated should therefore have been returned to him, but a large portion of his "property"—such as biscuits, candies, and alcohol—had been consumed by those who had carried it to the local government office.

This story, known to all the people in the area, seems to convey a message that whoever violated the birth control policy could not avoid punishment. It also demonstrates the power of confiscation of property; local people felt that resistance was impossible if one's property was taken away. As we have seen in chapters 2 and 3, their sense of self was tied to a material conception of life: one could not, for example, separate the notion of brotherhood from the actual building of the family house. The anthropological literature confirms that rural Chinese have always had practical concerns about the role of property in their life. In the past, property relations were always conceived as social relations— whether these were kin relations, as in the pre-Communist era, or political relations, as during the Maoist years. This sense of property relations continued into the 1990s; however, Jiancai's story of confiscation implies another and rather different sense, in which property relations are seen as being separated from specific hierarchies of social relations. In this new conception, property relations no longer stand as the other side of social relations; instead, any social force is conceived in material terms in a way that allows little room for another kind of ideological construction. Thus the message of this story—the impossibility of losing what is material—becomes clear. Given this ideology about society, everyone would choose whatever practical strategies are necessary to avoid having their property confiscated.

One ordinary early evening, when most people had returned from the fields, I was walking back to Dawa enjoying the atmosphere of tranquillity and peace. As I neared my host's house, only a hasty jump to one side kept me from being knocked over. Wanbin's daughter-in-law had run out, buttoning up her overcoat nervously. A little puzzled by what I saw, I tried but was unable to figure out what was going on. When I went inside, nothing unusual seemed to have taken place. My host had gone to town, and his wife was still in the field. The grandmother was playing with the two little babies as usual. I went out, looking around. It was hard not to begin feeling anxious or perhaps even afraid as I saw young women running silently from one house to another. Those women who had been sitting together in front of their houses disappeared. I saw my host's daughter-in-law again, as she appeared right in front of me from nowhere, carrying her younger baby in her arms. The grandmother shouted behind her, "Hurry up, fuck you!" The young woman vanished into the darkness in haste.

The next day I learned that a "birth control team" sent down from the local government had raided a certain number of houses. They were successful in catching some young pregnant wives who had refused to obey the policy: four had been taken to town to be sterilized. My host's daughter-in-law should have been among them, because she had given birth to two daughters but was still hoping for a son. She would not have known to leave Zhaojiahe just before the officials came, had she not been warned in advance by the village head, Yankai, who was married to her sister. In turn, she passed on this important message to some other families who were related.

The day after the raid, a woman commented to me, "I have never been against the birth control policy set by the state. It actually has nothing to do with me. But regarding this raid, I have to say something. In our community, the cadres always focus *on people but not on issues*. If something has gone wrong, I have no problem at all with the idea that people who do wrong should be punished. But one should not treat different people differently. Let's take Xiaoqing's case as an example. He has two daughters, and his wife was forced to have the operation. That's fine. But they came into his house in the night, shining their flashlights at everyone's face; they knocked the door down while the whole family was sleeping. Xiaoqing's wife therefore had to have the operation. Even so, the cadres still took his property away. His mother was begging them to stop, crying for the whole day. Nobody cared. On the other hand, look at Leikai; just because he used to work in town and has some political connections there. His son also has two daughters and his daughter-in-law also is getting ready to bear another child, but nobody dares get close to his house. Leikai said, 'Whoever dares to come into my house, I'll break his legs!' This is what I have to say. People are treated differently. The powerless are treated worse."

One may well argue that such disparity in everyday politics has always existed, throughout the years of the Maoist revolution and even before. However, during the Maoist years, "the five bad categories," such as landlords or rich peasants,[11] could always be used as the target of political campaigns; thus whenever any problems arose in a community, the local cadres turned to those "class enemies" as convenient victims (see Chan, Madsen, and Unger 1992). At present, there are no designated victims; the question of who is to be a victim, when the government demands that someone be punished, has no easy answer. Some local cadres told me that they could not predict what would happen when a birth control team was sent down. What they knew was that they *had to* find some cases of violation of the birth control policy to prove that they were working; otherwise they could not continue to be cadres. But at the same time, these cadres would try to avoid creating enemies within their own communities.

Who is to be punished now depends on contingent and changing circumstances. A man said that he was told by the party secretary that there would be a raid simply because he happened to meet the secretary at the market and invite him for a bowl of noodles. The birth control policy was said to be a "hard" policy, but the term "hard" referred more to the severity of punishment than to the thoroughness with which the policy was carried out. Punishment for noncompliance is very harsh—yet those with opportunities and connections need not comply. Coercion may continue to be seen as the most effective means of carrying out the birth control policy, but under the new rules of the game, it is wielded with a great deal of flexibility.

In effect, both parties—those who are supposed to implement the policy and those who are its target—have adopted a similar, situation-dependent political strategy; as a result, the state policy cannot be applied to its full extent. Table 4 shows the actual number of children of each household in Dawa. If we group Dawa households by the age of the head of household, we see that those who are over forty-five— Xinyun, Liucai, Yongsheng, and Wanbin—have on average more children: four, except for Xinyun (who has three). None of the rest has more than three children. This demographic change in the number of children that each couple bears also is visible in other parts of rural China. Even more interesting, however, is the breakdown in the children's sexes: no one does not have a son. People in this area would comply with the birth control policy—only under the condition that they have at least one son among their two or three children. Those with two daughters keep trying for a son. Of the four cases in which younger couples have three children, three have the same birth pattern: f, f, m. At forty Lucai, the exception (f, m, m), is to some extent between the two generations; it is clear that having a son is the primary concern for local farmers.

What makes a "hard" policy soft is the disappearance of an identifiable group of punishable subjects. This is the main characteristic of what I call "immoral politics," a kind of politics that picks and chooses, often quite randomly, the subjects on which it is exercised. Here, immoral politics has resulted from several converging influences on local life, including the retreat of the state from its dominance of local economic practices, the introduction of a market economy with its ideology of exchange, and some relaxation of political control over cultural and religious activities. The role of the local cadres has changed, indicating a fundamental departure from the mass politics of the Maoist kind.

TABLE 4.   Number of Children in Each Household in Dawa

Head of the Household	Age of the Husband and His Wife in 1992	Number of Children
Yangkai	38, 36	2: m, m, f°
Jinchang	34, 34	3: f, f, m
Jinkai	32, 34	2: m, m
Xinyun	48, 48	3: f, m, f
Jincang	31, 28	2: m, m
Liucai	65, 62	4: m, m, m, f
Shanghe	36, 35	2: f, m
Mannian	29, 29	2: m, f
Ruolin	40, 38	2: f, m
Yongsheng	64, 54	4: f, f, m, m
Wancheng	34, 34	2: m, m
Sanbao	39, 37	2: m, f
Xicai	35, 33	3: f, f, m
Wanbin	47, 45	4: m, m, f, m
Wanbao	42, 41	2: m, f
Moucai	29, 28	2: m, m
Gencai	33, 33	3: f, f, m
Xincai	36, 36	2: f, m
Lucai	40, 40	3: f, m, m

NOTE: °Yangkai's daughter was adopted.

Socialist Education?

A so-called second socialist education movement, intended to imitate the successful "first socialist education movement" of 1964–65,[12] was planned for the early 1990s; but before it even started it had begun to disappear from the official discourse—particularly after Deng Xiaoping's famous South China trip in 1992, which brought another round of propaganda urging further market reforms. Zhaojiahe was probably the last rural community in Shaanxi to undergo this education movement. By providing an ethnographic account of that experience, I will show how grassroots politics has taken a very different direction in post-reform China, from which it may be impossible ever to return to Maoist mass politics.

In Shaanxi province, the socialist education movement was supposed to move from one area to another. Although it had been a topic of gossip and conversation for a while, a work team of seven men was not sent to Zhaojiahe until March 1992. All the members of the team were from a neighboring township, Jiaodao; its leader was a township official. As soon as the team arrived, people in Zhaojiahe began to talk about who the members were and where they came from. Everyone wanted to know as much as he or she could about them. Disappointment spread quickly from one household to another: of the seven, three were simply peasants.[13]

The work team entered the community rather quietly. There was no meeting or any other kind of gathering to acknowledge them, beyond a very small group of cadres and party members who had been informed of their arrival. The purpose and goal of this socialist education movement were announced in writing on several blackboards that had been set up in a few public squares in Zhaojiahe. The team would "squat" (*dundian,* i.e., stay to work) in this community for 140 days, which meant remaining in Zhaojiahe at least through July. They were given three tasks, designed to be carried out in three stages. The first was to present propaganda reinforcing the socialist ideology and thereby demonstrate to the peasants the advantages of the socialist system in China. The second was to audit community accounts and to punish local criminals in order to produce social harmony. Finally, the team was to help people rebuild their roads and reshuffle the community leadership group. Each task was intended to take about forty days.

Each dwelling group was assigned one member from the team; although he stayed with one family, he would have his meals with each household in turn. Lao Fan was assigned to Dawa, and he stayed with Wangbao. People in Dawa were tremendously interested in knowing Lao Fan's background—who he was, what he had done, and how he had managed to become a team member. Stories about him passed from one household to another faster than any other gossip I'd observed. People soon discovered that Lao Fan was also a farmer, and the story about how he became a member of the socialist education team spread quickly: "Lao Fan is just a peasant! Because he lived a few yards away from the headquarters of his village committee, he got familiar with the cadres. When local officials from his township came to his community, Lao Fan was often asked to host these officials for lunch. This is how Lao Fan became familiar with some of the local officials. These officials felt that they should pay something to Lao Fan in return, so they have appointed him a member of the team. The members of the team are able to eat free meals as they move from one family to another, and they also have a salary of seventy-five yuan per month. Lao Fan should certainly be happy about that."

Lao Fan, in his fifties and with a gray beard, looked different from people in Dawa only in that two brand-new pens were always in his upper left pocket. He introduced himself as a schoolteacher, which made everyone in Dawa laugh. As my host said, "He is a joke. Lao Fan taught at a village school for a few years. But who didn't? I've taught there for several years. Everyone in this village has done so at some time or another. He is a shitty peasant!" This distrust or contempt was an early sign that Lao Fan, as well as his comrades, would have a difficult time in Zhaojiahe.

When nothing about Lao Fan's past and his secrets was left to be talked about, people in Dawa turned their attention to his behavior, particularly his manner of eating. As he took his meals in one household and then the next, Lao Fan met with everyone, and everyone had an opportunity to observe him in detail. Table manners were believed to mirror character, and in that mirror Lao Fan looked very bad.

Two particular complaints began circulating soon after he arrived. First, Lao Fan was said to be gluttonous: he ate too much, always taking more than he should have as a guest. The gossip had it that Lao Fan consumed food as if he had been starved for a long time. Everyone seemed to find his appetite particularly extraordinary because he sat all day long without engaging in any physical labor. Whenever the subject came up, women began to describe how unbelievable it was that an old man like Lao Fan could manage to gobble so many pieces of steamed bread. "You know my usual size of the bread, my sister. Three times bigger than the ordinary ones. But still, Lao Fan had no trouble at all in consuming half a dozen! I am so amazed by his appetite that I began to worry for him. He may catch some sort of stomach disease if he continues to eat this way. Well, that would be a good lesson for him." Second, people complained because Lao Fan required three meals a day rather than two, which was the norm at this time of the year. It was supposed to be very impolite for a guest to demand three meals a day, and thus he was believed to be very insensitive. "My sister, Lao Fan does nothing but he is really good at digestion. We don't see him going to the toilet very often; what a good stomach!" With much irony, Lao Fan was being portrayed as a greedy peasant.

Socialist propaganda, the focus of the first stage of this campaign, seemed to have little effect. All the team had done was plaster several walls with a few slogans, such as "Socialism is the best for China," "China must go on down a socialist road," "Contribute to the four modernizations," and "Continue the economic reform." The party members had been called together for several meetings. Otherwise, everything proceeded as it ordinarily did during this season. At several places in the village the team installed "mass opinion collecting boxes" (*yijianxiang*), in which residents were supposed to place criticisms of the community leaders. All that the work team could collect was one note complaining about a newly married bride who was having a dispute with her father-in-law.

During the second stage of this socialist education campaign, a few of the mass meetings that had been so popular during the years of the Maoist revolution were supposed to be organized. But as one man remarked, "In the past, everything was different. Whenever there was a mass meeting, even if you were having your meal, you would have to put down your bowl immediately to join the meeting. A meeting used to be an order." This was no longer the case.

One early evening in March, at about 6:30, while sitting inside my room organizing my field notes, I heard somebody beating a gong and shouting from the other side of Dawa: "There is a mass meeting tonight! There is a meeting tonight!" It was Wancheng, who had been the group leader for a couple of years, calling everyone to gather at his house to hear what Lao Fan had to say about this socialist education movement. About an hour or so later, the gong and shouting began again. I went to see my host in his room. Wanbin was enjoying his tea at leisure, with no sign of interest in attending anything soon. I retreated to my room, waited for another half hour and, after hearing the sound of the gong again, I went to see my host once more. He continued—without seeming to have changed his position at all—to be enjoying his tea. I could not hold back my question: "Are you going to attend the meeting after all?" His answer was certain and calm: "Not in a hurry. It is too early now." It was only after another two rounds of Wancheng's persuasion, which included his shouting from right outside each house, that my host began to move. Having followed him to Wancheng's house, I found that we were among the very first to arrive. Only one man looked like he had already been there for a while; he was sleeping in a corner. Wancheng went to each house again, and people gradually appeared, often with some reluctance.

Each family sent a representative, either male or female. The women sat on the bed, some carrying their children. Another half an hour later, the meeting finally began. Immediately after a brief introduction by Wancheng, Lao Fan took out a small notebook from his pocket and began to read. Lao Fan declared in a rather formal tone that this was a great political movement that would change the countryside, and went on to explain the purpose and goal of the movement. His speech was frequently interrupted by laughter, caused not by his speech but by a local opera that was playing on a television. Wancheng mentioned several times that the television should be turned off, but his suggestion was met with stubborn resistance. Lao Fan seemed to be indifferent to the disturbance and went on with his speech, ignoring everything else. Everyone, except Wancheng, seemed to have found something important to say to their neighbors. It apparently was a most delightful occasion for conversation and dialogue. There was so much information to be communicated while Lao Fan was giving his lecture. Small children were crying from time to time. Their mothers scolded them: "I'll screw your mother! Stop crying, fucking bastard! Fuck your grandmother, stop that nonsense! You little fuck!" These exclamations were part of the common language of women in this area. An outsider might have reacted differently, but Lao Fan was not disturbed by this. Seemingly deaf to all these noises, he continued his speech gracefully. It was Wancheng who, from time to time, appealed to the people at this meeting: "Could you keep quiet for a while when others are speaking?" He was completely ignored. The man sleeping in the corner had been making unpleasant snoring noises, and then he suddenly woke up. As soon as he realized what was going on, he stopped Lao Fan, appearing to be very angry, and asked why the local government had imposed a tobacco tax on those who did not grow tobacco.

Lao Fan had said nothing about such a tax, and he was shocked by the bold question. Wancheng saved Lao Fan by saying that it was not yet the time to discuss such issues.

Finally, after about thirty minutes, Lao Fan managed to finish his speech. Everyone was then asked for his or her opinion of the present situation of this community—what each thought of its problems and their possible solutions. It was as if everyone was suddenly without a tongue. Without a word, someone switched off the television. All the children seemed to have fallen in sleep within a few seconds. An incredible, and almost unbearable, silence froze the room. I thought I could have heard the sound of a hair falling. Nobody seemed even to breathe. Wancheng repeated his invitation for people to speak out, and it was answered with a heavier silence. People forthrightly criticized their leaders all the time, but this was certainly not a good occasion to do so. The silence had lasted for about an hour before some women began to make excuses to leave. The meeting was to continue for another hour, until midnight, but to no more effect.

A few weeks later there was another mass meeting in Dawa, but it ended in violence rather than silence. Two families were directly involved; one supported the idea of rebuilding the main road and the other opposed it. For those who owned tractors, improving the condition of the road seemed quite desirable. But others, who cared little about the road, were worried that they would be called on to contribute as much to the work as those who wanted it. A quarrel between two men quickly developed into a real fight, right inside Wancheng's house. After the meeting, everyone seemed to agree that Lao Fan should be blamed, because he had brought this issue up for discussion without the proper preparation.

After a series of group meetings, a mass meeting of the whole village was organized. One of its main purposes was to allow people to hear a report of public finance and expenditure from the executive committee of the community. The meeting was held in a very large courtyard that, during the Maoist years, had been the headquarters of the Zhaojiahe Brigade, part of Leijiawa People's Commune. A long table, covered in white, had been set at one side of the courtyard before people arrived. Three men were seated at the table: Xincai (the party secretary) and two members of the work team. One of the two team members leaned on the table, his head buried in his arms; and he remained in that position throughout the entire meeting, as if he had been forced to be there.

The huge courtyard was divided into seven segments by five lines marked on the ground, supposedly to segregate people from the seven dwelling groups. Men and women, of each group, tended to sit separately. Small children, who were playing, screaming, and crying, stayed with their mothers. Having failed to quiet down the audience, the party secretary, who was wearing a pair of sunglasses on this gloomy afternoon, began his speech by loudly announcing the progress of socialism in China. Nothing seemed unusual until two young men for some reason suddenly began wrestling with each other. Nobody seemed to be disturbed except the party secretary, who begged the audience to be quiet: "Could you wait for me to finish? Or do you intend to talk in my place? If you simply do not want to listen to me, you may as well tell me. We can ask another person to explain the party's policies. Would you please not talk so loudly now!?" He was completely ignored.

As soon as the party secretary finished his speech, the community accountant made a short report about public finance, to which no one paid any attention. An important task of this meeting was to organize a "mass group" to thoroughly examine public expenditures over the past few years. It would be composed of seven people: one representative from each dwelling group. Selecting them turned out to be difficult. Everybody had complained about "those corrupt cadres," but no one was willing to be part of the mass group. The nominations thus went in circles. Someone shouted from the crowd: "We don't know anything about accountancy; why don't you just do it yourselves!? You cadres get paid, you should be doing this!" Most groups settled the matter by appointing one of their members who was absent from the meeting.

The mass meetings did not achieve anything positive, and meanwhile Lao Fan's life in Dawa became more unbearable. Having dined with many families in Dawa in a period of two months, Lao Fan had collected a number of "mass opinions" (*qunzhong yijian*) and prepared to deal with them accordingly. Some told Lao Fan that Wanbin was a bad example, a corrupt man. The main part of the complaint was that although Wanbin's second son, Xincang, had moved his household registration record out of Zhaojiahe to another local community, Wanbin resisted returning any land to the collective. Xincang had two daughters; he had temporarily removed his registration record as part of his

plan for his wife to have one more child without being caught and punished. But because Xincang was no longer a member of this community, his share of land should have been returned to the village. Some
people encouraged Lao Fan to begin cleaning up corruption by investigating this case. Trying to find out whether this allegation was true
or not, Lao Fan went to the other village. Of course, Wanbin's family
heard everything about the investigation. Whenever Lao Fan was mentioned in the house, he would be cursed in the most animated language.
"What a *wanbadan* (literally, 'the egg of a turtle')!" would cry Yin'ai,
Wanbin's wife, always the most angry one. "How dare you investigate
us? There is so much corruption he does not see. A pig like he is! When
you come to my house to dine, I will feed you your own shit. I'll be
happy to see if you eat or not. There is nothing but shit for you! Damn
you, how dare you request three meals a day? Fuck yourself in your
ass! You will be fed with shit! Even that I won't feed you more than
twice a day. You have a salary, you can go to spend it on yourself. You
fucking shit!"

So the imprecations continued until Lao Fan came to dine with Wanbin's family. One would expect Lao Fan to be given a hard time, though
perhaps not literally forced to eat his own waste. But when he finally
came, an extraordinary family banquet was waiting for him. This was
the first time in a long while that meat, fried eggs, and plenty of vegetables were served for an ordinary daily lunch. The plate of fried eggs
was placed right in front of Lao Fan. Wanbin, sitting next to him,
demonstrated a hospitality that I had not seen before. Yin'ai was helping Lao Fan with extraordinary care and attention. Wanbin's family as
a rule never prepared three meals a day, except during the Chinese
New Year, but a special evening meal was prepared for Lao Fan. Lao
Fan stayed with Wanbin's family for five days, and each of these days
featured holiday meals. To curse someone does not necessarily mean
that one should act unfriendly toward him or her—if friendship was in
one's best interest.

The two most difficult tasks for the work team were to audit public
accounts and to reshuffle the community leadership group. There was
a great deal of complaining about public expenditures. Theoretically,
any public spending should be decided by a committee consisting of
at least three persons: the party secretary, the village head, and the vice
village head. The accountant should be in charge of making records;

and only a cashier should have access to the money. In reality, however, there had not been a cashier for many years. All final decisions on spending were believed to be made by Xincai, the party secretary, who alone had access to the collective fund. The work team found out there were no receipts for any of these outlays; in some cases there was simply a signature by Xincai himself.

One particular incident occasioned much grumbling. A few years back, in order to purchase some musical instruments for the village school, Xincai, Yankai (the village head), Longcai (the vice village head), and Wang (the schoolmaster) went on a trip to Xi'an, the capital of Shaanxi. They stayed in Xi'an for a couple of days and purchased the instruments. A considerable amount of money was spent on this trip, but none of them provided a single receipt. Collectively, they wrote down the total amount that they had spent for the trip, including the instruments they had purchased for the school. Everyone in this community seemed to be surprised by their ability to lose all records so completely. As one man said, "How could they lose all the receipts— not a single one kept? They must have stolen the money."

In fact, it is quite difficult to determine whether such allegations are true or not. There is always a great deal of exaggeration in these sorts of complaints. For instance, fingers were often pointed to the houses of the cadres as evidence of their corruption. But I could see very little difference in living standards between the "corrupt" cadres and other people in this community. Longcai built a new house while he was acting as the vice village head, as did a large number of families over a fifteen-year period. There was nothing extraordinary about Longcai's house, at least that I could see. But some people insisted that had Longcai not been a cadre, he would not have been able to build his new house. Longcai was said to have been one of the poorest among them, and it was only through being a cadre that he made himself a fortune. Sometimes the accusations could appear absurd. One day I followed a couple of young people to Yankai's house. After a brief visit, as soon as we had left, one of my companions immediately told me that a set of tea pottery on Yankai's table must have been stolen by him from the collective. It might have been true, but ordinary families often owned similar sets of pottery. The issue is not whether the cadres are corrupt or not; rather, it is the extent to which these allegations of corruption have become part of a larger force reconstituting the public sphere by way of a moral discourse. In other words, these allegations have a function: in post-reform Chinese society, when a considerable amount of space is left for local or individual determination, the discourse on corruption has become an important means of creating and maintaining a moral space.

A more controversial financial scandal concerned a special allocation of five thousand yuan provided for Zhaojiahe by the local government in the mid-1980s, under the category of the "Fund for Helping the Poor Area." This money had disappeared without a trace. Xincai insisted that it was used to bribe local officials for the benefit of all the people in this community. For instance, in order to install electricity in Zhaojiahe in 1989, one had to present "gifts" to the local officials in charge. A large amount of money was said to have been spent on hosting banquets for the officials. The local people agreed that nothing could have been done without bribery, but they did not believe what Xincai said about this fund.

Members of the work team, under considerable pressure to investigate this particular case further, went to the township to find out who had received the alleged bribes. Naturally, every official in the township denied receiving anything of the kind from Zhaojiahe. Moreover, their efforts caused the work team more trouble. The township government was unhappy, because its own officials were questioned. The work team's superiors intervened, demanding that members stop pressuring the officials; such investigations, it was said, did no good in maintaining the normal order of government office and the stability of the society. Soon after, the investigation was called off.

The final task that the work team was supposed to carry out was to help choose a new village head. An opinion poll had been taken before an election meeting was called; only a group of representatives, about twenty people, attended. All the party members and group leaders were invited to this election meeting. The nominees, who had been decided by the local government, were Yankai and Longcai. An anonymous vote was held, and Longcai was elected. At the same time, the township officials announced that they had decided to appoint Xincai as the party secretary for another four years. Very little was changed. Wancheng stood up after hearing this result, and shouted to the face of all the officials and cadres: "If there is another revolution, we will kill all the party members first!"

Not very much was left to be done after the reshuffle, but Lao Fan in Dawa was still in trouble. After falling short of success in his investigation of corruption, Lao Fan had turned his attention to more trivial aspects of daily conflicts in Dawa. In a group meeting he criticized Liuxia, a young wife, and her friends (though without mentioning their names) for gossiping too much about other families. Lao Fan said that Liuxia's gossip especially affected the relationship between Xinmin's wife and her daughter-in-law. Lao Fan had obtained his information from Xinmin's wife, who was universally known as a notorious gossipmonger. Liuxia did not attend the meeting, but she heard about it later from Wenfang, one of her close friends. Liuxia became angry and had an argument with Xinmin's wife—but the women united to blame Lao Fan, claiming that he had misunderstood the matter entirely. Hiding in his own room, Lao Fan was too scared to face them as they shouted, "Come out, Lao Fan, you bastard, we want to ask you about what you said!" Liuxia, encouraged by her husband, threatened to lock up Lao Fan's bicycle, in order to force him to apologize for his criticism. For many days, Lao Fan hardly ever left his room. If he had to, he climbed the hill, leaving Dawa by a very inconvenient route, to avoid being seen by those ferocious women.

There was another reason for Lao Fan to hide in his room. When he first arrived, Lao Fan supported the idea of rebuilding and widening the main road in Dawa, a task that required removing some trees. A few families actually cut down their own trees—but they demanded Lao Fan's bicycle to compensate them for having done so. People hardly caught sight of Lao Fan in April, though the work team was supposed to finish its work in July. In fact, this socialist education work team left Zhaojiahe much earlier than it had originally planned. The members disappeared in May without any announcement. The summer harvest was coming, and the work team was soon forgotten. One old man remarked, "It was just a waste. It helped nothing. It simply wasted money and time." As an attempted political adventure, the "socialist education movement" ended in nothingness. This result is a natural development of the wholly situational "immoral politics" in which local people are actively participating.

Conclusion:
A History of the Future

In the summer of 1992, when local farmers were preparing themselves for the coming harvest, it was time for me to leave this community. In the last few weeks of my fieldwork, I moved into an empty house left by one of Zunxi's brothers, who had found a job in town as a truck driver. The night before my departure, several groups of villagers came to see me, and everyone brought me some kind of gift—most commonly, hard-boiled eggs. I was given more than fifty eggs, and was encouraged to have them all on the train going back to Beijing.[1] My three main hosts, Wanbin, Zunxi, and Famin, were the last to leave. We talked until midnight. At one stage or another of my fieldwork, I had come into conflict with each of them. The most problematic relationship was with Wanbin, who at one time saw me as an ungrateful guest whose improper behavior brought disgrace to his host. However, at the moment of our parting, I felt I owed a great deal to each of them.

No longer can any ethnographer ignore the power relationship between the writing subject and the subject of writing, nor the conditions of power under which a particular mode of fieldwork is made possible;[2] however, understanding the framework in which fieldwork takes place does not reduce ethnography to a narration of the power relationship itself. The task of the anthropologist remains the same: to strive for a critical understanding of the subject of his or her writing. This entails situating oneself not only within a general theoretical orientation of the discipline but also, and perhaps more important, within a specific regional tradition of ethnographic writing (see Fardon 1990).

The ethnographic materials presented in this book articulate a theoretical position in response to two popular tendencies in writing about

contemporary Chinese society. First, I wished to write from the perspective *not* of the local cadres but of my hosts, ordinary villagers. One
may well argue that the local cadres are central in determining the
shape of social life in rural communities, but most ethnographic research of contemporary China, particularly that done by Western
scholars, has either focused largely on the role of the local cadres or
relied heavily on their assistance for research; it is also important to
investigate other possible ways of seeing and being. Second, the ethnographic materials in this book were examined from the perspective of
a worm, not from the bird's-eye view usually taken by those attempting to grasp the significance of rural transformation in China. It was
my intention to focus on an experiential—rather than functional or
statistical—understanding of post-reform rural China.

The notion of a "worm's-eye view" invokes an old epistemological
question in anthropology: to what extent can the large-scale social transformation be captured in the ethnographer's immediate experience of
fieldwork? How far can we see beyond what is happening in a specific
local setting? Or, to put the question more generally, what is the limit
of experience? There is no simple answer to such questions; unprob-
lematic empiricism is no longer an option. But I can say that my ethnographic involvement has created an experiential ground in which the
following thoughts are rooted.

"Immoral Economy"

The increasing economic stratification was the most obvious social phenomenon in China from the late 1970s on. It brought a large number
of newly emerged subject positions to which individuals or groups of
individuals may be temporarily assigned. Some of these positions, such
as "peasant entrepreneurs" (*nongmin qiyejian*), were defined within
the official discourse of development; others emerged at a growing rate
in nonofficial social space as the market economy expanded and
transnational capital and capitalism penetrated Chinese society. Whatever their location, these subject positions arose in ways that defied easy
classification in any master social categories: each was actually or theoretically *overdetermined* in the very articulation of its own conditions
of possible existence.

The modernizing process both generates knowledge and produces ignorance (see Hobart 1993): it presupposes that "backwardness" is out there waiting to be eliminated. The notion of "poor and backward areas" (*pinkun diqu*) was in fact an inevitable ideological product of a process in which people were divided according to their own economic and social conditions, which were undergoing constant change through development. By describing the experiences and performances of a particular group of people in rural Shaanxi, I have tried to grasp the transitional moment in the last decade of the twentieth century, of social being *as becoming*. This mode of social existence is embedded in a set of historically situated everyday practices, and through examining these practices—despite using only ethnographic materials drawn from a specific location at a specific time—we can significantly improve our understanding of the general conditions of life in Chinese society as a whole.

Two major points can be drawn from this study. First, in this time of transition, social life in northern rural Shaanxi was essentially characterized by the lack of any mode of moral economy. In Durkheimian terms, we might say that there was a lack of "collective representation," defined as a transcendental totality of social facts external to but conditioning individual consciousness. This is not to say that individuals were free from the communal constraints; but the rules and codes of such constraints could not be articulated in any coherent way. A sense of communality, an "order of things," or a hierarchy of meanings—that is, a moral economy or a common ground for reason and action—did not exist. In other words, there was no consistent "moral" order to guide and determine social action or cultural meaning; instead, the "*order* of things" rather than "things" already in an order became the subject of debate. Thus arguments about rules of the game have become the game itself, as the players constantly challenged and contested *how* this game should be played.

Second, ironically or not, in conjunction with the lack of any moral order at the local level, the widespread changes in Chinese society have formed a moral space at large, making possible a new grounding for social interaction and individual experience. This moral space was formed on the one hand by the socialist state's retreat from direct control over local and communal affairs and, on the other hand, by the rapid development of market-oriented economic reforms. As the state's overt penetration into communal life has lessened, so has the significance of the political dimension of local life. The process of decollectivization in the countryside has continued, and economic reforms have brought the question of social and economic differentiation—fundamentally an ethical or a moral issue—to the attention of every person. As we have seen in the preceding chapters, the local people always viewed money or economic transactions in general in terms of right or wrong, good or bad, moral or immoral, and so on. That is, economic transactions occupied the foreground of social life; behind them lay shifting moral judgments. In the 1990s, the lack of a moral economy in communal life in conjunction with the emergence of a moral space at large became a crucial condition of existence in post-reform rural China.

The Arbitrary Combination of Cultural Forms

I have argued that each moment of the recent past was characterized by a unique combination of elements derived from three main macro sociohistorical sources: the traditional, the revolutionary, and the modern. Crucial to understanding contemporary Chinese society, in my view, is tracing a series of ruptures in the constitution of certain cultural forms that reflect the significant conceptual shifts in the (re)organization of these sociohistorical elements. In rural China in the 1990s, arbitrariness in how these sociohistorical elements combined into cultural forms marked everyday experience and existence. Here I use the term "arbitrary" to mean three things. First, it has become increasingly difficult to identify individual elements in each hierarchy of meaning within each sociohistorical inventory. What is supposed to be a "sacred" element may now be employed in a "profane" part of practice, or the other way around. For example, the degree of violence at the wedding may be seen as a combination of the collective violence employed against class enemies during the years of the Maoist revolution *and* the traditional mood of celebration that required noises and exaggerated displays of physical strength. Second, the boundaries between these three major sociohistorical domains, from which reason for action is derived, have become blurred because they are being constantly mixed, conceptually and practically, in specific everyday practices. As I have shown in chapter 3, the marriage process has incorporated the traditional, the revolutionary, and the modern into a functioning whole that oriented only toward the practice of marriage itself. Third, the connection between a cultural symbol and its significance is practical rather than ideological. In other words, there is an arbitrary relationship between what a symbol does and what it is supposed to mean. To be sure, individuals engaged in particular social activities had motives and intentions; but a stable relationship between a cultural form and its content was no longer desirable for the agents—and was impossible for the anthropologist to identify. For example, as we saw in chapter 6, a pop song, recently learned from a soap opera on television, might be performed at a funeral ceremony as part of the celebration, despite having been originally created for a very different occasion.

As I have noted on a number of occasions, there were structural reasons why this sociohistorical experience formed in rural China when it did. In this regard, the key structural rearrangement of the past fifty years was the disappearance of the powerful elite group in communal life. The Maoist revolution removed the gentry class, who used to serve as an interpretive authority in managing cultural meanings and symbols. During the years of the people's communes, the state ideology had been channeled through the collective economic operation controlled and administered by the local cadres, whose role in interpreting official documents and ideologies was analogous to that of the vanished gentry. As far as northern rural Shaanxi was concerned, decollectivization greatly diminished the power and authority of the local cadres in the 1990s. Without such an elite group in rural communal society, it has become difficult if not entirely impossible to secure any systematic view on a particular symbol or a particular form of practice. One result has been the arbitrariness in cultural forms discussed above.

Two conclusions may follow. First, in rural China in the last decade of the twentieth century, cultural struggles were no longer carried out on the conventional battleground of meaning and interpretation. That is, individuals and interest groups no longer fought to secure a set of intrinsic meanings or to give certain cultural forms their proper interpretations. Instead, it became important to agents to determine one cultural expression from a multiplicity of possible choices in a particular situation. Therefore, the anthropologist must examine the relations among various possible choices rather than seek the intrinsic meaning of each possible cultural expression. Indeed, under such conditions the relationship of one cultural form to another determines the relationship of that cultural form to its content. Thus, to understand the meaning of sacrificing to ancestors, the anthropologist has to understand the reason for juxtaposing pictures of one's late husband, Chairman Mao, and some naked actresses together on a wall.

Second, despite great variation in access to different forms of cultural expressions, there seems to be everywhere remarkable skill in manipulating these forms. People in northern rural Shaanxi undoubtedly had less access to the symbols of a modern kind than those in Shanghai, Guangzhou, or any other coastal cities, where Western influences were strongest; but in the practices of everyday life, we can identify a general pattern of change across Chinese society. The people whom I have described did not enjoy strategic economic or political influence, but they—no less than any others—were great masters of cultural forms. There is a great deal of uncertainty about the future of China, but it will inevitably be shaped by a generation whose character is marked by their skill at detaching specific cultural forms from their contents. The very ability to weep without tears may enlighten us on the possible future of Chinese society.

Notes

Chapter 1. Exotic Familiarity

1. Qin Shihuang, the first emperor, defeated all other warring states and then established the Qin dynasty (221–206 B.C.E.), the first centralized empire in Chinese ancient history.

2. Local people more often refer to the Weihe Plain as the Guanzhong Plain.

3. Though I grew up in Beijing, I spent four college years in Taiyuan—the capital of Shanxi, a neighboring province on the other side of the Yellow River from Shaanxi.

4. This area is part of the northern Shaanxi loess plateau. T. R. Tregear, a geographer of China, described the topographic characteristics of the region: "an outstanding characteristic of the loess is its proneness to vertical cleavage, which results in the precipitous valleys and unique cliff landscape so typical of the area" (1965, 212).

5. "Get rich first" is a slogan that sets apart the post-Mao regime from its predecessor. When economic reform was launched in the late 1970s, the government encouraged people to accept an anti-egalitarian ideology. Economic development came to be seen as necessarily depending on a degree of social differentiation.

6. I refer here only to voluntary traveling. Of course, to facilitate their investment interests businessmen may have to travel from urban centers to rural areas. Another exception might be the tourists who wish to explore the unspoiled countryside. However, the majority of individual travelers were peasants trying to find temporary jobs in big cities. For a discussion of peasant traveling in the 1990s, see Zhao (1996).

7. The provincial government conducted a large-scale study, the "Shaanxi Rural Social and Economic Survey," in 1986. In the published results, rural communities in Shaanxi are said to have three characteristic features: "conservatism" (*baoshouxing*), "narrow-mindedness" (*xiaaixing*), and "self-containment" (*fengbixing*). See "Dui cun de sikao" (Some thoughts on village life), in *Shaanxi-*

sheng nongcun shehui jinji diaocha (1986, 284–97). In a more general theoretical framework, Wang (1992, 22–29) has categorized the "village family culture" in contemporary China as bearing eight character traits that contrast sharply with those of modern society.

8. Zhaojiahe is a Han village. A little more than one-third of all villages in this area are single-surname communities, and most have no more than two or three surnames among their residents. The people speak a Shaanxi dialect that is not very different from Mandarin, which is my native language. Within a couple of weeks, I was able to speak easily with them.

9. The notion of "descent group" is used here to describe a loosely connected group of agnates. For a discussion of functions and characteristics of lineage organization in North China, see Cohen (1990).

10. The communities range from one hundred to a few thousand residents; see *Chengcheng xianzhi* (1991, 8–9, 71–72).

11. Literary writers in this part of rural China, including both northern Shaanxi and Shanxi, have always devoted considerable attention to the problem of drought. In a recent short story, for instance, the popular novelist Tie Ning describes a scene in a village in this area: whenever there is a shower, people will jump out of their doors naked—men and women alike—to wash themselves in the rain.

12. As J. Gunnar Andersson once observed of this area:

[T]he most fatally incalculable factor of the seasons is the rainfall. Since reckless felling has destroyed the last remnants of the primeval forests, which, by evidence of the Stone Age deposits, once covered the land, the treeless loess plain has become exceptionally sensitive to changes in rainfall. If the normal light rainfall falls, there is no reverse of moisture in the plateau, which is drained by innumerable ravines. If, on the other hand, the summer rains come with the violence of a cloudburst, as not infrequently happens, the ravines are widened with catastrophic rapidity. New miniature ravines are formed in a single night of rain, houses are threatened and roads diverted. Most feared is drought, which is synonymous with famine. (quoted in Tregear 1965, 213).

13. I did not take a bath for six months when I was in Zhaojiahe, but less because of water shortages than because of custom. Bathing simply was not considered part of daily life; indeed, there were no bathing facilities, either public or private. J. Watson observes that it is standard procedure in Chinese funerals to first bathe the dead person one last time (1988, 12), but in northern rural Shaanxi there is only a "dry cleaning" of his or her face before the body is placed in a coffin. Even this fairly cursory procedure is often ignored.

14. Fei Xiaotong, a distinguished Chinese anthropologist, has pointed out the significance of soil for Chinese farmers and their communities: "We often say that country people are figuratively as well as literally 'soiled' (*tuqi*). Although this label may seem disrespectful, the character meaning 'soil' (*tu*) is appropriately used here. Country people cannot do without the soil because their very livelihood is based upon it" (1992, 37).

15. In the local dialect, "rancid" is *hala*. In particular, the term *hala* is applied to something, like leftover food, that has become rotten.

16. To follow E. P. Thompson, the moral economy is grounded "upon a consistent traditional view of social norms and obligations, of the proper economic functions of several parties within the community. . . . An outrage to these moral assumptions, quite as much as actual deprivation, was the usual occasion for direct action" (1993, 188).

17. Such a view is close to the Confucian notion of a person as continuously making progress through self-education; see Tu (1985).

18. A distinction should be made between those who receive salaries from the state (i.e., local officials) and those who are paid by the collective fund within their own community (i.e., cadres). For a very insightful discussion of the status and functions of the local officials and cadres in comparison to what has been called "Chinese gentry" in the pre-Communist era, see Shue (1988).

19. This nostalgia for the Maoist past contrasts sharply with the collective memories documented by Jing (1996) in his study of a Ningxia village in northwestern China. He found bitter images of starvation and desperate struggle, filled with nothing but agony and remorse. Nevertheless, people in Zhaojiahe were not unique in their attitude; Hinton (1990, 163) describes a similar kind of sentiment toward the revolutionary past.

20. At its core, the agricultural responsibility system constitutes the family as the unit of agricultural production. After almost three decades of collectivized agriculture, centered on the people's commune, production was once again organized primarily around the household. Land was redistributed or, more precisely, leased in long-term contracts to each household. Other communal or collective assets were similarly redistributed, rented, or sold to farmers. By the mid-1980s most rural families were operating in a political economy in which the local agents of state authority had less control over labor and land than at any time since the land reform in the early 1950s. For discussions and different interpretations of this process, see Riskin (1987, 284–315); Croll (1988); Howard (1988); Shue (1988, 148–52); Siu (1989, 273–90); Gittings (1990, 127–49); Hinton (1990); Nee and Su (1990); S. Potter and J. Potter (1990, 158–79).

21. Safety may not be an entirely new problem for Chinese farmers; on crop watching by peasants in the pre-Communist era, see M. C. Yang (1945, 148–50). But potential thieves at that time generally came from outside one's own community. In other words, it was a sign of conflicts between villages and lineages (Baker 1979, 149).

22. Today, anthropologists cannot avoid paying as much attention to writing as to fieldwork. For debates about writing and fieldwork since the early 1980s, see Fabian (1983); Sperber (1985); Clifford and Marcus (1986); Marcus and Fischer (1986); Clifford (1988b); Geertz (1988); Fardon (1990); R. G. Fox (1991); A. James, Hockey, and Dawson (1997).

23. I left Beijing in the winter of 1989, to enroll in the University of London's School of Oriental and African Studies for an M.A. in social anthropology; my Ph.D. training did not start until the winter of 1990.

24. For a classic discussion of the advantage of being a stranger to the community (or society) that one studies, see Evans-Pritchard (1951, 75–85); Srinivas (1966), a native scholar studying his own society, appropriated some of Evans-Pritchard's points. See also Fei's criticism (1993) of Leach, who similarly held that it was better for the ethnographer to be a naive stranger (1982, 122–27).

25. Ginzburg's study (1980) views the popular culture of sixteenth-century Italy through the eyes of a man known as Menocchio, who was brought to trial during the Inquisition. Though a common miller, Menocchio was surprisingly well-read; in his trial testimony he referred to more than a dozen books, including the Bible. His reading enabled him to recast a vision of the creation, using terms familiar to him: the cheese and the worms were metaphors for the earth and the angels.

26. The difficulties of scholars from the West doing field research in rural China are well known. For a general discussion of such problems, see Thurston and Pasternak (1983). Western scholars tend to picture rural life in China through the lens of local officials and cadres; e.g., see the field studies of Mosher (1983), Siu (1989), S. Potter and J. Potter (1990), and Chan, Madsen, and Unger (1992), to list only a few. These authors have provided extremely valuable materials and insightful discussions, but their partiality is also evident.

27. Wanbin's family was very conscious of their own status in the community. Two of his sons attended college, which is very unusual in this area, and Wanbin expected me to visibly demonstrate their power to make allies and connections outside the community. I was expected to dress differently from local people, for instance. I failed to meet Wanbin's expectations in many ways (see chapter 5), and ultimately I moved out of his house.

28. I do not mean that all individuals are reproduced in the same way; instead, each person occupies a specific place at a specific time in any given society. In life the reproduction of a person is never abstract; it is always concrete and particular (e.g., see Volosinov 1973). Everyday life is "heteroglossic," to use a Bakhtinian term, but each form of everyday power is historically identifiable.

29. Norbert Elias's study of the history of manners (1994) may serve as a good example of this kind of investigation; first published in German in 1939, it had to wait half a century for its English translation. Elias's work concentrates on certain aspects of social behavior—such as "table manners," "blowing one's nose," and "spitting"—in Western Europe, especially in the late Middle Ages. Pointing to major changes during the Renaissance, Elias argues that the handkerchief and the fork were instruments of "civilization," which he defines as a shift in the thresholds of embarrassment and shame. He further

links self-control, derived from such a civilizing process, to the formation of the absolute state. In turning sociological inquiry on such a long span of history, Elias has demonstrated that the forces behind such evolution in behavior are not linear. His main concern is to go beyond describing historical phenomena to explain how these changes took place. For his own view on sociology, see Elias (1970); see also Braudel on "history and sociology" (1958). On what is now called "historical sociology," see Skopcol (1984) and D. Smith (1991).

Within the discipline of anthropology, one recent example of historical ethnography is the work carried out by Jean Comaroff, first without (1985) and then with John Comaroff (1991, 1992). Although the Comaroffs' theoretical position is specifically tied to an account of cultural encounters in colonial situations—a topic that has been of anthropological interest for some time—their focus on notions such as ideology and hegemony, representation and consciousness, culture and history, and agency and practice is relevant to any attempt to study culture in history.

30. For an informative but brief account of the studies of Maoist politics, see Shue (1988, 12–25). For overviews of different regional traditions in writings about Chinese society, see Shambaugh (1993); Sidel (1995); Bianco (1995); Michio, Eades, and Christian (1995).

31. The claim that practice is always situated may seem novel, but its genesis can be better understood if one considers the intellectual life of French structuralism that provided Bourdieu's context. See P. Anderson (1983) for an interesting account of the rise of structuralism and the decline of Marxism in continental Europe.

32. As Bourdieu writes: "Bodily hexis is political mythology realised, *embodied,* turned into a permanent disposition, a durable manner of standing, speaking and thereby of *feeling* and *thinking*. . . . The principles embodied in this way are placed beyond the grasp of consciousness, and hence cannot be touched by voluntary, deliberate transformation, cannot even be made explicit" (1977, 93).

33. Such a notion of practice implies that in order to understand the meaning of representation or social organization, one must understand how each is "embodied" in practice. According to Certeau, "The presence and circulation of a representation (taught by preachers, educators, and popularizers as the key to socioeconomic advancement) tells us nothing about what it is for its users. We must first analyze its manipulation by users who are not its makers. Only then can we gauge the difference or similarity between the production of the image and the secondary production hidden in the process of its utilization" (1984, xiii).

34. The very notion of a "theory of practice" may be ironic. Bourdieu himself admits to "certain properties of the logic of practice which by definition escape theoretical apprehension" (1990, 86).

35. Interpreting Foucault, Certeau writes: "Instead of analyzing the apparatus exercising power (i.e., the localizable, expansionist, repressive, and legal institutions), Foucault analyzes the mechanisms (*dispositifs*) that have sapped the strength of these institutions and surreptitiously reorganized the functioning of power: 'minuscule' technical procedures acting on and with details, redistributing a discursive space in order to make it the means of a generalized 'discipline' (*surveillance*)" (1984, xiv).

36. Though there are valuable studies of Taiwan, Hong Kong, and other overseas Chinese communities, I am principally concerned with the literature on mainland China.

37. Many works are devoted to political organizations and ideologies while neglecting the social unconscious; see, e.g., Schurmann (1966); Lampton (1987); Schram (1987).

38. Some influential studies of rural China focusing on political relationships include Siu (1989); S. Potter and J. Potter (1990); Friedman, Pickowicz, and Selden (1991); Chan, Madsen, and Unger (1992).

Chapter 2. Resisting Ideology

1. The village genealogy, *Zhaoshi jiapu* (Zhao genealogy), consists of five volumes: one for the whole community and the others for its four different branches—the Eastern, the Western, the Southern, and the Northern Branch. In the local dialect, "branch" is written and pronounced as *yuan*, meaning "courtyard" or "compound." The last compilation was made in 1948, just before the Communists took control of this region. In recent years, no one has considered recompiling it. It records twenty generations of settlement since their old ancestor (*laoxianren*) came to this area from Luochuan, a place about two hundred kilometers northeast of Zhaojiahe. Allowing twenty years per generation, we can estimate that people bearing a surname of Zhao have been settled in this place for more than four hundred years. However, according to *Chengcheng xian dimingzhi* (Village names of Chengcheng county) (1984, 142), Zhaojiahe was established in the years of Jianlong, emperor of the Song dynasty, which means that it could have been a settlement as early as 960 C.E.

2. A more familiar term in anthropological literature of Chinese kinship is "ancestral hall." But in Zhaojiahe it is actually called *jiamiao*, literally "family temple." There had been a number of family temples in the past: one for the whole community and several for each branch and subbranch. The degree of segmentation had largely depended on the number of sons that a particular branch was able to produce.

3. On the emergence of the term "lineage" in the study of Chinese kinship, see Freedman (1979a, 335).

4. On Freedman's theory and his contribution to anthropological questioning in general, see Pasternak (1985a, 166–75).

5. The term "descent paradigm" was employed by R. Watson (1981, 593). Freedman's paradigm inspired a series of further investigations, covering a wide range of areas in the study of Chinese society and culture. See Cohen on family division and organization (1976); Baker on agnatic village and local organization (1968); J. Potter on corporate estates (1970); J. Watson on emigration (1975); Ahern on ancestor worship (1973). For discussions of alternative models of Chinese kinship organizations, see, e.g., Pasternak (1969); M. Wolf (1970); A. Wolf and Huang (1980); R. Watson (1981, 1982); Harrell (1982). For critiques of Freedman's model, see, e.g., Hallgren (1979); Q. Chen (1985); Chun (1996). For a critical review of lineage theory in anthropology, focusing on the earlier work of Evans-Pritchard and Fortes, see Kuper (1982); see also Fried (1957).

6. Some early materials that show the difference can be found in Hu (1948). Hu's survey of Gao'an county in Jiangxi province, South China, showed that 1,121 villages—i.e., 86.9 percent of the total number—were single-surname ones (1948, 14). Niida's investigation of Luancheng county in Shandong province, North China, yielded a quite different result. Communities in which there were one or two surnames constituted only 12.5 percent of the total number of villages investigated (Niida is cited in Y. Chen 1984, 425 n. 14).

7. Zhaojiahe's case fits into Cohen's general picture quite well. There is no evidence of corporate land holding that could have defined and determined subgroups of kin in the past. Before the 1950s there had been annual ancestral celebrations, both at the family temples and graveyards, but these activities were financed by contributions collected from each household rather than by profits derived from commonly owned properties.

8. Chun points to Hu's *Common Descent Group in China and Its Functions* (1948), which was a starting point in Freedman's paradigmatic monograph, *Lineage Organization in Southeastern China* (1958).

9. Freedman indeed made such an attempt, see his "Politics of an Old State: A View from the Chinese Lineage" (1979a). Freedman's scholarship continues to be honored; see, e.g., Baker and Feuchtwang, *An Old State in New Settings: Studies in the Social Anthropology of China in Memory of Maurice Freedman* (1991).

10. Q. Chen's article (1985) is a short version of his Ph.D. dissertation titled "Fang and Chia-tsu: The Chinese Kinship System in Rural Taiwan" (Yale University, 1983).

11. For a critique of Cohen on *jia* (family) and *jiachan* (family property), see Q. Chen (1985, 135–50); he also critiques Ahern on lineage membership and ancestor worship (158–63), and J. Watson as well as A. Wolf and Huang on adoption (165–67).

12. Y. Chen (1984) offers a similar critique of Western functional analysis of Chinese kinship. But the question is whether there is anything new in a claim that principles of descent precede functional operations. Does not their

view reflect an intellectual tradition that has existed among Chinese scholars for centuries—exactly what Freedman tried to avoid?

13. The notion of "practical kinship," in contrast to "official kinship," has been employed by Bourdieu. Official kinship serves primarily as a legitimating ideology that regulates social order; in contrast, practical kinship is the utilization of kinship—i.e., how kinship is actually manipulated in changing situations. Bourdieu explains: "Thus, to schematize, official kinship is opposed to practical kinship in terms of the official as opposed to the non-official (which includes the unofficial and the scandalous); the collective as opposed to the individual; the public, explicitly codified in a magical or quasi-juridical formalism, as opposed to the private, kept in an implicit, even hidden state; collective ritual, subjectless practice, amendable to performance by agents interchangeable because collectively mandated, as opposed to strategy, directed towards the satisfaction of the practical interests of an individual or group of individuals" (1977, 35).

14. The notion of the domestic group, not always but usually equivalent to "family," is more often represented by the Chinese term *jia*. But *jia* is seldom used alone in this region. For some early discussions of Chinese notion of family, see Fei (1939, 27); M. C. Yang (1945, 45); Lang (1946, 13); Hu (1948, 15–16).

15. In this sense, *wu* is equivalent to the more popular term *jia*. For instance, to ask "How many people are there in your *family?*" one would say, "Ni *wu* (jia) ji kou ren?" When talking about whether someone was back home, one would say, "Ta hui *wu* le." When talking about oneself and one's family, one would say, "Wo *wu* mei qian" (*We* are not rich). When referring to differences between households, one would say, "Yi *wu* (jia) yi yang" (It is different from one *household* to another).

16. For discussions of the significance of metaphors (by which we live) as a cognitive register of what we often unconsciously express, see Sapir and Crocker (1977); Sontag (1978); Ortony (1979); Sacks (1979); Lakoff and Johnson (1980).

17. Jakobson has often dealt with the difference between metaphor and metonymy in his writings; here I refer specifically to his essay "Two Aspects of Language and Two Types of Aphasic Disturbances," in *Fundamentals of Language* (Jakobson and Halle 1971, 69–96). For comments on and elaborations of Jakobson's discussion, see Jameson (1972, 122–23); Hawkes (1977, 78–79); Scholes (1982, 20–22).

18. Metonymic associations take a large number of forms. Scholes points to some of the more common examples: "Things which are logically related by cause and effect (*poverty* and *hut*) or whole and part (*hut* and *thatch*), as well as things that are habitually found together in familiar contexts (*hut* and *peasants*), are all in metonymic relationship to one another" (1982, 20).

19. I have replaced Hawkes's "associative" with "paradigmatic."

20. See, e.g., Jakobson's treatment of realism in art (1987, 19–27).

21. Further extensions in the meaning of *wu* are always associated with a concrete sense of space that one takes within a room. For instance, the terms *liwu* versus *waiwu* or *wuli* versus *wuwai* mean "inner room" versus "outer room" or "inside (a room)" versus "outside (a room)." A husband may refer to his wife as *wuli de,* which literally means the "inside (house) person." The meaning of *wu* can be extended but it is often done metonymically. That is, its extension is often based on contiguity rather than similarity.

22. A classic treatment of such context-bound words can be found in Evans-Pritchard's discussion of the Nuer notion of "home," *cieng:*

What does a Nuer mean when he says, "I am a man of such-and-such a *cieng?*" *Cieng* means "home," but its precise significance varies with the situation in which it is spoken. If one meets an Englishman in Germany and asks him where his home is, he may reply that it is England. If one meets the same man in London and asks him the same question he will tell one that his home is in Oxfordshire, whereas if one meets him in that county he will tell one the name of the town or village in which he lives. . . . So is it with the Nuer. . . . The variations in the meaning of the word *cieng* are not due to the inconsistencies of language, but to the relativity of the group-values to which it refers. ([1940] 1969, 136)

23. For a very insightful discussion of the inequality among brothers in South China, see R. Watson (1985).

24. See *Zhaoshi jiapu* (Zhao genealogy). Few people in Zhaojiahe were actually addressed by their official names.

25. For an overview of events in rural China in the 1950s, see Shue (1980). The land reform largely did away with the elite group. But one could argue that its replacement—i.e., the communist cadre system—was based on a very similar principle. On the role and function of the cadre vs. the gentry class, see Shue (1988).

26. For an earlier discussion of four types of families, see Kulp (1925, 24–25).

27. A. Wolf and Huang write:

In sum, we see that what is generally referred to as the Chinese family is a composite of three interdependent but analytically distinct organizations. Setting aside the women and looking at the family from the viewpoint of its place in the kinship system, one sees a core composed of the men linked by descent and rights in property. It was with reference to this core that men related to their dead ancestors and the past and to their children and the future. A shift from this kinship perspective to that taken by the community and the state brings together another aspect of the family into focus. The relevant institution is then the ke, the basic unit of production and consumption, which included women as well as men. Whereas the line spanned time and included the dead as well as the living, the ke located the family in space and regulated its relations with the community, the government, and the supernatural bureaucracy. Finally, when one gives life to these institutional views by admitting the bonds of sentiment formed in childhood, one sees that the family has still a third aspect. Crosscutting the jurally defined lines of the men are other solidary groups composed of women and their children. Though less obvious to the eye trained for ritual detail and the ear attuned to forms of address, these groups were nonetheless real and exerted a powerful impact on decisions concerning marriage and adoption. (1980, 64–65)

28. Such arrangements are not uncommon. A relatively large proportion of families share a courtyard with their *zijiawu* brothers.

29. In other parts of northern China, the brick bed used in the countryside is often called a *kang*.

30. On the domestic order as the world reversed, see, e.g., Bourdieu's description of the Kabyle House (1990, 271–83), which presents an exact symmetrical correspondence between the two.

31. This question about women's separate sphere has been asked by feminist scholars writing on Chinese society; e.g., see Croll (1983); Stacey (1983); M. Wolf (1985); Honig and Hershatter (1988).

32. Class struggle was introduced when land reform began in 1949–50. For a discussion of the process of building a new social order by giving everyone a class label, see S. Potter and J. Potter (1990, 37–58). On the definitions of each class, see Hinton (1966, 623–26).

33. The marriage crisis was by no means universal, nor even equally felt by rural communities in this area. However, what Raymond Williams calls a "structure of feelings," in Zhaojiahe best reflected in this issue, seemed to affect everyone in the region. Williams employs the phrase to define experiences in their moment of happening, which are distinguished "in two ways . . . from reduced senses of the social as the institutional and the formal: first, . . . they are *changes of presence* (while they are being lived this is obvious; when they have been lived it is still their substantial characteristic); second, . . . although they are emergent or pre-emergent, they do not have to await definition, classification, or rationalization before they exert palpable pressures and set effective limits on experience and on action" (1977, 131–32). This notion helps us define a social sphere in which meanings and values are actually lived, rather than fixed and explicit.

34. For instance, Croll writes: "It is generally accepted that there is a demonstrable tendency for it [i.e., mate selection] to occur within a bounded locality, with the likelihood of marriage decreasing markedly as the distance between the contracting parties increases" (1981, 85).

35. According to the Marriage Law of P.R.C., adopted at the Third Session of the Fifth National People's Congress, September 1980, "Marriage is not permitted in any of the following circumstances. a) Where the man and woman are lineal relatives by blood or collateral relatives by blood (up to the third degree of relationship) . . ." Local people's notion of "out of five generations" comes from the traditional idea of "five mourning grades," which used to be marked by five kinds of mourning dress that indicated a hierarchy of kin relations. For a discussion of *wufu*, see Baker (1979, 107–12).

Chapter 3. Marriage as a Mirror of Change

1. For overviews of the changes introduced by the post-Mao government in the name of economic reforms, see Feuchtwang and Hussain (1983); Griffin (1984); R. Hsu (1985); Leeming (1985); Perry and Wong (1985); Skinner (1985); Blecher (1986); Chossudovsky (1986); Feuchtwang, Hussain, and Pairault (1986); Riskin (1987); Croll (1988); Gittings (1989); Hinton (1990); Hussain (1994).

2. In general anthropological literature, the term "bridewealth" may be preferred in discussions of payment made by the bridegroom's side to the bride's side (Goody and Tambiah 1973). However, in the literature focusing on marriage in Chinese society, "bride-price" is more commonly employed (see Parish and Whyte 1978, 183; R. Watson 1981, 605; Siu 1993, 167).

3. Harrell's point, that changes are unlikely to occur in only one direction, suggests two possible approaches. The first is to look at how changes in marriage practice have resulted from changes in political and economic structure: for instance, to examine how collectivization or decollectivization has affected marriage. In such investigations, changes in marriage practice are often seen as consequences of modifications in government policies. The second approach is to compare China and other developing countries: for instance, to examine how marriage practice in each reacts to "the opening up of economic opportunities." The first mode of investigation is more familiar to scholars working on Chinese marriage; e.g., see C. Yang (1959); Whyte (1979); Croll (1981); M. Wolf (1984); Hsieh and Chuang (1985).

4. The Marriage Law of 1980 has affirmed a legal marriage age of twenty-two for men and twenty for women. On "late marriage" as practiced during the years of the Maoist revolution, see Croll (1981, 60–62); Banister (1987, 152–60).

5. Greenhalgh's study (1993) of three suburban Shaanxi villages and Selden's research (1993) in a Hebei village support this hypothesis of return to pre-Communist practice.

6. On uxorilocal marriage in rural China, see M. Wolf (1985, 196–98); see also Pasternak (1985b).

7. On bride-price and dowry in the 1980s, see, e.g., Siu (1993).

8. For a discussion of Goody's idea with reference to rural China, see Parish and Whyte (1978, 180–92).

9. Anthropologists have cast doubts on the validity of the principles and modes of classification that prevail in discussions of kinship and marriage. Rodney Needham, for instance, who draws on Wittgenstein's later philosophy, has argued: "To put it bluntly, then, there is no such thing as kinship and it follows that there can be no such thing as kinship theory" (1971, 5). In so doing, he rejects the ways that anthropologists conceptualize kinship and mar-

riage, which reflect what Wittgenstein would call "a craving for generality."
In urging anthropologists to pay attention to how different societies use kinship and marriage terms—a demand paralleling Wittgenstein's claim that philosophy should examine the uses of language in particular contexts, i.e., "language games"—Needham maintains that "there was no single word which
would be taken to stand for 'marriage,'"; but as a useful word, "it has all the
resources of meaning which its long history has conferred upon it, and we
should now find it hard to communicate without these" (7). Such critiques
underscore that one should not forget that meaning is dependent on its
specific historical context.

   10. I am indebted to Judith Farquhar for rightly pointing out that my original translation of *song* as "to send" was inadequate.

   11. *Jia,* the fourth tone, is "to marry"; *jia,* the first tone, means "family."

   12. The significance of language can hardly be exaggerated. On the one
hand, anthropologists have tended to build their theories on models of language, particularly since the rise of structuralism; on the other hand, linguistic anthropology, which focuses on the uses of language as social and cultural
practices, has a long history of its own (e.g., see Lévi-Strauss 1963; Leach 1964;
Tambiah 1968; Bloch 1975b; Douglas 1975b; Parkin 1982). As Bakhtin claims,
"all the diverse areas of human activity involve the use of language. Quite un-
derstandably, the nature and forms of this use are just as diverse as are the areas of human activity" (1986, 60). Concerned not with the monologic but the
dialogic, he emphasizes that utterance is always situational. As Emerson and
Holquist put it, "in Bakhtin's thought the place from which we speak plays an
important role in determining what we say" (1986, x), paralleling Volosinov's
insistence that "Verbal communication can never be understood and explained
outside of this connection with a concrete situation" (1973, 95). Speaking involves not only linguistic elements—the lexical, grammatical, and syntactic—
but also the positions that both the speaker and the listener take. These positions are first of all, in Bakhtin's terminology, "socioideological"; no utterance
is neutral. Stressing the *wholeness* of the utterance, Bakhtin argues that one
speaks only in generic forms—i.e., in "relatively stable types," which are
formed in relation to specific spheres of social life; "The forms of language
and the typical forms of utterances, that is, speech genres, enter our experience and our consciousness together, and in close connection with each other"
(1986, 78). Because speech genres are social, any individual's speech presupposes a socially constructed speech genre within his or her consciousness.
This is how we should understand the ways in which marriage is talked about
in Zhaojiahe.

   13. Taking an anthropological approach, David Parkin provides a good example of how rhetoric can be used as a means of instilling responsibility among
Kenya farmers. He first defines rhetoric as "a type of ritual: it says something
about the speaker, the spoken-to, and the situation, which goes beyond what

is contained in the surface message" (1975, 114). In his study of the Giriama people of Kenya, looking at how bureaucrats publicize the "need" for rural economic development and how other local groups react to such development, Parkin then argues that "rhetoric, like ritual, may be more than a symbolic reaffirmation of social relations. Through rhetoric people have licence, so to speak, to explain and evaluate the causes and consequences of social relations, sometimes to the point of distortion. Rhetoric is thereby dynamically involved in their organisation and perpetuation" (119). Maurice Bloch has generalized this position as he relates how people talk to each other to how authority is exercised in traditional societies:

> The process whereby one is caught by the formalisation of oratory into accepting without the possibility of question what is proposed is an everyday occurrence experienced whenever people stop and consider what they are doing. . . . On these occasions if you have allowed somebody to speak in an oratorical manner you have practically accepted his proposal. The reason is that the code adopted by the speaker contains within itself a set pattern of speech for the other party. What gets said, or rather cannot be said, is laid down by this polite, respectful, behaviour—both linguistic and non-linguistic. . . . The speaker and hearer have slipped into a highly structured situation which contains the hierarchical situation which only allows a one way relationship. (1975a, 9)

Thus we should not only look at what has been said but, more important, we should also examine *how* it is said. In the case of Zhaojiahe, a mode of conversation has been set up by the older generation's choice of a particular vocabulary.

14. *Mai* (to buy) and *mai* (to sell) are spelled in the same way in transliteration but written in completely different characters. The sound difference can be detected only from their different tones.

15. Did the Maoist revolution liberate women? This question has been central to a number of feminist studies: see, e.g., Davin (1976); Croll (1978); Stacey (1983); Wolf (1985); Honig and Hershatter (1988); Judd (1994).

16. In fact some young couples saw each other before the bride-price had been negotiated; see the section on matchmaking later in this chapter.

17. Sometimes the bridegroom's side reneges; but more often the bride's side takes advantage of the increasing difficulty in recent years in recruiting brides into Zhaojiahe to demand more from the bridegroom's side.

18. In other parts of northern rural China, bride-price is often called *caili:* as Yan explains, "The first character *cai* means color or colorful, indicating happiness in marriage, and the second character *li* means gifts. The term *caili* can thus be translated as 'marital gifts'" (1996, 180).

19. However, statistics may be deceptive. In considering how much a Chinese farmer earns and determining his standard of living, we often fail to take into account that many necessary daily supplies are free, such as the building materials for one's house.

20. *Li*, with the second tone ("to leave" or "to go away"), is different from *li* of the third tone ("gift money"), and the two words are written in completely different ways. *Niang* is "mother" and *fei* is "expense" or "compensation."

21. Similarly, Yan finds that beginning in the mid-1980s, a new category, *ganzhe*, was introduced into marriage transactions in Xiajia. *Ganzhe* is the value of all supposed payment, in its various forms, converted into a certain amount of cash (1996, 180).

22. To be sure, a wide range of materials, including nylon and silk, were available in the 1990s. But comparisons between materials were almost always made in terms of local categories, which were based on the distinction between the machine-made and the hand- or homemade. In judging machine-made materials, only price mattered.

23. For an interesting discussion of the case of Guangdong and its place in anthropologists' debates about the function of dowry, see Parish and Whyte (1978, 180–83); cf. Goody 1973; see also Yan (1996, 178–79).

24. One should note that any gift received at the wedding from any person will be displayed in public, though perhaps not so long and so obviously as the dowry.

25. Weber's study (1964) may be taken as an early example of this kind of analysis of social relationships. In what he called "the religion of China," a central element was familism, whose principles were derived from the Confucian ethics. The view that personal relationships in China fundamentally rest on the family has been further developed in recent discussions of the nature of Chinese capitalism. See, e.g., Redding (1990); Hamilton (1991).

26. For more on the function of go-betweens in communal life, see chapter 5.

27. Because of differences of pronunciation between the Mandarin and local dialect, the local spelling should be *shuehalue*.

28. The woman whom Rongcai's wife consulted was referred to as a *shenpozi*—that is, an old woman who is supposed to possess a certain dark, supernatural power.

29. Such a mixture need not contradict a primarily structural view of the Maoist revolution. Elizabeth Croll has pointed out that the authority of the older generation and the degree to which they continued to exercise control over marriage negotiations in the Maoist era could be related to "a) the structure and function of the household and b) the degree to which households encapsulated by overlapping primary groups" (1981, 184).

Chapter 4. Meaning and Eating

1. Robin Fox wrote, "Kinship is to anthropology what logic is to philosophy or the nude is to art" (1967, 10). K. C. Chang (1977) suggests that one of the best ways of getting to a culture's heart is through its stomach. This echoes

a general view laid out in more scientific terms by Audrey Richards: "Nutrition as a biological process is more fundamental than sex. In the life of the individual organism it is the more primary and recurrent want, while in the wider sphere of human society it determines, more largely than any other physiological function, the nature of social groupings, and the form their activities take" (1932, 1).

2. The anthropological study of food is almost as old as anthropology itself. For example, as Sidney Mintz has reminded us, Robertson Smith (a founding father of the discipline) took eating to be a special social act: "Those who sit at meat together are united for all social effects; those who do not eat together are aliens to one another, without fellowship in religion and without reciprocal social duties" (quoted in Mintz 1985, 4).

3. My definition of food as a system of signification is similar to Saussure's idea of language. See Saussure ([1916] 1983, 9, 19) and also Barthes (1967, 13–15).

4. Wanbin's mother, who married in the late 1940s, was comparing the pre-Communist and Communist eras.

5. In the early 1990s, three families in Zhaojiahe were operating electric mills for processing wheat.

6. Often, the variety of dishes seen as typical of the Chinese meal is interpreted as resulting from a long history of "undernourishment, drought and famines," which compelled the Chinese people to "make judicious use of every possible kind of edible vegetable and insect, as well as offal" (Gernet 1962, 135; quoted in Chang 1977, 13). Or as Eugene Anderson said, "Chinese cooking is a cooking of scarcity" (1988, 149). But the variety may also be explained, without reference to external factors, as due to the development of a basic principle of cooking. As Chang argues, "At the base of this complex is the division between *fan,* grains and other starch food, and *cai,* vegetable and meat dishes" (1977, 6). This division provides the fundamental possibility of allowing people to enjoy as many different dishes (*cai*) as possible at one meal.

7. For many local people, "meat" means pork, simply because they find beef too expensive. Their reasoning is quite different than that of people in Taitou, as described by M. C. Yang half a century ago. In that village, in Shandong province, people were reluctant to eat beef and disliked butchers because the ox was related to farming and had a significant practical function in their life: "The feeling is so strong that [a man] may feel worse about the loss of his ox than he would about the death of his infant child, for the loss of the animal endangers the life of the whole family" (1945, 47).

8. Other industrial goods, such as watches and radios, became popular during the Cultural Revolution, but especially since the late 1970s. It was not until 1989 that electricity became available in Zhaojiahe, and then the age of television arrived in this community. Electricity has changed many aspects of life. Different kinds of machines followed, including those to process

wheat, cotton, and so forth, though electricity was largely used for nonproductive purposes.

9. I am indebted to Judith Farquhar for pointing out some missing links in figure 6. I have no intention of denying that in thus reconstructing the nature of agricultural life in this part of rural Shaanxi, I—as an ethnographer working from an outsider's insider perspective—may have reduced the villagers' much richer reality to a skeleton of what I consider to be essential.

10. For a discussion of the organization of these three calendars, see Fei (1939, 144–48). On social employment of the traditional Chinese calendar, see also M. C. Yang (1945, 90).

11. The following table shows the agricultural production of different households in Dawa in 1991–92:

Crop	No. of households (N = 20)	Percentage of households
wheat	20	100
cotton	20	100
corn	6	30
sweet potatoes	11	55
hot peppers	17	85
watermelons	2	10
soybeans	3	15

12. The rate of exchange depends on several elements, including the bargaining ability of the participants. In 1992, six *jin* of unhusked wheat (not flour) could be exchanged for one *jin* of cooking oil. I was told that this rate was slightly higher than the previous year.

13. With no difference in tone and pronunciation, *hui* was also employed to refer to the mass meetings of the Maoist era. This suggests that the term fundamentally denotes the activity of coming together, regardless of purpose.

14. For a detailed discussion of the lunar *xun* (*hsun*) system and its importance in scheduling market days, see Skinner (1964–65, 14).

15. The circle of local markets that a group of villagers frequently visit defines one sense of neighborhood; the two others in this area of China are marriage locality and administrative region.

16. Lévi-Strauss's "culinary triangle" is too powerful to be forgotten; see Leach (1970, 21–35). Barthes's writings on the semiology of food (1967, 27–28; 1973, 58–64; 1979) have been very influential. See also Douglas on food (1975, 1982, 1984); Passariello (1990) provides a review essay on her contribution in this area of study.

17. See M. Harris (1985, 1987); Goody (1982); Mintz (1985, 1996); Bourdieu (1984); Mennell (1996); Finkelstein (1989).

18. The classic structuralist stance insists on three fundamental points: "[t]he human world as it appears to us is defined essentially as the world of

signification" (Greimas 1983, 3), the best means of understanding it is the structural analysis developed in linguistics, and that structural analysis presupposes that meaning is a quality of relations. For the original articulation of structural linguistics, which provided a theoretical foundation for later structural analysis, see Saussure ([1916] 1983); see also Culler (1976); R. Harris (1987). For further developments in and critiques of the structuralist paradigm, see Jameson (1972); Ricoeur (1974); Culler (1975); Hawkes (1977); Scholes (1982); Merquior (1986); Caws (1988); Pavel (1989); Sturrock (1993). For a very illuminating, thorough historical analysis of the paradigmatic shift from structuralism to poststructuralism, see Mosse (1997a, 1997b).

19. On the different kinds of oppositions employed and developed in linguistics and semiology, see Barthes (1967, 75–85).

20. This list of calendrical food is not derived from the official discourse—either local or provincial—on what should be consumed; rather, it presents what local farmers said they commonly consumed. For a discussion of local festivals, as registered in the official records, see *Chengcheng xianzhi* (Records of Chengcheng County) (1990).

21. *Zongzi* is a pyramid-shaped dumpling made of glutinous rice wrapped in bamboo or reed leaves.

22. *Hunton* is a kind of dumpling-like food served with soup.

23. There are three major steps in making steamed bread. First a piece of leavened dough is prepared two or three days in advance. This is the most difficult stage and requires experience. Second, the dough is given various shapes; and third, the bread is steamed.

24. The local people never clearly defined what *hundun* is, though some women described it as something that had not yet produced a shape. In Chinese folklore, the word refers to the primeval state of the universe, before the earth had separated from the heaven. It is different from *hunton,* which is a kind of dumpling, usually served with soup.

25. As some readers may have noticed, the heading of this section is taken from the title of a chapter in Sindey Mintz's *Sweetness and Power* (1985), but my theoretical approach is quite different from his.

26. On ceremonial occasions, men will take charge of both cooking and serving, leaving the women to look after tea (if they are needed at all).

27. Local people commonly refer to the relationship between a married-out daughter and her natal family as the mother-daughter relationship. In the anthropological literature on this subject, it is sometimes discussed as relations defined by the notion of "uterine family." See, e.g., M. Wolf (1970); A. Wolf and Huang (1980, 58–59).

28. According to the Mandarin pronunciation, the latter should be spelled "Mangba."

29. For instance, in the case of a married-out daughter, a parent would say *gaigei wa songdian mo le* (It is time to send some steamed bread to our child).

30. Such terms as "ordinary" and "extraordinary" are by no means alien to anthropologists. For example, Bourdieu (1977, 52–59) discusses marriage strategies in these terms. In a more recent effort, F. N. Pieke has taken up this dichotomy in his analysis of the people's movement in contemporary China (1996).

31. Some readers may find my use of the term "spatial" unsatisfactory and question why social relations, such as those of affinal ties, should be viewed as spatial relations. In rural China, particularly in regions where there are lineage organizations or common descent groups, social relations are always at the same time relations of a geographic (spatial) sort. In other words, kin groups are always at the same time community groups; the village and the lineage often coincide. It is in this sense that a "relative" is identified both as an affinal kin and as a person from a neighboring community. Distance in social relationship is indeed often construed in terms of distance in space. For an original discussion of the embodiment of social relations in space, see Freedman (1958, 1–8).

32. For an undoubtedly classic treatment of this topic, see E. E. Evans-Pritchard on the Nuer ([1940] 1969).

33. The term "modes of time" may imply a link to the work of such theorists as Georges Gurvitch (1961), who has distinguished several types of social time. For a recent discussion of Gurvitch's typology of time in relation to the condition of postmodernity, see Harvey (1990, 223–25). Alfred Gell's critique (1992) of Gurvitch and many others in their treatment of time finds all the errors in the anthropological study of time to be rooted in the Durkheimian ontology based on a strong version of cultural relativism. I use the phrase simply to refer to several coexisting rhythms in the local people's conceptualization of social life.

34. Scholars interested in the question of primitive mentality (see, e.g., Lévy-Bruhl [1923] 1966, [1949] 1975; Evans-Pritchard 1934, 1937; Durkheim and Mauss 1963; Lévi-Strauss 1964, 1966; Needham 1972) commonly argue that the primitive conceptualization of time generally bears a spatial character (see Hallpike 1979, 340–65). This may be true; but their framing of the argument presupposes the dichotomies so popular in the Durkheimian era: the primitive versus the modern, the concrete versus the abstract, and so on. My emphasis here is on showing the possible articulation of the temporal with the spatial in a system of food, stressing how these categories of space and time function in daily practice—not on the abstract character of thought itself.

Chapter 5. The Practice of Everyday Life

1. I had brought my host two cartons of cigarettes (as well as some other things) as a gift for his kindness in allowing me to stay with his family.

2. There was great regional variation in the development of local market systems, particularly between North and South China, both during and after the Maoist years.

3. In 1992, 1 dollar = 5.5 yuan; in 1997, 1 dollar = 8.4 yuan. Each yuan is divided into ten *mao*, and each *mao* in turn is divided into ten *fen*.

4. I am grateful to Judith Farquhar for suggesting this very interesting translation of Wanyou's statement.

5. For example, in analyzing the colonial encounter between a South African people and the Nonconformist missionaries in the nineteenth century, Jean and John Comaroff (1991) argue that even though the ideology of Christianity may be refused by the South African people, the European hegemony of a certain historical vision has inevitably penetrated South Africa. As they put it, the framework of conversation was set up by the colonial force, although individual arguments may favor the indigenous people.

6. Sulamith and Jack Potter (1990) deal particularly with Chinese peasants in Guangdong; my more general application of the explanation that they provide in no way emphasizes the cultural differences between the West and China.

7. As Lévi-Strauss explains the French term, "In its old sense the verb 'bricoler' applied to ball games and billiards, to hunting, shooting and riding. It was however always used with reference to some extraneous movement: a ball rebounding, a dog straying or a horse swerving from its direct course to avoid an obstacle. And in our own time the 'bricoleur' is still someone who works with his hands and uses devious means compared to those of a craftsman" (1966, 16–17).

8. Bourdieu is most often invoked when the idea of practice surfaces. However, my point is not to theorize the notion of practice in order to rethink social theory; rather, my purpose here is to stress that for this group of people in rural Shaanxi, "work" is experienced as an endless practice rather than as an organized mode of production that aims at efficiency and output.

Chapter 6. The Pliable Emotions

1. In anthropological writing, the term "ritual" may invoke Victor Turner's work (1982), where it is understood as performance in a theatrical sense. However, I must make clear that local people do not speak of "ritual." Moreover, the English term implies a fixed routine; as Renato Rosaldo writes, "Ritual itself is defined by its formality and routine; under such descriptions, it more nearly resembles a recipe, a fixed program, or a book of etiquette than an open-ended human process" (1993, 12). Because that is not my meaning here, I have used the term in quotation marks.

2. There is another kind of celebration: *shangliang*, the crucial moment in building a cave house when the arched framework is to be completed. A

small ceremony always accompanies this event. However, it by no means compares with weddings or funerals either in cost or as performance.

3. In 1990 the village committee announced that those who spent extravagantly on weddings or funerals would be punished; violators were to be fined. But nobody seemed to have obeyed these regulations.

4. A natural death may be taken as happy; it is a "happy thing" for the family, because the death of an elder increases the economic strength of the family as a whole.

5. Throughout this analysis, I use "rites of passage" very much in the sense that Arnold van Gennep (1960) used it—i.e., to stress "passage" as transition in a series of life crises.

6. I use FBSS (father's brother's son's sister) to indicate that the daughter of FB is married out—as distinguished from FBD (father's brother's daughter), a designation indicating that the daughter is unmarried (still living with her father). Wanbin counts Honglu's mother as Yangkai's sister, but not as Wanbin's father's brother's daughter.

7. For a very good ethnographic account of how seriously people in rural China treat the gifts they receive and those they give, see Yan (1996).

8. The Chinese character used for this task is *tao*, which means to take gifts out of the basket.

9. After the truck went to pick up the bride, the road also was blocked by a few ropes. In order to leave the bride's natal village, the best man, on behalf of the bridegroom's family, had to present gifts such as cigarettes and sweets to those who had positioned those ropes.

10. For a discussion of the notion of *wufu* (i.e., "five grades of mourning dress") in traditional Chinese society, see Baker (1979, 107–13).

11. On the basic kinship categories in this part of rural China, see chapter 2.

12. In his argument, James Watson implies a reorientation of the study of Chinese ritual toward anthropological rather than historical or literary approaches. For a historian's response, see Rawski 1988.

13. For an anthropological treatment of the meaning of violence in different cultural contexts, see Riches (1986). The problem of violence has become a popular topic in anthropology in recent years, and in these discussions several different theoretical orientations have emerged. For a focus on the political economy of everyday life, see Scheper-Hughes (1992); for a focus on danger, risk, and respect, see Bourgois (1995).

14. This pattern—members of different segments fighting with each other, while they unite into larger groups such as lineages in order to fight with other lineages—has been discussed by Evans-Pritchard with reference to the Nuer and by Freedman with reference to southeastern China. See Evans-Pritchard ([1940] 1969); Freedman (1958, 110–11; 1966, 106–17). On intralineage hostility, see also Baker (1979, 149–52).

15. This picture of the traditional Chinese family system has been challenged by some anthropologists; see, e.g., A. Wolf and Huang (1980); R. Watson (1985).

16. The coincidence is slightly less than it first appears; though the transliterated term has the same spelling as the English verb, it is pronounced [de].

17. What is (an) emotion? Such a question cannot be answered easily, and philosophers offer different approaches to defining it (see, e.g., Calhoun and Solomon 1984). By here espousing a popular view that defines emotion as a physiological reaction (e.g., see W. James [1890] 1950), I mean to emphasize that in the context of ceremonial celebrations in northern rural Shaanxi, these emotional elements concerned physiology more than abstract concepts.

Chapter 7. Immoral Politics

1. To be sure, some excellent studies of village politics have been done. For instance, Chan, Madsen, and Unger (1992), in one of the best examples of this kind, provide a detailed account of community politics in a Guangdong village throughout the years of Mao and Deng. See also Siu (1989); S. Potter and J. Potter (1990). However, more often than not such studies focus on the structure of rural politics at large, without employing any specific local perspective. For a survey of the studies of Chinese politics, see Halpern (1993). For a critical sketch of different approaches employed in analyses of state and society under Mao, see Shue (1988, 12–29).

2. Foucault has discussed two senses of the term "subject": "subject to someone else by control and dependence, and tied to his own identity by a conscience or self-knowledge. Both meanings suggest a form of power which subjugates and makes subject to" (1982, 212).

3. For a classic discussion of Communist ideology and organization in China, see Schurmann (1966); on the nature of the Maoist politics, see Solomon (1971); on political participation in Communist China, see Townsend (1967).

4. As a consequence of this redistribution, land has been divided into very small pieces. For example, Wanbin had roughly twenty *mu* of land made up of eleven pieces, the smallest being only about five meters square.

5. Distribution by lot is a practice not unique to this community. Chan, Madsen, and Unger found in Chen village (1992, 31) that lotteries were used to distribute land among either families or production teams during the land reform in the early 1950s; but in Chen village the cadre who was in charge of the drawing cheated in order to benefit his own relatives and neighbors.

6. On the problem of corruption, see Oi (1989a); Gong (1994). On peasant complaints and resistance, see, e.g., Li and O'Brien (1996).

7. I had an embarrassing experience tied to this assumption that the state is the ultimate source of wealth. One afternoon, when I was walking around

in the neighborhood, I came across a group of young people who were sitting in front of Famin's door, chatting and enjoying the sunshine. A young man in his late twenties smiled at me and asked, "Is your jacket provided by the government?" Looking at his serious expression, I hesitated to answer; I could not imagine why he thought that the government would have given me something like that. Later I tried to explain to them that I was simply a college teacher who received nothing from the government except for my salary. From their reaction, I could see that they were not at all convinced by my explanation. Such encounters helped give me a reputation in this community for not being honest about my own earnings and my relationship with the government.

8. Foster describes the cognitive orientation in Tzintzuntzan (in rural Mexico) by a model that he calls the "image of limited good." He explains:

> By *Image of Limited Good* I mean that behavior in these and other broad areas is patterned in such fashion as to suggest that Tzintzuntzeños see their social, economic, and natural universes—their total environment—as one in which almost all desired things in life such as land, respect, power, influence, security, and safety *exist in absolute quantities insufficient to fill even minimal needs of villagers.* Not only "good things" exist in strictly limited quantities, but in addition *there is no way directly with the Tzintzuntzeño's power to increase the available supplies.* It is as if the obvious fact of land shortage in the municipio applied to all other desired things: not enough to go around. "Good," like land, is seen as something inherent in nature, there to be divided and redivided if necessary, to be passed around, but not to be augmented. This view, it may be noted parenthetically, seems to me to characterize peasants in general, and it is found in other societies as well. (1967, 123–24).

Such a broad generalization, which fails to recognize the historical particularities faced by each rural community, is clearly problematic; I am by no means defending it here.

9. On China's changing population and population policies, see Banister (1987); on the one-child policy and its impact, see Croll, Davin, and Kane (1985).

10. The term that I have translated "thugs" was *erdan*, which literally means "secondary eggs." *Erdan* are those who loathe work and follow no rules in their relationships with other people.

11. The "bad" social categories, created during the land reform in the early 1950s and applied through the radical years of the Maoist revolution, were landlords, rich peasants, counterrevolutionaries, bad people, and rightists.

12. For translations of the documents of the first socialist education movement, see Baum and Teiwes (1968). Chan, Madsen, and Unger (1992, 41–73) give an ethnographic account of how this movement was carried out in a Cantonese village.

13. According to Chan, Madsen, and Unger, members of the work team that came to Chen village in Guangdong in 1965 during the first socialist education movement insisted on not being known personally by the villagers.

One of the three reasons anonymity was important was that "since most of the work-team members were from nearby counties or communes, anonymity would render them less vulnerable to rumour mongering" (1992, 42).

Conclusion: A History of the Future

1. Fortunately, I was able to distribute these eggs to children the following morning before I left.

2. For the debates on fieldwork and writing in the past two decades in anthropology, see, e.g., Boon (1982); Fabian (1983); Sperber (1985); Clifford and Marcus (1986); Marcus and Fischer (1986); Rabinow (1986); Clifford (1986, 1988a, 1988b, 1988c); Geertz (1988); Sangren (1988); Fardon (1990); Stocking (1992); A. James, Hockey, and Dawson (1997).

Glossary

baishi	白事
bangmangde	帮忙的
banlang	伴郎
baoshouxing	保守性
bucheng buweimei	不成不为媒
bu weisheng	不卫生
cai	菜
caili	彩礼
chi	尺
chixi	吃席
chiyan	吃烟
Chuyi	初一
Dan	担
Dawa	大洼
Dayuhe	大浴河
dazao	大早
dianjiao	奠轿
die	跌
dinghun	订婚
Dongzhi	冬至

Duanwu	端午
dui	队
duilian	对联
dundian	蹲点
erdan	二蛋
fan	饭
fangyingdui	放映队
fei	费
fen (cent)	分
fen (share)	份
fengbixing	封闭性
ganma	干妈
ganmo	干馍
ganbu	干部
guanxi	关系
Guanzhong	关中
guoshi	过事
Han	汉
hongbai xishi	红白喜事
hongshi	红事
huamo	花馍
huan	换
huangse huapian	黄色画片
hui	会
hundun	混沌
hunton	馄饨
huoke	货客
jia	家
jianjianmo	尖尖馍

jiao	轿
jiaozi	饺子
jie	姐
jieqi	节气
jin	斤
kanwu	看屋
Laba	腊八
laohumo	老虎馍
laoxianren	老先人
Leijiawa	雷家洼
li	礼
li/wai	里-外
liniangfei	离娘费
liwu/waiwu	里屋-外屋
luohou	落后
mainuzi	卖女子
Mangpa (ba)	忙罢
Mangqian	忙前
mao	毛
maozi	茅子
meiren	媒人
menhe	门合
minzhu	民主
mo	馍
mu	亩
niang	娘
nongmin qiyejia	农民企业家
pei (bei)	被
pianhan (xian)	谝闲

pinkun diqu	贫困地区
pochan	破产
Powu	破五
pusu	朴素
Qifeng	七峰
Qin	秦
Qincheng	秦城
Qingming	清明
qinqi	亲戚
qunzhong yijian	群众意见
renjia xiaohua	人家笑话
renwu	任务
ruan	软
Shaanxi	陕西
shangliang	上梁
shangou	山沟
shangwufan	晌午饭
shangwufan houshang	晌午饭后晌
shangwufan toushang	晌午饭头晌
shaozhi	烧纸
shaozhiqian	烧纸钱
shenpozi	神婆子
shixian sihua	实现四化
Shiwu	十五
shuiyandai	水烟袋
shuoxiala	说下了
shuren	熟人
sinaojin	死脑筋
songxifu	送媳妇

tanhua	谈话
tao	掏
tuyao	土窑
Weihe	渭河
weijia	魏家
weisheng	卫生
wu	屋
wufu	五服
wuli/wuwai	屋里-屋外
xiaaixing	狭隘性
Xi'an	西安
xianfu qilai	先富起来
xifu	媳妇
xinfang	新房
xingmenhe	行门合
xinke	新客
xitang	喜糖
xiyan	喜烟
xun	旬
Yan'an	延安
yao	窑
yijianxiang	意见箱
yimaoqi	一毛七
yingqinde	迎亲的
yuanshang	塬上
yuanxia	塬下
yuanzi	院子
zeiwazi	贼娃子
Zhao	赵

Zhaojiahe	赵家河
zhengshu	整数
zhiqian	纸钱
zhishi	执事
zhishibu	执事簿
zhongjianren	中间人
zhuanyao	砖窑
zhuazidan	抓子弹
zhuwei	主位
zijiawu	自家屋
zong	宗
zongzi	粽子
zongzu	宗族
zu (clan)	族
zu (group)	组

Bibliography

Ahern, E. M. 1973. *The cult of the dead in a Chinese village.* Stanford: Stanford University Press.

————. 1976. Segmentation in Chinese lineages: A view from written genealogies. *American Ethnologist* 3, no. 1:1–16.

Anderson, E. N. 1988. *The food of China.* New Haven: Yale University Press.

Anderson, E. N., and M. L. Anderson. 1977. Modern China: South. In *Food in Chinese culture,* ed. K. C. Chang, 317–82. New Haven: Yale University Press.

Anderson, P. 1983. *In the tracks of historical materialism.* London: Verso.

Appadurai, A. 1981. The past as a scarce resource. *Man,* n.s., 16, no. 2:201–19.

Ardener, E. 1971. Introductory essay: Social anthropology and language. In *Social anthropology and language,* ed. E. Ardener, ix–cii. London: Tavistock.

Arkush, R. D. 1981. *Fei Xiaotong and sociology in revolutionary China.* Cambridge, Mass.: Harvard University Press.

Asad, T. 1987. Are there histories of people without Europe? *Comparative Studies in Society and History* 29, no. 3:594–607.

————. 1993. *Genealogies of religion—Discipline and reasons of power in Christianity and Islam.* Baltimore: Johns Hopkins University Press.

Baker, H. D. R. 1968. *A Chinese lineage village: Sheung Shui.* Stanford: Stanford University Press.

————. 1979. *Chinese family and kinship.* London: Macmillan.

Baker, H. D. R., and S. Feuchtwang, eds. 1991. *An old state in new settings: Studies in the social anthropology of China: In memory of Maurice Freedman.* Oxford: JASO.

Bakhtin, M. M. 1986. The problem of speech genres. In *Speech genres and other late essays,* 65–102. Ed. C. Emerson and M. Holquist, trans. V. W. Mcgee. Austin: University of Texas Press.

Banister, J. 1984. Population policy and trends in China—1978–1983. *China Quarterly,* no. 100:714–41.

————. 1987. *China's changing population.* Stanford: Stanford University Press.

Barthes, R. 1967. *Elements of semiology.* Trans. A. Lavers and C. Smith. London: Cape.

———. 1973. *Mythologies.* Ed. and trans. A. Lavers. London: Paladin.

———. 1979. Towards a psychosociology of contemporary food consumption. In *Food and drink in history,* ed. R. Forster and O. Ranum, 166–73. Baltimore: Johns Hopkins University Press.

———. 1983. *The fashion system.* Trans. M. Ward and R. Howard. New York: Hill and Wang.

Baum, R., and F. Teiwes. 1968. *Ssu-Ch'ing: The socialist education movement of 1962–1966.* China Research Monographs 2. Berkeley: Center for Chinese Studies, University of California.

Best, S., and D. Kellner. 1991. *Postmodern theory—critical interrogations.* London: Macmillan.

Bianco, L. 1995. French studies of contemporary China. *China Quarterly,* no. 142:509–20.

Blecher, M. J. 1986. *China, politics, economics, and society: Iconoclasm and innovation in a revolutionary socialist country.* London: F. Pinter.

Bloch, M. 1975a. Introduction to *Political language and oratory in traditional society,* ed. M. Bloch, 1–28. London: Academic Press.

———, ed. 1975b. *Political language and oratory in traditional society.* London: Academic Press.

———. 1977. The past and the present in the present. *Man* 13, no. 2:21–33.

Boon, J. A. 1982. *Other tribes, other scribes—Symbolic anthropology in the comparative study of cultures, histories, religions, and texts.* Cambridge: Cambridge University Press.

Bourdieu, P. 1977. *Outline of a theory of practice.* Trans. R. Nice. Cambridge: Cambridge University Press.

———. 1984. *Distinction: A social critique of the judgement of taste.* Trans. R. Nice. London: Routledge and Kegan Paul.

———. 1990. *The logic of practice.* Trans. R. Nice. Cambridge: Polity.

Bourdieu, P., and L. J. D. Wacquant. 1992. *An invitation to reflexive sociology.* Chicago: University of Chicago Press.

Bourgois, P. I. 1995. *In search of respect: Selling crack in El Barrio.* Cambridge: Cambridge University Press.

Braudel, F. 1980. History and sociology. In *On history,* 64–82. Trans. S. Matthews. Chicago: University of Chicago Press.

Calhoun, C., E. LiPuma, and M. Postone, eds. 1993. *Bourdieu: Critical perspectives.* Cambridge: Polity.

Calhoun, C., and R. C. Solomon, eds. 1984. *What is an emotion?—Classic readings in philosophical psychology.* Oxford: Oxford University Press.

Caws, P. 1988. *Structuralism: The art of the intelligible.* Atlantic Highlands, N.J.: Humanities.

Certeau, M. de. 1984. *The practice of everyday life*. Trans. S. F. Rendall. Berkeley: University of California Press.

Chan, A., R. Madsen, and J. Unger. 1992. *Chen Village under Mao and Deng.* Berkeley: University of California Press.

Chang, K. C. 1977. Introduction to *Food in Chinese culture*, ed. K. C. Chang, 1–21. New Haven: Yale University Press.

Chao, P. 1983. *Chinese kinship*. London: Kegan Paul.

Chen, Q-N. 1985. Fang yu chuantong Zhongguo jiazu zhidu (Fang and the traditional Chinese kinship system). *Hanxue Yanjiu* (Chinese Studies) 3, no. 1:127–83.

Chen, Y-L. 1984. Chongxin sikao "lineage theory" yu Zhongguo shehui (Rethinking "lineage theory" and Chinese society). *Hanxue Yanjiu* (Chinese Studies) 2, no. 2:403–45.

Chengcheng xian dimingzhi (Village names of Chengcheng county). 1984. Xi'an: Shaanxi Remin Press.

Chengcheng xianzhi (Records of Chengcheng county). 1991. Xi'an: Shaanxi Remin Press.

Chossudovsky, M. 1986. *Towards capitalist restoration? Chinese socialism after Mao*. New York: St. Martin's Press.

Chun, A. 1996. The lineage-village complex in southeastern China: A long footnote in the anthropology of kinship. *Current Anthropology* 37, no. 3:429–50.

Clammer, J. 1996. Comments. *Current Anthropology* 37, no. 3:440–41.

Clifford, J. 1986. Introduction: Partial truth. In *Writing culture: The poetics and politics of ethnography*, ed. J. Clifford and G. E. Marcus, 1–26. Berkeley: University of California Press.

———. 1988a. Introduction: The pure products go crazy. In *The predicament of culture: Twentieth-century ethnography, literature, and art*, 1–18. Cambridge, Mass.: Harvard University Press.

———. 1988b. On ethnographic authority. In *The predicament of culture: Twentieth-century ethnography, literature, and art*, 21–54. Cambridge, Mass.: Harvard University Press.

———. 1988c. On ethnographic self-fashioning: Conrad and Malinowski. In *The predicament of culture: Twentieth-century ethnography, literature, and art*, 92–113. Cambridge, Mass.: Harvard University Press.

Clifford, J., and G. E. Marcus, eds. 1986. *Writing culture: The poetics and politics of ethnography*. Berkeley: University of California Press.

Cohen, M. L. 1969. Agnatic kinship in south Taiwan. *Ethnology* 8, no. 2:167–82.

———. 1970. Developmental process in the Chinese domestic group. In *Family and kinship in Chinese society*, ed. M. Freedman, 21–36. Stanford: Stanford University Press.

———. 1976. *House united, house divided: The Chinese family in Taiwan*. London: Macmillan.

————. 1985. Lineage development and the family in China. In *The Chinese family and its ritual behaviour*, ed. J-C. Hsieh and Y-C. Chuang, 210–18. Taipei, Taiwan: Institute of Ethnology, Academia Sinica.

————. 1990. Lineage organization in North China. *Journal of Asian Studies* 49, no. 4:509–34.

————. 1993. Cultural and political inventions in modern China: The case of Chinese peasants. *Daedalus* 122, no. 2:151–70.

Collingwood, R. G. 1942. *The new Leviathan: or, Man, society, civilization, and barbarism.* Oxford: Clarendon.

Comaroff, J. 1985. *Body of power, spirit of resistance: The culture and history of a South African people.* Chicago: University of Chicago Press.

Comaroff, J., and J. L. Comaroff. 1991. *Of revelation and revolution.* Vol. 1, *Christianity, colonialism, and consciousness in South Africa.* Chicago: University of Chicago Press.

————. 1992. *Ethnography and the historical imagination.* Boulder, Colo.: Westview.

Croll, E. 1978. *Feminism and socialism in China.* London: Routledge and Kegan Paul.

————. 1981. *The politics of marriage in contemporary China.* Cambridge: Cambridge University Press.

————. 1983. *Chinese women since Mao.* London: Zed.

————. 1985. Introduction: Fertility norms and family size in China. In *China's One Child Policy*, ed. E. Croll, D. Daven, and P. Kane, 1–36. London: Macmillan.

————. 1987. Some implications of the rural economic reforms for the Chinese peasant household. In *The re-emergence of the Chinese peasantry*, ed. A. Saith, 105–36. London: Croom Helm.

————. 1988. The new peasant economy in China. In *Transforming China's economy in the eighties*, ed. S. Feuchtwang, A. Hussain, and T. Pairault, 1:77–100. London: Zed.

————. 1994. *From heaven to earth — Images and experiences of development in China.* London: Routledge.

Croll, E., D. Davin, and P. Kane, eds. 1985. *China's one-child family policy.* London: Macmillan.

Crook, I., and D. Crook. 1959. *Revolution in a Chinese village: Ten Mile Inn.* London: Routledge and Kegan Paul.

————. 1966. *The first years of Yangyi Commune.* London: Routledge and Kegan Paul.

————. 1979. *Mass movement in a Chinese village: Ten Mile Inn.* London: Routledge and Kegan Paul.

Culler, J. 1975. *Structuralist poetics: Structuralism, linguistics, and the study of literature.* London: Routledge and Kegan Paul.

————. 1976. *Saussure.* London: Fontana.

Dangdai Zhongguo de Shaanxi (The book of contemporary China: Shaanxi). 1991. Beijing: Contemporary China Press.

Davin, D. 1976. *Woman-work: Women and the Party in revolutionary China*. Oxford: Clarendon.

Davis, D., and S. Harrell, eds. 1993. *Chinese families in the post-Mao era*. Berkeley: University of California Press.

Davis-Friedmann, D. 1991. *Long lives—Chinese elderly and the Communist revolution*. Stanford: Stanford University Press.

Donnithorne, A. 1972. China's cellular economy: Some economic trends since the Cultural Revolution. *China Quarterly*, no. 52:605–19.

Douglas, M. 1975a. Deciphering a meal. In *Implicit meanings: Essays in anthropology*, 249–75. London: Routledge and Kegan Paul.

———. 1975b. *Implicit meanings: Essays in anthropology*. London: Routledge and Kegan Paul.

———. 1982. Food as a system of communication. In *In the active voice*, 82–104. London: Routledge and Kegan Paul.

———. 1984. Standard social use of food. In *Food in the social order: Studies of food and festivities in three American communities*, ed. M. Douglas, 18–39. New York: Russell Sage Foundation.

Dreyfus, H., and P. Rabinow. 1982. *Michel Foucault: Beyond structuralism and hermeneutics*. Chicago: University of Chicago Press.

Duara, P. 1988. *Culture, power, and the state: Rural North China, 1900–1942*. Stanford: Stanford University Press.

Durkheim, E., and M. Mauss. 1963. *Primitive classification.* Chicago: University of Chicago Press.

Ebrey, P. B., and J. L. Watson, eds. 1986. *Kinship organization in late imperial China, 1000–1940*. Berkeley: University of California Press.

Elias, N. 1978. *What is sociology?* Trans. S. Mennell and G. Morrissey. New York: Columbia University Press.

———. 1994. *The civilizing process*. Trans. E. Jephcott. Oxford: Blackwell. (First published in 1939 in German.)

Emerson, C., and M. Holquist. 1986. Introduction to *Speech genres and other late essays*, by M. M. Bakhtin, ix–xxiii. Austin: University of Texas Press.

Erikson, K. 1989. Sociological prose. *Yale Review*, no. 78:525–38.

Evans-Pritchard, E. E. 1934. Levy-Bruhl's theory of primitive mentality. *Bulletin of the Faculty of Arts* 2, no. 1:1–26.

———. 1937. *Witchcraft, oracles, and magic among the Azande*. Abridged by E. Gillies. Oxford: Clarendon.

———. 1951. *Social anthropology*. London: Cohen and West.

———. [1940] 1969. *The Nuer: A description of the modes of livelihood and political institutions of a Nilotic people*. Oxford: Oxford University Press.

Fabian, J. 1983. *Time and the other: How anthropology makes its object*. New York: Columbia University Press.

Fardon, R., ed. 1990. *Localizing strategies: Regional traditions of ethnographic writing*. Edinburgh: Scottish Academic Press.

Farquhar, J. 1994. *Knowing practice: The clinical encounter of Chinese medicine*. Boulder, Colo.: Westview.

Faure, D. 1986. *The structure of Chinese rural society: lineage and village in the eastern New Territories, Hong Kong*. Hong Kong: Oxford University Press.

————. 1989. The lineage as a cultural invention. *Modern China* 15, no. 1:4–36.

Fei, X-T. 1939. *Peasant life in China: A field study of country life in the Yangtze valley*. London: Kegan Paul, Trench, and Trubner.

————. 1946. Peasantry and gentry: An interpretation of Chinese class structure and its changes. *American Journal of Sociology* 52, no. 1:1–17.

————. 1988. *Fei Xiaotong xuanji* (Selected works of Fei Xiaotong). Tianjing: Tianjing Remin Press.

————. 1992. *From the soil: The foundations of Chinese society*. Trans. G. G. Hamilton and W. Zhang. Berkeley: University of California Press.

————. 1993. *Ren de yanjiu zai Zhongguo* (The study of man in China). Tianjin: Tianjin Remin Press.

Feng, H-Y. 1948. *The Chinese kinship system*. Cambridge: Cambridge University Press.

Feuchtwang, S. 1974. *An anthropological analysis of Chinese geomancy*. Vientiane, Laos: Vithagna.

————. 1992. *The imperial metaphor—Popular religion in China*. London: Routledge.

Feuchtwang, S., and A. Hussain, eds. 1983. *The Chinese economic reforms*. London: Croom Helm.

Feuchtwang, S., A. Hussain, and T. Pairault, eds. 1988. *Transforming China's economy in the eighties*. 2 vols. Boulder, Colo.: Westview; London: Zed.

Finkelstein, J. 1989. *Dining out: A sociology of modern manners*. New York: New York University Press.

Firth, R. 1936. *We, the Tikopia: A sociological study of kinship in primitive Polynesia*. London: Allen and Unwin.

————, ed. 1957. *Man and culture: An evaluation of the work of Bronislaw Malinowski*. London: Routledge and Kegan Paul.

Fortes, M. 1945. *The dynamics of clanship among the Tallensi*. Oxford: Oxford University Press.

————. 1953. The structure of unilineal descent groups. *American Anthropologist* 55, no. 1:17–41.

Foster, G. M. 1967. *Tzintzuntzan: Mexican peasants in a changing world*. Boston: Little, Brown.

Foucault, M. 1972. *The archaeology of knowledge: and The discourse on language*. Trans. A. M. Sheridan Smith. New York: Pantheon.

————. 1973. *Madness and civilization.* Trans. R. Howard. New York: Vintage.

————. 1977. *Language, counter-memory, practice.* Ed. D. F. Bouchard, trans. D. F. Bouchard and S. Simon. Ithaca, N.Y.: Cornell University Press.

————. 1979. *Discipline and punish: The birth of the prison.* Trans. A. Sheridan. Harmondsworth: Penguin.

————. 1980. *The history of sexuality.* Vol. 1, *An introduction.* Trans. R. Hurley. New York: Vintage.

————. 1982. Afterword: The subject and power. In *Michel Foucault: Beyond structuralism and hermeneutics,* by H. Dreyfus and P. Rabinow, 208–26. Chicago: University of Chicago Press.

————. 1988. *The history of sexuality.* Vol. 3, *The care of the self.* Trans. R. Hurley. New York: Vintage.

Fox, R. 1967. *Kinship and marriage: An anthropological perspective.* Harmondsworth: Penguin.

Fox, R. G., ed. 1991. *Recapturing anthropology: Working in the present.* Santa Fe, N.M.: School of American Research Press.

Freedman, M. 1958. *Lineage organization in southeastern China.* London: Athlone.

————. 1966. *Chinese lineage and society: Fukien and Kwangtung.* London: Athlone.

————. 1970. Introduction to *Family and kinship in Chinese society,* ed. M. Freedman, 1–20. Stanford: Stanford University Press.

————. 1979a. The politics of an old state: A view from the Chinese lineage. In *The study of Chinese society—Essays by Maurice Freedman,* 334–50. Ed. G. W. Skinner. Stanford: Stanford University Press.

————. 1979b. Rites and duties, or Chinese marriage. In *The study of Chinese society—Essays by Maurice Freedman,* 255–72. Ed. G. W. Skinner. Stanford: Stanford University Press.

Fried, M. H. 1957. The classification of corporate unilineal descent groups. *Journal of Royal Institute* 87, part I:1–29.

Friedman, E., P. G. Pickowicz, and M. Selden. 1991. *Chinese village, socialist state.* New Haven: Yale University Press.

Fung, Y-L. 1948. *A short history of Chinese philosophy.* Ed. D. Bodde. New York: Macmillan.

Gallin, B. 1966. *Hsin hsing, Taiwan: A Chinese village in change.* Berkeley: University of California Press.

Geertz, C. 1973. *The interpretation of cultures.* New York: Basic Books.

————. 1976. From the native's point of view: On the nature of anthropological understanding. In *Meaning in anthropology,* ed. K. Basso and H. Selby, 221–36. Albuquerque: University of New Mexico Press.

————. 1988. *Works and lives—The anthropologist as author.* Stanford: Stanford University Press.

Gell, A. 1992. *The anthropology of time: Cultural constructions of temporal maps and images.* New York: Berg.

Gennep, A. van. 1960. *The rites of passage.* Trans. M. B. Vizedom and G. L. Caffee. Chicago: University of Chicago Press.

Gernet, J. 1962. *Daily life in China on the eve of the Mongol invasion, 1250–76.* Trans. H. M. Wright. Stanford: Stanford University Press.

———. 1982. *A history of Chinese civilization.* Trans. J. R. Foster. Cambridge: Cambridge University Press.

Giddens, A. 1984. *The constitution of society: Outline of the theory of structuration.* Cambridge: Polity.

Ginzburg, C. 1980. *The cheese and the worms: The cosmos of a sixteenth-century miller.* Trans. J. and A. Tedeschi. Baltimore: Johns Hopkins University Press.

Gittings, J. 1989. *China changes face—The road from revolution, 1949–1989.* Oxford: Oxford University Press.

Gold, T. B. 1993. The study of Chinese society. In *American studies of contemporary China,* ed. D. Shambaugh, 43–64. Washington, D.C.: Woodrow Wilson Center Press; Armonk, N.Y.: M. E. Sharpe.

Gong, T. 1994. *The politics of corruption in contemporary China: An analysis of policy outcomes.* Westport, Conn.: Praeger.

Goody, J. 1973. Bridewealth and dowry in Africa and Eurasia. In *Bridewealth and dowry,* by J. Goody and S. J. Tambiah, 1–58. Cambridge: Cambridge University Press.

———. 1982. *Cooking, cuisine, and class: A study in comparative sociology.* Cambridge: Cambridge University Press.

Goody, J., and S. J. Tambiah. 1973. *Bridewealth and dowry.* Cambridge: Cambridge University Press.

Greenhalgh, S. 1993. The peasantization of population policy in Shaanxi. In *Chinese families in the post-Mao era,* ed. D. Davis and S. Harrell, 219–50. Berkeley: University of California Press.

Greimas, A-J. 1983. *Structural semantics: An attempt at a method.* Trans. D. McDowell, R. Schleiter, and A. Velie. Lincoln: University of Nebraska Press.

Griffin, K., ed. 1984. *Institutional reform and economic development in the Chinese countryside.* New York: M. E. Sharpe.

Gurvitch, G. 1964. *The spectrum of social time.* Ed. and trans. Myrtle Korenbaum, with P. Bosserman. Dordrecht: D. Reidel.

Hacking, I. 1982. Language, truth, and reason. In *Rationality and Relativism,* ed. R. Hollis and S. Lukes, 185–203. Cambridge, Mass.: MIT Press.

———. 1990. *The taming of chance.* Cambridge: Cambridge University Press.

Hallgren, C. 1979. The code of Chinese kinship: A critique of the work of Maurice Freedman. *Ethnos* 44, no. 1:7–33.

Hallpike, C. 1979. *The foundation of primitive thought.* Oxford: Blackwell.

Halpern, N. P. 1993. Studies of Chinese politics. In *American studies of contemporary China,* ed. D. Shambaugh, 120–37. Washington, D.C.: Woodrow Wilson Center Press; Armonk, N.Y.: M. E. Sharpe.

Hamilton, G., ed. 1991. *Business networks and economic development in East and Southeast Asia.* Hong Kong: Centre of Asian Studies, University of Hong Kong.

Hamilton, G., and Z. Wang. 1992. Introduction: Fei Xiaotong and the beginnings of a Chinese sociology. In *From the soil—The foundations of Chinese society,* by Fei X-T., 1–34. Berkeley: University of California Press.

Harari, J. V., ed. 1979. *Textual strategies: Perspectives in post-structuralist criticism.* London: Methuen.

Harré, R., ed. 1986. *The social construction of emotions.* Oxford: Blackwell.

Harrell, S. 1982. *Ploughshare village: Culture and context in Taiwan.* Seattle: University of Washington Press.

————. 1990. Introduction. In *Violence in China: Essays in culture and counterculture,* ed. J. N. Lipman and S. Harrell, 1–25. Albany: State University of New York Press.

————. 1992. Aspects of marriage in three south-western villages. *China Quarterly,* no. 130:323–37.

Harris, M. 1985. *Good to eat: Riddles of food and culture.* New York: Simon and Schuster.

————. 1987. Foodways: Historical overview and theoretical prolegomenon. In *Food and evolution: Toward a theory of human food habits,* ed. M. Harris and E. B. Ross, 57–90. Philadelphia: Temple University Press.

Harris, R. 1987. *Reading Saussure.* La Salle, Ill.: Open Court.

Harvey, D. 1990. *The condition of postmodernity—An enquiry into the origins of cultural change.* Cambridge: Blackwell.

Hawkes, T. 1977. *Structuralism and semiotics.* Berkeley: University of California Press.

Hinton, W. 1966. *Fenshen: A documentary of revolution in a Chinese village.* New York: Monthly Review.

————. 1990. *The great reversal—The privatization of China, 1978–1989.* New York: Monthly Review.

Hobart, M. 1979. A Balinese village and its field of social relations. Ph.D. diss., University of London.

————. 1990a. The patience of plants: A note on agency in Bali. *Review of Indonesian and Malaysian Affairs* 24, no. 2:90–135.

————. 1990b. Who do you think you are? The authorized Balinese. In *Localizing strategies: Regional traditions of ethnographic writing,* ed. R. Fardon, 303–38. Edinburgh: Scottish Academic Press.

————. 1993. *An anthropological critique of development: The growth of ignorance?* London: Routledge.

Honig, E., and G. Hershatter. 1988. *Personal voices: Chinese women in the 1980's.* Stanford: Stanford University Press.

Howard, P. 1988. *Breaking the iron rice bowl—Prospects for socialism in China's countryside.* New York: M. E. Sharpe.

Hsieh, J-C., and Y-C. Chuang, eds. 1985. *The Chinese family and its ritual behavior.* Taipei, Taiwan: Institute of Ethnology, Academia Sinica.

Hsu, F. L. K. 1948. *Under the ancestors' shadow: Chinese culture and personality.* New York: Columbia University Press.

———. 1971. *Under the ancestors' shadow: Kinship, personality, and social mobility in China.* Stanford: Stanford University Press.

Hsu, R. C. 1985. Conceptions of the market in post-Mao China: An interpretative essay. *Modern China* 2, no. 4:436–60.

Hsu, V. Y. N., and F. L. K. Hsu 1977. Modern China: North. In *Food in Chinese Culture,* ed. K. C. Chang, 295–316. New Haven: Yale University Press.

Hu, H-C. 1948. *The common descent group in China and its functions.* New York: Viking Fund.

Hussain, A. 1994. The Chinese economic reform: An assessment. In *China: The next decade,* ed. D. Dwyer, 11–30. Essex: Longman.

Jakobson, R. 1987. *Language in literature.* Ed. K. Pomorska and S. Rudy. Cambridge, Mass.: Belknap Press of Harvard University Press.

Jakobson, R., and M. Halle. 1971. *Fundamentals of language.* 2nd ed. The Hague: Mouton.

James, A., J. Hockey, and A. Dawson, eds. 1997. *After writing culture: Epistemology and praxis in contemporary anthropology.* London: Routledge.

James, W. [1890] 1950. *Principles of psychology.* Vol. 2. New York: Dover.

Jameson, F. 1972. *The prison-house of language: A critical account of structuralism and Russian formalism.* Princeton: Princeton University Press.

Jenkins, R. 1992. *Pierre Bourdieu.* London: Routledge.

Jing, J. 1996. *The temple of memories: History, power, and morality in a Chinese village.* Stanford: Stanford University Press.

Judd, E. R. 1994. *Gender and power in rural North China.* Stanford: Stanford University Press.

Kapferer, B. 1990. From the periphery to the centre: Ethnography and the critique of anthropology in Sri Lanka. In *Localizing strategies: Regional traditions of ethnographic writing,* ed. R. Fardon, 280–302. Edinburgh: Scottish Academic Press.

Kipnis, A. B. 1997. *Producing guanxi: Sentiment, self, and subculture in a North China village.* Durham, N.C.: Duke University Press.

Kleinman, A., and B. Good. 1985. *Culture and depression: Studies in the anthropology and cross-cultural psychiatry of affect and disorder.* Berkeley: University of California Press.

Kulp, D. H. 1925. *Country life in South China: The sociology of familism.* Vol. 1, *Phoenix Village, Kwangtung, China.* New York: Bureau of Publications, Teachers College, Columbia University.

Kuper, A. 1982. Lineage theory: A critical retrospect. *Annual Review of Anthropology* 11:71–95.

———. 1983. *Anthropology and anthropologists: The modern British school.* London: Routledge and Kegan Paul.

Lakoff, G., and M. Johnson. 1980. *Metaphors we live by.* Chicago: University of Chicago Press.

Lampton, D. M., ed. 1987. *Policy implementation in post-Mao China.* Berkeley: University of California Press.

Lang, O. 1946. *Chinese family and society.* New Haven: Yale University Press.

Leach, E. R. 1961. *Rethinking anthropology.* London: Athlone.

———. 1964. Anthropological aspects of language: animal categories and verbal abuse. In *New directions in the study of language,* ed. E. Lenneberg, 23–64. Cambridge, Mass.: MIT Press.

———. 1970. *Lévi-Strauss.* London: Fontana/Collins.

———. 1982. *Social anthropology.* Oxford: Oxford University Press.

Leeming, F. 1985. *Rural China today.* London: Longman.

Lévi-Strauss, C. 1963. *Structural anthropology.* Vol. 1. Trans. C. Jacobson and B. G. Schoepf. New York: Basic Books.

———. 1964. *Totemism.* Trans. R. Needham. London: Merlin.

———. 1966. *The savage mind.* London: Weidenfeld and Nicolson.

Lévy-Bruhl, L. [1923] 1966. *Primitive mentality.* Trans. L. A. Clare. Boston: Beacon.

———. [1949] 1975. *The notebooks on primitive mentality.* Trans. P. Rivière. New York: Harper Torchbooks.

Li, L-J., and K. J. O'Brien. 1996. Villagers and popular resistance in contemporary China. *Modern China* 22, no. 1:28–61.

Lin, Y-H. 1947. *The golden wing: A sociological study of Chinese familism.* London: Kegan Paul, Trench, Trubner.

Liu, L-G. 1989. *Chinese architecture.* London: Academy.

Lu, X-Y., ed. 1992. *Gaige zhong de nongcun yu nongmin* (Villages and peasants during the period of the economic reforms). Beijing: Remin Press.

MacFarquhar, R. 1983. *The origins of the Cultural Revolution.* Vol. 2, *The Great Leap Forward, 1958–1960.* Oxford: Oxford University Press.

Madsen, R. 1984. *Morality and power in a Chinese village.* Berkeley: University of California Press.

Malinowski, B. [1923] 1956. The problem of meaning in primitive languages. In *The meaning of meaning: A study of the influence of language upon thought and of the science of symbolism,* by C. K. Ogden and I. A. Richards, 296–336. New York: Harcourt, Brace; London: Routledge and Kegan Paul.

———. [1922] 1961. *Argonauts of the Western Pacific.* New York: E. P. Dutton.

Marcus, G. E. 1986a. Afterword: Ethnographic writing and anthropological careers. In *Writing culture: The poetics and politics of ethnography,* ed. J. Clifford and G. E. Marcus, 262–66. Berkeley: University of California Press.

———. 1986b. Contemporary problems of ethnography in the modern world system. In *Writing culture: The poetics and politics of ethnography,* ed. J. Clifford and G. E. Marcus, 165–93. Berkeley: University of California Press.

Marcus, G. E., and M. M. J. Fischer. 1986. *Anthropology as cultural critique — An experimental moment in the human sciences.* Chicago: University of Chicago Press.

Massey, D. 1994. *Space, place, and gender.* Minneapolis: University of Minnesota Press.

McCoy, J. 1970. Chinese kin terms of reference and address. In *Family and kinship in Chinese society,* ed. M. Freedman, 209–26. Stanford: Stanford University Press.

Mead, M. 1943. *The problem of changing food habits: Report of the committee on food habits, 1941–43.* National Research Council, bulletin 108. Washington, D.C.: National Academy of Sciences.

———. 1964. *Food habits research: Problems of the 1960s.* Washington, D.C.: National Academy of Sciences.

———. 1965. *Manual for the study of food habits: Report of the committee on food habits.* National Research Council, bulletin 111. Washington, D.C.: National Academy of Sciences.

Meijer, M. J. 1971. *Marriage law and policy in the Chinese People's Republic.* Hong Kong: Hong Kong University Press.

Mennell, S. 1996. *All manners of food: Eating and taste in England and France from the Middle Ages to the present.* 2nd ed. Urbana: University of Illinois Press.

Merquior, J. G. 1985. *Foucault.* London: Fontana.

———. 1986. *From Prague to Paris: A critique of structuralist and post-structuralist thought.* London: Verso.

Michio, S., J. S. Eades, and D. Christian, eds. 1995. *Perspectives on Chinese society — Anthropological views from Japan.* Canterbury: Center for Social Anthropology and Computing, University of Kent.

Mintz, S. W. 1985. *Sweetness and power: The place of sugar in modern history.* New York: Viking.

———. 1996. *Tasting food, tasting freedom: Excursions into eating, culture, and the past.* Boston: Beacon.

Monteiro, A., and K. P. Jayasankar. 1994. The spectator-Indian: An exploratory study on the reception of news. *Cultural Studies* 8, no. 1:162–82.

Mosher, S. 1983. *Broken earth: The rural Chinese.* New York: Free Press; London: Collier-Macmillan.

Mosse, F. 1997a. *History of structuralism.* Vol. 1, *The rising sign, 1945–1966.* Minneapolis: University of Minnesota Press.

———. 1997b. *History of structuralism.* Vol. 2, *The sign sets, 1967–present.* Minneapolis: University of Minnesota Press.

Murcott, A., ed. 1983. *The sociology of food and eating: Essays on the sociological significance of food.* Aldershot, Hants.: Gower.

———. 1988. Sociological and social anthropological approaches to food and eating. *World Review of Nutrition and Dietetics,* no. 55:1–40.

Nee, V. 1989. A theory of market transition: From redistribution to markets in state socialism. *American Sociological Review* 54, no. 5:663–81.

———. 1991. Social inequalities in reforming state socialism: Between redistribution and markets in China. *American Sociological Review* 56, no. 3:276–82.

Nee, V., and S-J. Su. 1990. Institutional change and economic growth in China. *Journal of Asian Studies* 49, no. 1:3–25.

Needham, R. 1971. Remarks on the analysis of kinship and marriage. In *Rethinking kinship and marriage,* ed. R. Needham, 1–33. London: Tavistock.

———. 1972. *Belief, language, and experience.* Oxford: Blackwell.

Oi, J. 1985. Communism and clientelism: Rural politics in China. *World Politics* 37, no 2:238–66.

———. 1989a. Market reform and corruption in rural China. *Studies in Comparative Communism* 22, nos. 2/3:221–23.

———. 1989b. *State and peasant in contemporary China: The political economy of village government.* Berkeley: University of California Press.

Ong, A. 1993. On the edge of empires: Flexible citizenship among Chinese in diaspora. *Positions* 1, no. 4:745–78.

Ortner, S. 1984. Theory in anthropology since the sixties. *Comparative Studies of Society and History* 26, no. 1:126–66.

Ortony, A., ed. 1979. *Metaphor and thought.* Cambridge: Cambridge University Press.

Parish, W. L., and M. K. Whyte. 1978. *Village and family in contemporary China.* Chicago: University of Chicago Press.

Parkin, D. 1975. The rhetoric of responsibility: bureaucratic communications in a Kenya farming area. In *Political language and oratory in traditional society,* ed. M. Bloch, 113–39. London: Academic Press.

———, ed. 1982. *Semantic anthropology.* London: Academic Press.

Passariello, P. 1990. Anomalies, analogies, and sacred profanities: Mary Douglas on food and culture, 1957–1989. *Food and Foodways* 4, no. 1:53–71.

Pasternak, B. 1969. The role of the frontier in Chinese lineage development. *Journal of Asian Studies* 28, no. 3:551–61.

———. 1972. *Kinship and community in two Chinese villages*. California: Stanford University Press.

———. 1985a. The disquieting Chinese lineage and its anthropological relevance. In *The Chinese family and its ritual behaviour*, ed. J-C. Hsieh and Y-C. Chuang, 165–91. Taipei, Taiwan: Institute of Ethnology, Academia Sinica.

———. 1985b. On the causes and consequences of uxorilocal marriage. In *Family and population in East Asian history*, ed. S. B. Hanley and A. P. Wolf, 309–36. Stanford: Stanford University Press.

Pavel, T. G. 1989. *The feud of language: A history of structuralist thought*. New York: Blackwell.

Perry, E. J. 1985. Rural violence in socialist China. *China Quarterly*, no. 103:414–40.

Perry, E. J., and C. Wong, eds. 1985. *The political economy of reform in post-Mao China*. Cambridge, Mass.: Council on East Asian Studies/Harvard University, distributed by Harvard University Press.

Pieke, F. N. 1996. *The ordinary and the extraordinary: An anthropological study of Chinese reform and the 1989 people's movement in Beijing*. London: Kegan Paul International.

Pospisil, L. J. 1963. *Kapauku Papuan economy*. Yale University Publications in Anthropology 67. New Haven: Department of Anthropology, Yale University.

Potter, J. M. 1968. *Capitalism and Chinese peasants: Social and economic change in a Hong Kong village*. Berkeley: University of California Press.

———. 1970. Land and lineage in traditional China. In *Family and Kinship in Chinese Society*, ed. M. Freedman, 121–38. Stanford: Stanford University Press.

Potter, S. H., and J. Potter. 1990. *China's peasants: The anthropology of a revolution*. Cambridge: Cambridge University Press.

Pye, L. W. 1988. *The mandarin and the cadre — China's political culture*. Ann Arbor: Centre for Chinese Studies, University of Michigan.

Rabinow, P. 1977. *Reflections on fieldwork in Morocco*. Berkeley: University of California Press.

———. 1986. Representations are social facts: Modernity and post-modernity in anthropology. In *Writing culture: The poetics and politics of ethnography*, ed. J. Clifford and G. E. Marcus, 234–61. Berkeley: University of California Press.

———. 1991. Introduction to *The Foucault reader*, ed. P. Rabinow, 3–29. London: Penguin.

Rabinow, P., and W. Sullivan, eds. 1979. *Interpretive social science: A reader*. Berkeley: University of California Press.

Rawski, E. S. 1988. A historian's approach to Chinese death ritual. In *Death ritual in late imperial and modern China*, ed. J. L. Watson and E. S. Rawski, 20–34. Berkeley: University of California Press.

Redding, S. G. 1990. *The spirit of Chinese capitalism.* New York: W. de Gruyter.

Richards, A. I. 1932. *Hunger and work in a savage tribe: A functional study of nutrition among the southern Bantu.* London: Geo. Routledge and Sons.

Riches, D. 1986. The phenomenon of violence. In *The anthropology of violence,* ed. D. Riches, 1–27. Oxford: Blackwell.

Ricoeur, P. 1971. The model of the text: Meaningful action considered as a text. *Social Research,* no. 38:529–62.

———. 1974. Structure, word, event. In *The conflict of interpretations: Essays in hermeneutics,* ed. D. Ihde, 79–96. Evanston, Ill.: Northwestern University Press.

Riskin, C. 1987. *China's political economy: The quest for development since 1949.* Oxford: Oxford University Press.

Rorty, R. 1979. *Philosophy and the mirror of nature.* Princeton: Princeton University Press.

Rosaldo, R. 1993. *Culture and truth—The remaking of social analysis.* London: Routledge.

Sacks, S., ed. 1979. *On metaphor.* Chicago: University of Chicago Press.

Sahlins, M. 1976. *Culture and practical reason.* Chicago: University of Chicago Press.

———. 1985. *Islands of history.* London: Tavistock.

Said, E. W. 1978. *Orientalism.* London: Routledge and Kegan Paul.

Saith, A., ed. 1987. *The re-emergence of the Chinese peasantry.* London: Croom Helm.

Sangren, P. S. 1987. *History and magic power in a Chinese community.* Stanford: Stanford University Press.

———. 1988. Rhetoric and the authority of ethnography: Postmodernism and the social reproduction of texts. *Current Anthropology* 29, no. 3:415–24.

———. 1995. "Power" against ideology: A critique of Foucaultian usage. *Cultural Anthropology* 10, no. 1:3–40.

Sanjek, R. 1991. The ethnographic present. *Man* 26, no. 4:609–28.

Sapir, J. D., and J. C. Crocker, eds. 1977. *The social use of metaphor: Essays on the anthropology of rhetoric.* Philadelphia: University of Pennsylvania Press.

Saussure, F. de. [1916] 1983. *Course in general linguistics.* Ed. C. Bally and A. Sechehaye, with A. Riedlinger; trans. R. Harris. New York: Philosophical Library.

Scheper-Hughes, N. 1992. *Death without weeping: The violence of everyday life in Brazil.* Berkeley: University of Berkeley Press.

Scholes, R. E. 1982. *Semiotics and interpretation.* New Haven: Yale University Press.

Schram, S. R., ed. 1987. *Foundations and limits of state power in China.* London: Published on behalf of the European Science Foundation by School of Oriental and African Studies, University of London.

Schurmann, F. 1966. *Ideology and organization in Communist China.* Berkeley: University of California Press.

Scott, J. C. 1976. *The moral economy of the peasant: Rebellion and subsistence in Southeast Asia.* New Haven: Yale University Press.

———. 1990. *Domination and the arts of resistance: Hidden transcript.* New Haven: Yale University Press.

Searle, J. 1971. What is a speech act? In *The philosophy of language,* ed. J. Searle, 39–53. Oxford: Oxford University Press.

Selden, M. 1993. Familial strategies and structures in rural north China. In *Chinese families in the post-Mao era,* ed. D. Davis and S. Harrell, 139–64. Berkeley: University of California Press.

Shaanxisheng nongcun shehui jing ji diaocha (Shaanxi: Rural social and economic survey). 1986. Xi'an: Shaanxi People's Press.

Shaanxi tong ji nianjian (Shaanxi statistical yearbook). 1991. Beijing: Statistics Press.

Shabad, T. 1972. *China's changing map — National and regional development, 1949–71.* London: Methuen.

Shack, W. A. 1966. *The Gurage: A people of the Ensete culture.* London: published for the International African Institute by Oxford University Press.

Shambaugh, D., ed. 1993. *American studies of contemporary China.* Washington, D.C.: Woodrow Wilson Center Press; Armonk, N.Y.: M. E. Sharpe.

Shue, V. 1980. *Peasant China in transition: The dynamics of development toward socialism, 1949–1956.* Berkeley: University of California Press.

———. 1988. *The reach of the state — Sketches of the Chinese body politic.* Stanford: Stanford University Press.

Sidel, M. 1995. The re-emergence of China studies in Vietnam. *China Quarterly,* no. 142:521–40.

Siu, H. F. 1989. *Agents and victims in South China: Accomplices in rural revolution.* New Haven: Yale University Press.

———. 1993. Reconstituting dowry and brideprice in South China. In *Chinese families in the post-Mao era,* ed. D. Davis and S. Harrell, 165–88. Berkeley: University of California Press.

Skinner, G. W. 1964–65. Marketing and social structure in rural China (three parts). *Journal of Asian Studies* 24, no. 1:3–24; no. 2:195–228; no. 3:363–99.

———. 1985. Rural marketing in China: Repression and revival. *China Quarterly,* no. 103:393–413.

Skocpol, T., ed. 1984. *Vision and method in historical sociology.* Cambridge: Cambridge University Press.

Smith, A. H. 1894. *Chinese characteristics.* 2nd ed. New York: Revell.

Smith, D. 1991. *The rise of historical sociology.* Philadelphia: Temple University Press.

Solomon, R. H. 1971. *Mao's revolution and the Chinese political culture.* Berkeley: University of California Press.

Sontag, S. 1978. *Illness as metaphor.* New York: Farrar, Straus, and Giroux.

Sperber, D. 1985. *On anthropological knowledge: Three essays.* Cambridge: Cambridge University Press.

Srinivas, M. N. 1966. Some thoughts on the study of one's own society. In *Social change in modern India,* 147–63. Berkeley: University of California Press.

Stacey, J. 1983. *Patriarchy and socialist revolution in China.* Berkeley: University of California Press.

Stocking, G. W., Jr. 1983. The ethnographer's magic: Fieldwork in British anthropology from Tylor to Malinowski. In *History of anthropology.* Vol. 1, *Observers observed: Essays on ethnographic fieldwork,* ed. G. W. Stocking Jr., 70–119. Madison: University of Wisconsin Press.

———. 1992. *The ethnographer's magic and other essays in the history of anthropology.* Madison: University of Wisconsin Press.

Sturrock, J. 1993. *Structuralism.* 2nd ed. London: Fontana.

Strathern, M. 1991. *Partial connections.* Sabage, Md.: Rowman and Littlefield.

Tambiah, S. J. 1968. The magical power of words. *Man* 3, no. 2:175–208.

Taylor, C. 1985. *Human agency and language.* Philosophical papers 1. Cambridge: Cambridge University Press.

———. 1993. To follow a rule . . . In *Bourdieu: Critical perspectives,* ed. C. Calhoun, E. LiPuma, and M. Postone, 45–60. Cambridge: Polity.

Thompson, E. P. 1993. *Customs in common: Studies in traditional popular culture.* New York: New Press.

Thompson, J. B. 1991. Editor's introduction to *Language and Symbolic Power,* by P. Bourdieu, 1–31. Cambridge: Polity.

Thompson, S. E. 1988. Death, food, and fertility. In *Death ritual in late imperial and modern China,* ed. J. L. Watson and E. S. Rawski, 71–108. Berkeley: University of California Press.

———. 1990. Metaphors the Chinese age by. In *Anthropology and the riddle of the Sphinx—Paradox of change in the life course,* ed. P. Spencer, 102–20. ASA Monographs 28. London: Routledge.

Thurston, A. F., and B. Pasternak, eds. 1983. *The social sciences and fieldwork in China: Views from the field.* Boulder, Colo.: Westview.

Townsend, J. R. 1967. *Political participation in Communist China.* Berkeley: University of California Press.

Tregear, T. R. 1965. *A geography of China.* London: University of London Press.

Tu, W-M. 1985. Selfhood and otherness in Confucian thought. In *Culture and self—Asian and Western perspectives,* ed. A. J. Marsella, G. DeVos, and F. L. K. Hsu, 231–35. New York: Tavistock.

Turner, V. W. 1982. *From ritual to theatre: The human seriousness of play.* New York: Performing Arts Journal Publications.

Vermeer, E. 1987. Collectivisation and decollectivisation in Guanzhong, central Shaanxi, 1934–1984. In *The re-emergence of the Chinese peasantry,* ed. A. Saith, 1–34. London: Croom Helm.

————. 1988. *Economic development in provincial China—The central Shaanxi since 1930.* Cambridge: Cambridge University Press.

Vitebsky, P. 1993. *Dialogues with the dead: The discussion of mortality among the Sora of eastern India.* Cambridge: Cambridge University Press.

Vogt, E. Z. 1976. *Tortillas for the gods: A symbolic analysis of Zinacantecan rituals.* Cambridge, Mass.: Harvard University Press.

Volosinov, V. N. 1973. *Marxism and the philosophy of language.* Trans. L. Matejka and I. R. Titunik. New York: Seminar Press.

Wagner, R. 1980. *The invention of culture.* Chicago: University of Chicago Press.

Walder, A. 1989. Social change in post-revolution China. *Annual Review of Sociology* 15: 405–24.

Wang, H-N. 1992. *Dangdai Zhongguo cunlo jiazu wenhua* (The culture of lineage villages in contemporary China). Shanghai: Science Press.

Watson, J. L. 1975. *Emigration and the Chinese lineage: The Mans in Hong Kong and London.* Berkeley: University of California Press.

————. 1982. Chinese kinship reconsidered: Anthropological perspectives on historical research. *China Quarterly,* no. 92:589–622.

————. 1986. An anthropological overview: The development of Chinese descent groups. In *Kinship organization in late imperial China: 1000–1940,* ed. P. B. Ebrey and J. Watson, 274–92. Berkeley: University of California Press.

————. 1988. The structure of Chinese funeral rites: Elementary forms, ritual sequence, and the primacy of performance. In *Death ritual in late imperial and modern China,* ed. J. L. Watson and E. S. Rawski, 3–19. Berkeley: University of California Press.

Watson, J. L., and E. S. Rawski, eds. 1988. *Death ritual in late imperial and modern China.* Berkeley: University of California Press.

Watson, R. S. 1981. Class differences and affinal relations in South China. *Man* 16, no. 4:593–615.

————. 1982. The creation of a Chinese lineage: The Teng of Ha Tsuen, 1669–1751. *Modern Asian Studies* 16, part 1:69–100.

————. 1985. *Inequality among brothers: Class and kinship in South China.* Cambridge: Cambridge University Press.

————. 1986. The named and the nameless: Gender and person in Chinese society. *American Ethnologist* 13, no. 4:619–32.

Weber, M. 1964. *The religion of China: Confucianism and Taoism.* New York: Free Press.

White, G. 1987. Riding the tiger: Grass-roots rural politics in the wake of the Chinese economic reforms. In *The re-emergence of the Chinese peasantry,* ed. A. Saith, 250–69. London: Croom Helm.

White, H. V. 1987. *The content of the form: Narrative discourse and historical representation.* Baltimore: John Hopkins University Press.

Whyte, M. K. 1979. Revolutionary change and patrilocal residence in China. *Ethnology* 18, no. 3:221–27.

———. 1992. Introduction: Rural economic reforms and Chinese family patterns. *China Quarterly*, no. 130:317–22.

Williams, R. 1977. *Marxism and literature.* Oxford: Oxford University Press.

Wolf, A. P. 1970. Chinese kinship and mourning dress. In *Family and kinship in Chinese society,* ed. M. Freedman, 189–207. Stanford: Stanford University Press.

Wolf, A. P., and C-S. Huang. 1980. *Marriage and adoption in China, 1845–1945.* Stanford: Stanford University Press.

Wolf, E. 1982. *Europe and the people without history.* Berkeley: University of California Press.

Wolf, M. 1970. Child training and the Chinese family. In *Family and kinship in Chinese society,* ed. M. Freedman, 37–62. Stanford: Stanford University Press.

———. 1984. Marriage, family, and state in contemporary China. *Pacific Affairs* 57, no. 2:213–24.

———. 1985. *Revolution postponed: Women in contemporary China.* Stanford: Stanford University Press.

Wong, S-L. 1979. *Sociology and socialism in contemporary China.* London: Routledge and Kegan Paul.

Yan, Y-X. 1992. The impact of rural reform on economic and social stratification in a Chinese village. *Australian Journal of Chinese Affairs,* no. 27:1–24.

———. 1996. *The flow of gifts: Reciprocity and social networks in a Chinese village.* Stanford: Stanford University Press.

Yang, C. K. 1959. *The Chinese family in the communist revolution.* Cambridge, Mass.: MIT Press.

Yang, M. C. 1945. *A Chinese village: Taitou, Shantung province.* New York: Columbia University Press.

Yang, M. M. 1988. The modernity of power in the Chinese socialist order. *Cultural Anthropology* 3, no. 4:408–27.

———. 1989. The gift economy and state power in China. *Comparative Studies in Society and History* 31, no. 1:25–54.

———. 1994. *Gifts, favors, and banquets—The art of social relationships in China.* Ithaca, N.Y.: Cornell University Press.

Zhao S. K. 1996. Yijiu jiuwu nian nongmin liudong: taishi yu jiaodian (Rural-urban migration in 1995). In *Zhongguo shehui xing fenxi yu yuce: 1995–1996* (Forecast and analysis of China's social development: 1995–1996), ed. Liu J. et al., 78–96. Beijing: Social Science Press.

Index

affinal relations, 35, 37. *See also* marriage
age: marriage, 59, 75–76, 197n4; old, 153–54
agents, 25, 184
agnates, 8, 31, 33, 38, 149, 188n9
agricultural production: calendar for, 86, 87, 88*table*, 96, 97–98, 102, 103*fig;* cotton crops, 8, 84–85; Dawa, 202n11*table;* draft animals, 116–17, 127–28; fruit crops, 160; money making with, 85; necessary but not central, 98; people's commune, 46, 56, 189n20; robbery in, 15, 189n21; sexual division of labor, 46; soil concerns beyond, 11; water for, 8–11, 56; wheat crops, 8, 11, 83–84, 85–86. *See also* "agricultural responsibility system"
"agricultural responsibility system" (household production), xii, 14–15, 189n20. *See also* households
Ahern, Emily, 32
ancestor worship, 32, 33, 152, 185, 193n7
Andersson, J. Gunnar, 188n12
animals: draft, 116–17, 127–28; in *yao*, 46
anthropology: and endogamy, 55–56; and food, 201n2; and gifts, 70; and kinship, 33, 34, 39, 82, 197–98n9; and language, 198n12; and practice, 25; and time, 99; and violence, 206n13. *See also* ethnography
articulation: everyday practice as, 26; ideology as, 34; of time, 86–87, 99–106, 103*fig,* 104*fig,* 204nn33,34
audience: funeral, 152, 153, 156; wedding, 143–44. *See also* entertainment
authority: interpretive, 145, 146, 150, 156, 184; over violence, 149–50. *See also* control; local authority; state

bachelorhood, 75–78
backward people, "poor and backward areas" (*pinkun diqu*), xi, 6–7, 16, 27, 182

Baker, Hugh, 100
Bakhtin, M. M., 198n12
Baocheng, wedding, 128, 146–50
bargaining, 114–18
Barthes, Roland, 91–92, 202n16
bathing, 11, 188n13
bed: brick (*pei*), 43–44, 45–46, 45*fig,* 196n29; heating, 45–46, 84; wedding "new room," 138, 144
"best man" (*banlang*), wedding, 134, 135, 136, 137–38
birth control, 8, 27, 164–69
Bloch, Maurice, 121, 158, 199n13
body, 131; individual, 27, 51; indocile, 122–25; in practice, 23, 191nn32,33; social, 27, 50–51; violence conveyed by, 122–24, 148, 149, 150
Bourdieu, Pierre, 91, 205n8; embodiment in practice, 23, 191nn32,33; "intellectualism," 34; logic of practice, 146, 191n34; ordinary and extraordinary oppositions, 204n30; practical vs. official kinship, 194n13; situated practice, 23, 191n31; theory of practice, 22–24, 191n34
bride: Baocheng, 146–48; Honglu's, 135, 136–37; and language of marriage, 60; in marriage process, 62–71, 74–75, 199n17; recruiting, 51–57, 52–53*table,* 54*table,* 75–76, 199n17. *See also* bride-price
bridegroom, 96–97; Baocheng, 148; cooking equipment, 96–97; Honglu, 135–37; *huoke* related to, 143; and language of marriage, 60; in marriage process, 62–71, 74–75, 199n17
bride-price, 46, 59, 63–64, 65, 197n2, 199n18; gift money (cash portion), 66–68, 200n20; Jinhua's remarriage for, 78
brotherhood, 15, 35, 36–37. *See also zijiawu*

237

Text and Display: Caledonia
Composition: Integrated Composition Systems, Inc.
Printing and binding: Thomson-Shore, Inc.
Illustrations: Bill Nelson
Index: Barbara Roos